Microsoft Power Automate Essentials

Automate Your Day-to-Day Tasks

Kiet Huynh

Table of Contents

PART I
Introduction to Microsoft Power Automate

1.1 What is Power Automate?

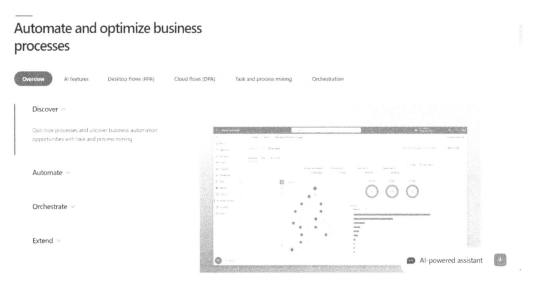

Introduction

In today's fast-paced digital environment, efficiency and automation are key drivers of success. Businesses and individuals alike seek ways to reduce manual tasks, streamline workflows, and improve productivity. This is where **Microsoft Power Automate** comes in.

Power Automate is a cloud-based automation tool from Microsoft that enables users to create automated workflows between applications and services. By leveraging triggers, actions, and conditions, Power Automate helps users eliminate repetitive tasks, integrate various tools, and optimize their daily processes without needing advanced coding skills.

This section will explore what Power Automate is, how it works, and why it is a valuable tool for both personal and business productivity.

Understanding Power Automate

1. Power Automate as a Workflow Automation Tool

Microsoft Power Automate is designed to help users **automate workflows** by connecting different applications and services. These automated processes, called **flows**, can be triggered by specific events and perform a series of actions without manual intervention.

With Power Automate, users can:

- **Automate repetitive tasks** such as sending emails, approvals, and data entry.

- **Integrate multiple applications** across Microsoft 365, third-party tools, and business software.

- **Enhance productivity** by reducing human errors and streamlining operations.

2. The Evolution of Power Automate

Power Automate was initially introduced as **Microsoft Flow** in 2016 and later rebranded as Power Automate in 2019 to align with Microsoft's Power Platform ecosystem, which includes **Power BI, Power Apps, and Power Virtual Agents**.

Since its inception, Power Automate has expanded its capabilities, adding features like **Robotic Process Automation (RPA)** through **Power Automate Desktop**, AI-driven automation with **AI Builder**, and seamless integrations with business applications.

3. How Power Automate Works

At its core, Power Automate operates based on a **trigger-action model**.

1. **Trigger**: An event that starts the automation (e.g., receiving an email, adding a file to a folder, or a scheduled time).

2. **Action**: The step(s) that follow once the trigger is activated (e.g., sending a notification, updating a database, or creating a report).

3. **Conditions and Loops**: Additional logic can be added to refine workflows, such as **conditional branching, approvals, and iterations**.

For example:

- A **trigger** could be "When a new email arrives in Outlook with an attachment."

- The **action** could be "Save the attachment to OneDrive."

- A **condition** could be "If the email is from a specific sender, forward it to a colleague."

Power Automate simplifies complex business processes by enabling **no-code or low-code automation**, making it accessible to both technical and non-technical users.

Key Components of Power Automate

1. Flows

Flows are the core automation element in Power Automate. There are different types of flows, including:

- **Cloud Flows** – Automate workflows between cloud-based applications.

- **Desktop Flows** – Automate tasks on a local computer using **Robotic Process Automation (RPA)**.

- **Business Process Flows** – Guide users through predefined steps in a process.

2. Connectors

Connectors act as bridges between different applications, enabling Power Automate to interact with services like **Outlook, SharePoint, OneDrive, Google Drive, Slack, Twitter, Salesforce, and hundreds more**.

There are three types of connectors:

- **Standard Connectors** – Free and widely used (e.g., Outlook, Excel, Teams).

- **Premium Connectors** – Require a paid plan (e.g., Salesforce, SAP).

- **Custom Connectors** – Created to connect with APIs for proprietary apps.

3. Triggers and Actions

- **Triggers** initiate workflows (e.g., "When a new email arrives").

- **Actions** define what the flow does (e.g., "Save the email to SharePoint").

4. Conditions and Branching

Users can set **conditional logic** to customize workflows. For example:

- If an invoice is above $1,000 → Send for manager approval.

- If a new customer is added → Send a welcome email.

5. Templates and AI Builder

Power Automate provides **pre-built templates** to quickly deploy workflows. Additionally, AI Builder allows users to incorporate **AI-powered automation**, such as extracting data from documents and predicting business outcomes.

Use Cases of Power Automate

Power Automate is widely used across industries, including:

1. Business Process Automation

- Automating employee onboarding by collecting and distributing information.

- Streamlining expense approvals by routing requests automatically.

2. IT and Operations Automation

- Automatically assigning help desk tickets based on keywords.

- Monitoring server logs and sending alerts for critical issues.

3. Sales and Marketing Automation

- Syncing leads from web forms to CRM systems.

- Sending personalized emails to customers based on purchase history.

4. HR and Employee Management

- Tracking employee leave requests.

- Automating reminders for performance reviews.

5. Personal Productivity

- Saving email attachments to cloud storage.

- Sending automatic birthday reminders to contacts.

Benefits of Power Automate

1. Increased Efficiency

- Automates repetitive tasks, reducing manual work.
- Speeds up approval processes and data handling.

2. Cost Savings

- Reduces dependency on IT for workflow automation.
- Minimizes errors, leading to better resource utilization.

3. Scalability

- Works across small businesses to large enterprises.
- Can be expanded with **AI, Power Apps, and Power BI**.

4. Accessibility and Ease of Use

- **No-code/low-code platform**, making automation accessible to non-developers.
- Works across desktop, mobile, and web platforms.

5. Security and Compliance

- **Microsoft security integration** ensures data protection.
- **GDPR and ISO compliance** for enterprise-level security.

Challenges and Limitations of Power Automate

While Power Automate is powerful, it has certain limitations:

1. Learning Curve

- Although it is a low-code platform, some **technical knowledge** is required for complex workflows.

2. API and Licensing Constraints

- Some premium connectors require additional licensing.

- API limits may restrict high-volume automation.

3. Execution and Performance

- **Delays in execution** if multiple flows are running simultaneously.

- **Monitoring required** to ensure workflows operate smoothly.

Conclusion

Microsoft Power Automate is a **versatile, user-friendly, and powerful automation tool** that enhances productivity, reduces manual tasks, and streamlines business processes. By automating workflows, organizations can **save time, reduce errors, and improve efficiency**.

In the next section, we will explore **why Power Automate is essential for businesses and individuals** and how it can transform the way we work.

1.2 Why Use Power Automate?

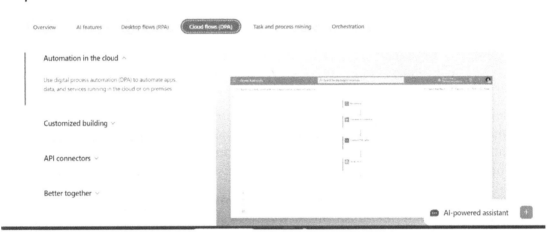

Introduction

In today's fast-paced digital world, automation has become a key driver of efficiency, productivity, and innovation. Microsoft Power Automate is a powerful tool that enables users to automate repetitive tasks, streamline workflows, and integrate various applications without requiring extensive coding knowledge. But why should individuals and businesses invest time in learning and implementing Power Automate?

This chapter explores the major benefits of Power Automate, demonstrating how it helps organizations save time, reduce manual work, improve accuracy, and enhance collaboration. Whether you are an individual professional, a small business owner, or part of a large enterprise, Power Automate provides immense value in automating day-to-day tasks.

Increasing Productivity and Efficiency

One of the primary reasons for using Power Automate is **increased productivity**. Many tasks in business operations involve repetitive manual work, such as data entry, sending notifications, or approving requests. These tasks consume time and effort, reducing overall efficiency.

With Power Automate, you can:

- **Eliminate manual processes** – Automate repetitive tasks like email notifications, approvals, and document processing.

- **Speed up workflows** – Ensure tasks are completed quickly without waiting for manual intervention.

- **Reduce human errors** – Automation eliminates the risk of mistakes that can occur in manual processes.

Real-World Example

A marketing team needs to update a customer database whenever a new lead fills out a contact form. Instead of manually copying data from the form to a CRM system, Power Automate can automatically extract the data and update the CRM, saving time and reducing errors.

Automating Repetitive Tasks

Many business operations involve tasks that require **consistent repetition**, such as:

- Sending email reminders for upcoming meetings.

- Backing up files from email attachments to cloud storage.

- Collecting responses from Microsoft Forms and storing them in an Excel sheet.

Power Automate allows you to set up **triggers and actions** that execute these tasks automatically. Once configured, these processes run in the background without human intervention.

Example Use Cases

Task	Traditional Method	Power Automate Solution
Save email attachments to OneDrive	Manually downloading each attachment	Automatically saving attachments to a designated folder
Collect survey responses	Copying responses from emails to Excel	Storing responses in a SharePoint list in real-time

Notify team members of new leads	Sending emails manually	Automated email notifications whenever a new lead is added to CRM

By leveraging automation, teams can focus on strategic tasks instead of spending time on low-value activities.

Enhancing Collaboration Across Teams

In modern workplaces, employees use multiple applications such as Microsoft Teams, SharePoint, Outlook, and third-party platforms like Slack and Trello. Power Automate acts as a **bridge** between these applications, ensuring smooth collaboration across different tools.

Benefits of Enhanced Collaboration

- **Instant updates** – Notify team members automatically when tasks are assigned or completed.

- **Seamless integration** – Connect different apps to ensure smooth data flow.

- **Faster approvals** – Speed up business processes by automating approval workflows.

Example Use Case

A project manager wants to track task assignments in Microsoft Planner. Instead of manually updating the team, Power Automate can send automated notifications to a Microsoft Teams channel whenever a new task is added.

Reducing Human Errors and Improving Accuracy

Human errors are common in manual tasks, especially in data entry, financial calculations, and report generation. Even small mistakes can have significant consequences. Power Automate **minimizes errors** by ensuring:

- **Data consistency** – Automated workflows follow predefined rules, reducing inconsistencies.

- **Error-free calculations** – Automating reports ensures accuracy in financial and operational data.

- **Standardized processes** – Ensures that every workflow follows a uniform process, reducing risks of miscommunication.

Real-World Example

An HR department manually tracks employee leave requests and updates them in an Excel sheet. Mistakes in tracking could lead to incorrect payroll calculations. By automating the process, Power Automate ensures that every approved leave request is recorded correctly, reducing payroll discrepancies.

Seamless Integration with Microsoft and Third-Party Apps

Power Automate seamlessly connects with over **500+ applications**, including:

- **Microsoft 365 Apps** – Outlook, Teams, SharePoint, Excel, OneDrive, Dynamics 365.

- **Third-Party Tools** – Google Drive, Slack, Trello, Salesforce, Twitter, Dropbox.

- **Databases and APIs** – SQL Server, Azure, HTTP requests for API integration.

This flexibility allows organizations to automate processes **without switching between multiple apps** manually.

Example Use Case: Automating Social Media Posts

A digital marketing team wants to post updates on Twitter and LinkedIn whenever a new blog is published. Instead of manually logging into each platform, Power Automate can detect new blog posts and trigger an automated social media update.

Saving Time and Reducing Costs

By automating repetitive processes, businesses can save **thousands of hours** per year, leading to significant cost reductions. Power Automate helps in:

- **Reducing labor costs** – Automation reduces the need for manual data entry and administrative work.

- **Faster processing times** – Automated workflows execute tasks instantly, improving turnaround times.

- **Optimizing resource allocation** – Employees can focus on high-value activities instead of routine tasks.

Real-World Example: Automating Invoice Processing

A finance team receives **hundreds of invoices** via email. Instead of manually extracting data, Power Automate can:

1. Scan email attachments for invoices.

2. Extract relevant data (invoice number, amount, due date).

3. Enter the details into an accounting system automatically.

This reduces processing time from **hours to minutes**, allowing employees to focus on financial analysis rather than manual data entry.

Enabling No-Code and Low-Code Development

One of the biggest advantages of Power Automate is its **no-code/low-code** approach. Users without programming experience can create powerful workflows using a **drag-and-drop interface**.

Who Can Use Power Automate?

- **Non-technical users** – Business professionals who want to automate tasks without writing code.

- **IT administrators** – To automate complex workflows and integrate systems.

- **Developers** – To create custom connectors and advanced automation scenarios.

Power Automate democratizes automation, making it accessible to a **wider audience** beyond traditional software developers.

Conclusion

Microsoft Power Automate is a game-changer for individuals and businesses looking to improve efficiency, accuracy, and collaboration. By eliminating manual tasks, integrating multiple applications, and reducing human errors, Power Automate allows teams to work smarter, not harder.

In the next chapter, we will explore how to **get started with Power Automate**, including setting up an account, navigating the interface, and creating your first automation workflow.

1.3 Key Features and Capabilities

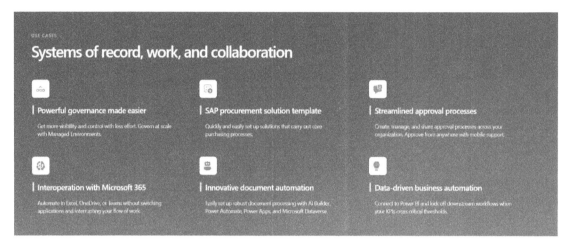

Microsoft Power Automate is a powerful automation tool that helps users streamline repetitive tasks, integrate various applications, and improve productivity. With its robust set of features, Power Automate allows both individuals and businesses to automate workflows efficiently without extensive coding knowledge. In this section, we will explore the key features and capabilities that make Power Automate a valuable tool for process automation.

No-Code/Low-Code Automation

One of the most significant advantages of Power Automate is its **no-code/low-code approach**, allowing users of all technical backgrounds to create automated workflows. The drag-and-drop interface and pre-built connectors make it easy to design automation without writing complex code.

Benefits of No-Code/Low-Code Automation:

- **Accessibility:** Non-developers can create workflows without programming expertise.

- **Speed:** Users can quickly build, test, and deploy automation.

- **Cost-Effective:** Reduces dependency on developers, lowering costs for businesses.

By enabling a **visual, intuitive workflow design**, Power Automate empowers users across departments, from IT professionals to HR teams and marketing specialists, to create solutions tailored to their needs.

Cloud-Based and Desktop Automation

Power Automate supports both **cloud-based automation** and **desktop automation**, making it a versatile tool for different use cases.

Cloud Flows:

Cloud flows allow users to automate tasks that involve cloud services, web applications, and APIs. These workflows run in the cloud and can trigger actions based on events occurring in connected applications such as **Microsoft 365, SharePoint, Outlook, Teams, and third-party services like Slack, Trello, and Dropbox.**

Desktop Flows (RPA - Robotic Process Automation):

For tasks that require **interacting with desktop applications**, Power Automate provides **Robotic Process Automation (RPA)** capabilities through **Power Automate Desktop.** This feature allows users to automate manual tasks such as:

- Filling out forms in desktop applications.

- Extracting data from legacy systems.

- Automating repetitive keystrokes and mouse clicks.

Benefits of Combining Cloud and Desktop Automation:

- Automate processes across both **cloud-based and on-premises applications.**

- Reduce the need for manual intervention in **legacy applications that lack APIs.**

- Increase efficiency by **bridging automation between modern and traditional systems.**

With cloud and desktop flows, Power Automate provides **comprehensive automation coverage**, making it a suitable solution for businesses operating in hybrid environments.

Pre-Built Connectors for Seamless Integration

Power Automate comes with **hundreds of pre-built connectors** that enable seamless integration between different applications and services. These connectors allow users to automate workflows across a wide range of platforms without extensive coding.

Commonly Used Connectors:

- **Microsoft 365 Apps:** Outlook, Teams, SharePoint, OneDrive, Excel, Planner

- **Business Applications:** Dynamics 365, Salesforce, HubSpot, SAP

- **Productivity Tools:** Trello, Asana, Slack, Zoom

- **Social Media:** Twitter, LinkedIn, Facebook

- **Cloud Storage:** Dropbox, Google Drive, Box

- **Databases:** SQL Server, Azure, MySQL, PostgreSQL

Benefits of Pre-Built Connectors:

- **Simplifies automation** by reducing the need for custom integrations.

- **Ensures compatibility** with widely used business applications.

- **Accelerates workflow deployment** by providing ready-to-use components.

For businesses that require additional functionality, Power Automate allows users to **create custom connectors** to interact with internal APIs and services.

AI-Powered Automation with AI Builder

Power Automate includes **AI Builder**, a feature that enables users to incorporate artificial intelligence into workflows without requiring data science expertise. AI Builder allows users to **automate data extraction, document processing, and decision-making** using AI models.

Key AI Capabilities in Power Automate:

- **Form Processing:** Extracts data from invoices, receipts, and documents.

- **Text Recognition (OCR):** Converts scanned documents and images into editable text.

- **Sentiment Analysis:** Analyzes customer feedback to determine positive or negative sentiment.

- **Object Detection:** Identifies objects in images for automated categorization.

Use Cases of AI-Powered Automation:

- Automatically **extract invoice details** and store them in an accounting system.

- Categorize customer emails based on **sentiment analysis.**

- Use OCR to **convert scanned contracts into searchable documents.**

By integrating **AI capabilities into automation workflows**, Power Automate helps businesses reduce manual data entry and improve accuracy in decision-making processes.

Scheduled, Event-Triggered, and Instant Flows

Power Automate provides **multiple trigger types**, allowing users to build automation that suits different business needs.

1. Scheduled Flows

- Runs at specific times (daily, weekly, monthly).

- Example: Send automated reports to a manager every Monday morning.

2. Event-Triggered Flows

- Executes when a specific event occurs.

- Example: Automatically move email attachments to a SharePoint folder when received.

3. Instant Flows

- Manually triggered by a user via a button.

- Example: A user clicks a button to send an approval request to a manager.

Benefits of Different Flow Types:

- **Flexibility:** Choose the right trigger based on workflow requirements.

- **Efficiency:** Reduces manual intervention by automating responses to events.

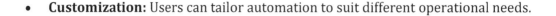

- **Customization:** Users can tailor automation to suit different operational needs.

Secure and Scalable Automation

Security is a top priority for businesses using automation tools. Power Automate provides enterprise-grade security features to ensure data protection, compliance, and governance.

Key Security Features:

- **Data Loss Prevention (DLP) Policies:** Prevents sensitive data from being shared across unauthorized apps.

- **Role-Based Access Control (RBAC):** Limits user access to specific automation processes.

- **Audit Logging and Monitoring:** Tracks workflow executions and detects anomalies.

- **Encryption and Compliance Standards:** Adheres to GDPR, ISO, and other security regulations.

Scalability for Business Growth:

Power Automate is designed to scale with business needs, allowing organizations to:

- Expand automation across **departments and teams.**

- Handle increasing workloads with **robust performance.**

- Integrate with **Power BI, Power Apps, and Dataverse** for advanced analytics and automation.

By ensuring **high security and scalability**, Power Automate is suitable for both small businesses and large enterprises.

Conclusion

Microsoft Power Automate offers a comprehensive set of features that enable users to automate repetitive tasks, integrate applications, and improve productivity without requiring extensive coding knowledge. From cloud-based and desktop automation to AI-powered capabilities, pre-built connectors, and secure workflows, Power Automate is a robust tool that can transform the way businesses operate.

Understanding these key features will help users leverage the full potential of automation to save time, reduce errors, and enhance operational efficiency. In the next section, we will explore how to set up your Power Automate account and start building workflows.

1.4 Power Automate vs. Other Automation Tools

Enhance productivity with automation

Learn how customers save time, lower costs, and foster a culture of innovation with Power Automate.

Read the Forrester study

248%	200	20%
ROI over three years by improving end-user and developer efficiency while reducing legacy system costs.¹	hours saved per year by employees involved in high-impact use cases for robotic process automation (RPA)¹	reduction in developer time on automated workflows¹

Automation has become a critical aspect of modern business operations, helping organizations improve efficiency, reduce human error, and enhance productivity. Microsoft Power Automate is one of the leading automation tools in the market, but how does it compare to other automation platforms? In this section, we will explore Power Automate in comparison with other popular automation tools, including Zapier, UiPath, and Automate.io. We will analyze their strengths, weaknesses, and best-use scenarios to help users make an informed decision about which tool best suits their needs.

Overview of Power Automate

Microsoft Power Automate, previously known as Microsoft Flow, is a cloud-based service that enables users to create automated workflows between applications and services. It is a key component of the Microsoft Power Platform and integrates seamlessly with Microsoft 365, Dynamics 365, Azure, and numerous third-party applications.

Key Advantages of Power Automate:

- **Deep Integration with Microsoft Ecosystem:** Power Automate works natively with Microsoft apps such as Outlook, SharePoint, Teams, Excel, and OneDrive, making it an excellent choice for organizations using Microsoft products.

- **No-Code and Low-Code Automation:** Users with little to no programming experience can build workflows using a visual drag-and-drop interface.

- **AI-Enhanced Automation:** Power Automate includes AI Builder, which enables intelligent automation features such as document processing, object detection, and text recognition.

- **Robotic Process Automation (RPA):** With Power Automate Desktop, users can automate tasks on their local computers by interacting with applications through UI automation.

- **Enterprise-Grade Security and Compliance:** Microsoft provides built-in security, governance, and compliance features that meet enterprise standards.

However, Power Automate also has some **limitations**, including its learning curve for complex workflows, dependency on Microsoft products, and pricing model that can be costly for advanced automation needs.

Comparison with Other Automation Tools

To understand Power Automate's position in the market, let's compare it to three major automation tools: **Zapier, UiPath, and Automate.io**.

Power Automate vs. Zapier

Feature	Power Automate	Zapier
Best For	Microsoft 365 users, enterprises, and organizations needing deep integrations	Small businesses, startups, and users who need quick automation between web apps
Ease of Use	Moderate learning curve, especially for complex workflows	Very user-friendly, designed for non-technical users
Integration	Best for Microsoft services, also supports third-party apps	Supports thousands of third-party web applications
Automation Type	Cloud-based workflows, RPA, AI-based automation	Cloud-based automation only (no RPA)
Pricing	Based on number of runs and premium connectors; can be expensive for advanced users	More affordable for smaller-scale automation
AI & Advanced Features	Includes AI Builder and RPA capabilities	No AI features, limited workflow complexity

Conclusion:

- **Use Power Automate** if you are in the Microsoft ecosystem and need robust automation with RPA and AI capabilities.

- **Use Zapier** if you want an easy-to-use tool for connecting various third-party web apps without deep technical knowledge.

Power Automate vs. UiPath

Feature	Power Automate	UiPath
Best For	Business process automation, Microsoft users, cloud-based workflows	Advanced robotic process automation (RPA) for enterprises
Ease of Use	User-friendly for basic automation but requires knowledge for advanced features	Steeper learning curve, designed for developers and automation engineers
Integration	Seamless Microsoft integration and third-party connectors	Extensive RPA capabilities for automating both web and desktop applications
Automation Type	Cloud-based workflows, RPA, AI-based automation	Full RPA platform for automating complex enterprise processes
Pricing	More affordable for Microsoft users, but can be expensive for enterprise features	Higher cost, mainly targeting large enterprises
AI & Advanced Features	AI-powered automation with AI Builder	Strong AI and machine learning capabilities for intelligent automation

Conclusion:

- **Use Power Automate** if you need cloud-based automation and some RPA capabilities within Microsoft 365.

- **Use UiPath** if you require advanced RPA solutions for automating desktop applications, legacy systems, and AI-driven workflows.

Power Automate vs. Automate.io

Feature	Power Automate	Automate.io
Best For	Microsoft users, business process automation	Startups and small businesses looking for affordable automation
Ease of Use	Moderate, but offers low-code/no-code options	Easier to use, designed for simple automation
Integration	Microsoft 365, enterprise applications	Supports third-party applications but fewer than Zapier

Automation Type	Cloud-based workflows, RPA	Cloud-based automation only
Pricing	Can be costly for enterprise users	More budget-friendly
AI & Advanced Features	AI-powered automation available	No AI features

Conclusion:

- **Use Power Automate** if you need enterprise-level automation with AI and RPA.

- **Use Automate.io** if you need basic, cost-effective automation for startups or small businesses.

Choosing the Right Automation Tool

Each automation tool serves different needs, so choosing the right one depends on several factors:

1. Your Ecosystem:

- If you are heavily invested in **Microsoft 365**, Power Automate is the best choice.

- If you rely on **third-party web applications**, Zapier or Automate.io may be more suitable.

- If you need **advanced RPA capabilities**, UiPath is the better option.

2. Your Use Case:

- **Simple Web Automation?** Zapier or Automate.io.

- **Enterprise-Level Workflow Automation?** Power Automate.

- **Complex RPA Needs?** UiPath.

3. Budget Considerations:

- **Power Automate's free tier** is useful for basic automation, but enterprise features require additional costs.

- **Zapier and Automate.io** offer cheaper plans for small businesses.

- **UiPath** is the most expensive, targeting enterprise clients.

Final Thoughts

Power Automate stands out due to its seamless Microsoft integration, AI-powered automation, and RPA capabilities. However, depending on your business needs, other tools like Zapier, UiPath, or Automate.io may be better suited.

If you work primarily with Microsoft products and need automation beyond simple web-based workflows, **Power Automate is an excellent choice**. On the other hand, if your focus is third-party app integration, Zapier may be a better fit. If you require **heavy-duty robotic process automation**, UiPath is the industry leader.

Ultimately, understanding your requirements, workflow complexity, and budget will help you select the best automation tool for your needs.

1.5 Understanding the Power Automate Ecosystem

Introduction

Microsoft Power Automate is more than just an automation tool—it is an integral part of the Microsoft Power Platform and connects with various Microsoft 365 services, third-party applications, and cloud-based tools. To effectively use Power Automate, it's essential to understand its ecosystem, including its integration capabilities, security framework, and the role it plays in modern business automation.

This section will explore the different components of the Power Automate ecosystem, how it integrates with other Microsoft services, and the types of users who benefit from it. We will also discuss its extensibility through connectors, APIs, and artificial intelligence (AI) capabilities.

The Role of Power Automate in the Microsoft Power Platform

Power Automate is a core component of the **Microsoft Power Platform**, which includes:

- **Power BI** – A business intelligence tool for data visualization and analytics.

- **Power Apps** – A platform for building custom applications without extensive coding knowledge.

- **Power Automate** – A tool for automating workflows between applications and services.

- **Power Virtual Agents** – A chatbot development tool for automating customer and employee interactions.

How Power Automate Fits into the Power Platform

Power Automate serves as the automation engine for the Power Platform, allowing users to:

- **Automate repetitive tasks** across different applications.

- **Connect Power Apps with external data sources** to enable dynamic workflows.

- **Integrate with Power BI** to trigger actions based on data analytics.

- **Use AI Builder** to automate document processing and intelligent decision-making.

This seamless integration allows businesses to create end-to-end automated solutions with minimal coding effort.

Integration with Microsoft 365 and Other Microsoft Services

Power Automate is deeply integrated with **Microsoft 365** applications, allowing users to automate workflows within familiar productivity tools like Outlook, SharePoint, OneDrive, Teams, and Excel.

Key Integrations with Microsoft 365

- **Outlook** – Automate email responses, manage calendar events, and track emails.

- **SharePoint** – Automate document approval processes and content management.

- **OneDrive** – Synchronize files across cloud storage and automate file-sharing workflows.

- **Microsoft Teams** – Send automated notifications, schedule meetings, and integrate bots.

- **Excel** – Automate data extraction, entry, and transformation processes.

Power Automate and Dynamics 365

Beyond Microsoft 365, Power Automate is also integrated with **Dynamics 365**, allowing businesses to automate customer relationship management (CRM) and enterprise resource planning (ERP) tasks. This includes automating sales follow-ups, customer support responses, and inventory management.

Integration with Microsoft Azure

For advanced users and developers, Power Automate connects with **Azure services** to enable:

- **Azure Logic Apps** – More advanced automation workflows with enterprise-scale capabilities.

- **Azure AI Services** – AI-driven automation for document scanning, sentiment analysis, and chatbots.

- **Azure SQL Database** – Automating data updates and reporting workflows.

These integrations help organizations leverage Power Automate as a bridge between their business applications and cloud services.

Connecting with Third-Party Applications

While Power Automate is tightly integrated with Microsoft products, it also supports over **1,000 third-party connectors**, allowing users to automate workflows with external apps such as:

- **Google Workspace** – Sync with Gmail, Google Drive, Google Sheets, and Google Calendar.

- **Salesforce** – Automate CRM updates and customer follow-ups.

- **Slack and Trello** – Manage notifications and task assignments.

- **Twitter, Facebook, and LinkedIn** – Automate social media interactions.

- **Dropbox and Box** – Automate file transfers and cloud storage management.

Using Custom Connectors

If an application is not natively supported, Power Automate allows users to build **custom connectors** to integrate with external APIs. This enables businesses to create tailored automation solutions that meet their specific needs.

Security, Compliance, and Governance in Power Automate

As organizations automate business processes, data security and compliance become critical. Microsoft Power Automate follows industry-standard security protocols to ensure data protection and regulatory compliance.

Data Security in Power Automate

- **Role-Based Access Control (RBAC)** – Limits user permissions based on roles and responsibilities.

- **Data Loss Prevention (DLP) Policies** – Prevents unauthorized data transfers between applications.

- **Encryption** – Ensures data is encrypted both in transit and at rest.
- **Audit Logs** – Tracks automation activities for compliance and monitoring.

Compliance Standards

Power Automate complies with major industry regulations, including:

- **GDPR** (General Data Protection Regulation)
- **ISO 27001** (Information Security Management)
- **HIPAA** (Health Insurance Portability and Accountability Act)
- **SOC 2** (Service Organization Control)

These compliance measures make Power Automate a secure choice for enterprises handling sensitive data.

AI and Power Automate: Enhancing Automation with AI Builder

Microsoft Power Automate integrates with **AI Builder**, an artificial intelligence tool that allows users to add machine learning capabilities to their workflows.

AI-Powered Automation Examples

- **Document Processing** – Extracting text from PDFs and invoices.
- **Sentiment Analysis** – Analyzing customer feedback for insights.
- **Object Detection** – Identifying items in images and automating categorization.
- **Predictive Analytics** – Automating decision-making based on historical data.

By incorporating AI into automation workflows, businesses can enhance efficiency and intelligence in their processes.

Who Can Benefit from Power Automate?

Power Automate is designed for users across various roles and industries, including:

1. Business Users (No-Code Users)

- Automate repetitive administrative tasks.

- Improve document management and approvals.

- Enhance team collaboration with automated notifications.

2. IT Professionals and Developers

- Create complex automation flows with custom scripts.

- Integrate Power Automate with APIs and enterprise systems.

- Implement advanced security policies and governance.

3. Small Business Owners

- Automate invoicing and customer service processes.

- Sync customer data across platforms.

- Reduce manual work in daily operations.

4. Enterprise Organizations

- Streamline HR processes such as employee onboarding.

- Automate IT help desk ticketing systems.

- Enhance compliance tracking and reporting.

No matter the industry or skill level, Power Automate provides automation solutions that improve efficiency and reduce manual workload.

Conclusion

The Power Automate ecosystem is vast and highly flexible, allowing users to automate tasks across Microsoft 365, third-party applications, and enterprise systems. Whether you're a business professional looking to save time on repetitive tasks or a developer seeking to build advanced workflows, Power Automate provides the tools needed to streamline operations efficiently.

Understanding this ecosystem is crucial for maximizing Power Automate's potential and ensuring seamless integration with other technologies. In the next chapters, we will explore how to set up Power Automate and create powerful workflows to enhance productivity.

PART II
Getting Started with Power Automate

2.1 Setting Up Your Power Automate Account

Before you can start automating workflows with Microsoft Power Automate, you need to set up your account. This section will walk you through the process of creating a Microsoft account, accessing Power Automate, and familiarizing yourself with its interface.

2.1.1 Creating a Microsoft Account

A Microsoft account is required to use Power Automate. This account gives you access to various Microsoft services, including Power Automate, OneDrive, Outlook, and more. If you already have a Microsoft account, you can skip this section and proceed to **2.1.2 Accessing Power Automate**. Otherwise, follow the steps below to create a new account.

Step 1: Visit the Microsoft Account Sign-Up Page

To create a Microsoft account, go to the official sign-up page:

🔗 https://signup.live.com

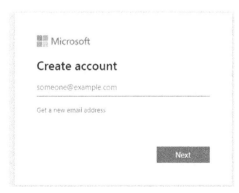

You will see a screen prompting you to enter an email address, phone number, or create a new email for your Microsoft account.

Step 2: Choose Your Sign-Up Method

You have three options for creating a Microsoft account:

1. Using an existing email address (e.g., Gmail, Yahoo, or any other provider)

2. Creating a new Outlook.com or Hotmail.com email address

3. Using a phone number instead of an email

Option 1: Sign Up with an Existing Email

- Enter your current email address in the provided field.

- Click **Next** and create a password for your Microsoft account.

- Follow the verification steps to confirm your email address.

Option 2: Create a New Outlook Email

- Click on **Get a new email address** if you want a Microsoft email (e.g., yourname@outlook.com).

- Choose your preferred domain: **@outlook.com** or **@hotmail.com**.

- Create a strong password and proceed with verification.

Option 3: Sign Up with a Phone Number

- Click **Use a phone number instead** and enter your phone number.

- Microsoft will send a verification code via SMS.

- Enter the code and set up your account details.

Step 3: Create a Strong Password

When creating a password, make sure it meets security requirements:

✓ At least 8 characters long

✓ Includes uppercase and lowercase letters

✓ Contains numbers or symbols for added security

After setting your password, click **Next** to continue.

Step 4: Provide Your Personal Information

Microsoft will ask for some basic details:

- First Name and Last Name – Enter your full legal name.
- Country/Region – Select your country from the dropdown list.
- Birthdate – Provide your date of birth.

Click **Next** to proceed.

Step 5: Verify Your Identity

Microsoft will send a **verification email** (if you signed up with an email) or a **verification code via SMS** (if you used a phone number).

- Open your email inbox or SMS messages.
- Find the **verification code** sent by Microsoft.
- Enter the code into the verification field and click **Next**.

If you don't receive the email or SMS, check your spam folder or request another code.

Step 6: Complete CAPTCHA Verification

Microsoft may ask you to complete a CAPTCHA test to confirm that you're not a bot.

- Enter the characters displayed on the screen.
- Click **Next** to finalize the account creation.

Step 7: Set Up Account Preferences

Once your account is verified, Microsoft may ask you to configure account preferences such as:

- Backup Email or Phone Number (optional but recommended for security)
- Privacy and Security Settings
- Newsletter or Promotional Emails Preferences

Adjust these settings as needed, then click **Next** to finish setting up your Microsoft account.

Signing In to Your New Microsoft Account

Now that your Microsoft account is created, you can sign in anytime:

1. Go to https://account.microsoft.com.

2. Click **Sign In**.

3. Enter your email/phone and password.

4. Click **Next** to access your Microsoft account dashboard.

Troubleshooting Common Issues

If you encounter problems during account creation, here are some possible solutions:

Issue 1: "This email is already associated with a Microsoft account."

- If you receive this error, try signing in instead of creating a new account.

- Reset your password if you have forgotten it.

Issue 2: "Verification email not received."

- Check your **spam/junk folder**.

- Ensure you entered the correct email address.

- Request a new verification email.

Issue 3: "Phone number already in use."

- A phone number can only be linked to a limited number of accounts.

- Use a different phone number or sign up with an email instead.

Next Steps: Accessing Power Automate

Now that you have successfully created your Microsoft account, you are ready to access Power Automate. Proceed to **2.1.2 Accessing Power Automate**, where you will learn how to sign in and navigate the Power Automate dashboard.

2.1.2 Accessing Power Automate

Introduction

Once you have created a Microsoft account, the next step is to access Power Automate. Power Automate is a cloud-based service that can be accessed through a web browser or a mobile application. In this section, we will walk through different ways to access Power Automate, including using the web portal, Microsoft 365, mobile apps, and desktop applications. We will also cover how to navigate the Power Automate interface once you log in.

1. Accessing Power Automate via the Web Portal

1.1 Using a Web Browser

The most common way to access Power Automate is through a web browser. Microsoft provides a dedicated web portal where users can create, manage, and monitor their workflows.

To access Power Automate via a web browser, follow these steps:

1. Open your preferred web browser (Google Chrome, Microsoft Edge, Mozilla Firefox, or Safari).

2. In the address bar, type the following URL and press **Enter**:
   ☞ https://flow.microsoft.com

3. You will be redirected to the **Microsoft Power Automate homepage**.

4. Click on **Sign in** in the upper-right corner of the page.

5. Enter your **Microsoft account credentials** (email and password).

6. Once authenticated, you will be taken to the **Power Automate dashboard**, where you can start creating and managing your workflows.

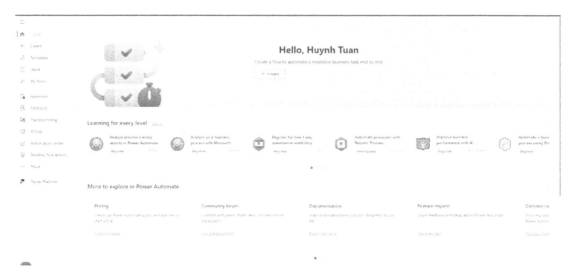

1.2 Microsoft 365 Integration

If you are using Power Automate as part of **Microsoft 365 (formerly Office 365)**, you can access it directly from the Microsoft 365 portal:

1. Open a web browser and go to ☞ https://www.office.com.

2. Sign in with your **Microsoft 365 credentials**.

3. Click on the **App Launcher** (the grid icon in the top-left corner).

4. Scroll down and select **Power Automate** from the list of Microsoft apps.

5. You will be redirected to the Power Automate dashboard.

If you do not see Power Automate in the app list, you can search for it using the search bar at the top.

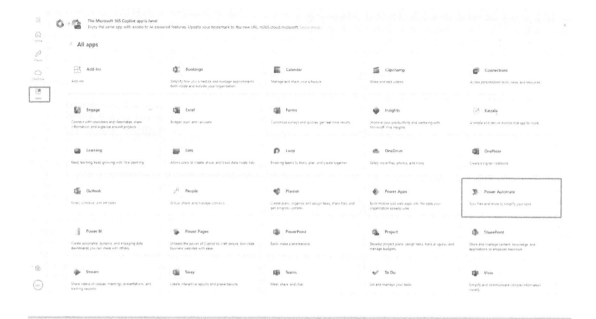

2. Accessing Power Automate via Mobile App

Microsoft provides a **mobile app** for Power Automate, allowing users to monitor, manage, and trigger flows on the go. The app is available for both **Android** and **iOS** devices.

2.1 Installing the Power Automate Mobile App

To install the mobile app:

For Android Users:

- Open **Google Play Store**.
- Search for **"Power Automate"**.
- Tap **Install** and wait for the installation to complete.

For iOS Users:

- Open the **App Store**.
- Search for **"Power Automate"**.
- Tap **Download** and install the app.

2.2 Signing In to Power Automate Mobile

Once the app is installed:

1. Open the **Power Automate app** on your phone.

2. Tap **Sign in**.

3. Enter your **Microsoft account credentials**.

4. After signing in, you will see the **dashboard**, where you can manage your existing flows or create new ones.

2.3 Features Available in the Mobile App

The Power Automate mobile app provides several features:

- **View and manage flows**: See all your created flows and their status.

- **Trigger manual flows**: Start flows that require user interaction.

- **Receive notifications**: Get alerts when a flow runs or fails.

- **Edit simple flows**: Modify certain aspects of your automation.

While the mobile app is useful for managing flows, it does not provide the full functionality available in the web version, such as creating complex workflows.

3. Accessing Power Automate via Desktop App (Power Automate for Windows)

3.1 Installing the Power Automate Desktop App

If you need to automate desktop tasks (such as interacting with Windows applications), you will need **Power Automate for Windows**.

To install Power Automate Desktop:

1. Open a web browser and go to ☞ https://powerautomate.microsoft.com/.

2. Navigate to the **Power Automate Desktop** section.

3. Click on **Download** and wait for the setup file to be downloaded.

4. Open the downloaded **.exe** file and follow the installation instructions.

5. Once installed, open **Power Automate Desktop** from the Start menu.

3.2 Signing In to Power Automate Desktop

Once you launch the app:

1. Click **Sign in**.

2. Enter your **Microsoft account credentials**.

3. After signing in, you will see the **Power Automate Desktop dashboard**, where you can start creating and managing desktop flows.

3.3 Features of Power Automate Desktop

- **Create and run desktop flows** (for automating Windows applications).

- **Record user interactions** and replay them automatically.

- **Integrate with cloud-based Power Automate flows**.

Power Automate Desktop is essential for users who need **Robotic Process Automation (RPA)** to automate repetitive tasks in local applications.

---

4. Troubleshooting Access Issues

Forgot Password?

If you forgot your Microsoft account password:

1. Go to Microsoft Account Recovery.

2. Follow the steps to reset your password.

No Power Automate License?

If you cannot access Power Automate, it may be due to licensing restrictions:

- Check if your **Microsoft 365 subscription** includes Power Automate.

- If using a free account, verify your **Power Automate trial period**.

Browser Compatibility Issues

If Power Automate does not load properly in a browser:

- **Use Microsoft Edge or Google Chrome** for best performance.

- **Clear cache and cookies** from your browser settings.

- **Disable browser extensions** that may interfere with Power Automate.

Mobile App Login Issues

If you cannot sign in on the mobile app:

- Ensure your **internet connection** is stable.

- Update to the **latest version** of the app.

- Restart your device and try logging in again.

Conclusion

Accessing Power Automate is straightforward and can be done through multiple platforms, including web browsers, mobile devices, and desktop applications. The web version provides the most functionality, while the mobile and desktop apps allow flexibility in managing and running flows. By following the steps outlined in this section, you can successfully log in and start automating your workflows with Power Automate.

2.1.3 Navigating the Power Automate Interface

Microsoft Power Automate provides a user-friendly interface that allows users to create, manage, and monitor automation workflows efficiently. Understanding how to navigate the interface is crucial for effectively using Power Automate, whether you're a beginner or an advanced user. This section will provide a detailed walkthrough of the Power Automate interface, explaining its various components and how to use them effectively.

1. Accessing Power Automate Interface

To start using Power Automate, you need to access the platform through a web browser or desktop application. The web version is the most commonly used interface.

1.1 Accessing Power Automate via the Web

1. Open a web browser (Google Chrome, Microsoft Edge, or Firefox).

2. Navigate to https://flow.microsoft.com.

3. Log in using your **Microsoft account** (Work, School, or Personal).

4. Once logged in, you will be directed to the **Power Automate home page**.

1.2 Accessing Power Automate via Microsoft 365

If you are already signed into Microsoft 365:

1. Go to https://office.com.

2. Click on the **App Launcher** (the grid icon in the upper-left corner).

3. Select **Power Automate** from the list of available applications.

1.3 Accessing Power Automate via Desktop (Power Automate for Windows)

For users who want to create **desktop flows**, Power Automate also offers a **desktop application** called **Power Automate for Windows**.

1. Download and install **Power Automate for Windows** from the **Microsoft Store**.

2. Launch the application and log in with your Microsoft credentials.

3. The desktop version provides additional functionality for automating tasks on a local machine.

2. Overview of the Power Automate Interface

Once you have accessed Power Automate, the interface is divided into several key sections. Each section plays a crucial role in managing your automation workflows.

2.1 Power Automate Dashboard (Home Page)

The **Home Page** is the first screen you see when you log in. It provides an overview of your workflows and quick access to essential tools.

Key Features of the Home Page

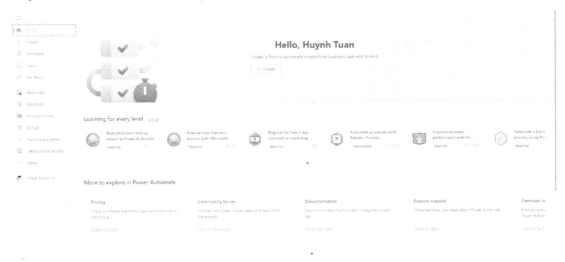

- **Search Bar** – Quickly search for existing flows.

- **Start from Blank** – Create a new flow from scratch.

- **Start from a Template** – Browse and use pre-built automation templates.

- **Recent Flows** – View a list of your recently used flows.

- **Learning Resources** – Get tutorials, documentation, and guides to help you get started.

2.2 The Left Navigation Pane

The **left navigation pane** provides access to all main features of Power Automate.

Menu Option	Description
Home	Returns to the dashboard.
Create	Start creating new flows from scratch or using templates.
Templates	Browse a collection of pre-built flows.
My Flows	View, manage, and edit your existing flows.
Approvals	Manage approval requests sent or received via flows.
Solutions	Access and manage Power Automate solutions (for advanced users).
Monitor	View analytics, performance, and flow history.
AI Builder	Use AI-powered automation tools.
Process Advisor	Analyze processes and get recommendations for automation.
Learn	Access tutorials and Microsoft documentation.

2.3 My Flows Section

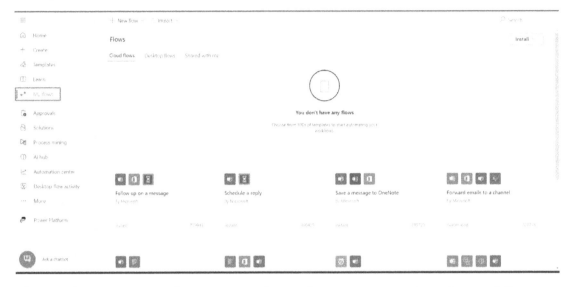

The **My Flows** section is where you can view and manage your automation workflows.

Flow Categories in "My Flows"

1. **Cloud Flows** – Workflows running in the cloud.

2. **Desktop Flows** – Local automation using Power Automate Desktop.

3. **Business Process Flows** – Multi-step business automation processes.

4. **Shared Flows** – Flows shared with your team or colleagues.

You can filter and search for flows easily using the **search bar** or sorting options.

2.4 The Flow Editor (Building a Flow)

The **Flow Editor** is the core component where you design and modify automation workflows.

Key Components of the Flow Editor

- **Flow Name** – The title of your automation (editable at the top).

- **Trigger** – The event that starts the flow (e.g., receiving an email).

- **Actions** – Steps that execute based on the trigger (e.g., sending an email).

- **Conditions** – Logic that controls when specific actions are executed.

- **Parallel Branching** – Running multiple actions simultaneously.

- **Dynamic Content Panel** – Allows you to use variables, inputs, and outputs dynamically.

To **edit a flow**, simply click on any step to modify its parameters.

2.5 Flow Details Page

After creating a flow, the **Flow Details Page** provides insights into its execution and performance.

Key Features on the Flow Details Page

- **Run History** – View past executions and status (Success, Failed, Running).

- **Edit Flow** – Modify and update your workflow.

- **Turn On/Off** – Enable or disable the flow.

- **Share Flow** – Grant access to others.

- **Delete Flow** – Remove an unwanted flow.

2.6 Monitoring and Debugging Flows

The **Monitor** section allows you to track the performance of your flows and troubleshoot errors.

How to Monitor a Flow Execution

1. Navigate to **Monitor > Flow Runs**.

2. Click on a specific **run instance** to view detailed logs.

3. Identify **errors or bottlenecks** and fix them accordingly.

3. Customizing the Power Automate Interface

Power Automate allows for **personalization** to improve usability.

Changing the Theme

1. Click on your **profile icon** (top-right corner).

2. Select **Settings > Theme**.

3. Choose from **Light Mode, Dark Mode, or High Contrast**.

4. Best Practices for Navigating Power Automate Efficiently

To work efficiently in Power Automate, follow these best practices:

1. **Use Search and Filters** – Quickly locate flows by name or category.

2. **Organize Flows into Solutions** – For better management of complex automations.

3. **Leverage Templates** – Save time by modifying existing workflows instead of starting from scratch.

4. **Bookmark Frequently Used Pages** – Save direct links to "My Flows" and "Monitor" for quick access.

5. **Use Power Automate Mobile App** – Manage and monitor flows on the go.

5. Summary

Navigating the Power Automate interface is essential for creating and managing automation workflows effectively. By understanding the dashboard, flow editor, monitoring tools, and customization options, users can streamline their experience and maximize productivity.

In the next section, we will explore **Understanding Flows (2.2)**, where we will dive deeper into the different types of flows and their core components.

2.2 Understanding Flows

Microsoft Power Automate enables users to automate repetitive tasks and streamline business processes by creating **flows**. A **flow** is a series of steps that execute automatically based on specific triggers and conditions. Understanding how flows work is fundamental to using Power Automate effectively.

Flows in Power Automate can be categorized into three main types:

1. **Cloud Flows** – These are automated processes that run in the cloud and integrate with various online services.

2. **Desktop Flows** – These are designed for robotic process automation (RPA), enabling automation of tasks on a local machine.

3. **Business Process Flows** – These guide users through predefined processes to ensure consistency in business operations.

In this section, we will explore each type of flow, its use cases, and how to create and manage them.

2.2.1 Types of Flows: Cloud, Desktop, and Business Process Flows

1. Cloud Flows

Cloud Flows are the most commonly used type of flow in Power Automate. They run on Microsoft's cloud infrastructure and integrate with Microsoft 365, SharePoint, Outlook, OneDrive, Teams, as well as third-party services like Google Drive, Slack, and Salesforce.

1.1 Types of Cloud Flows

Cloud flows are categorized into three subtypes:

- **Automated Flows** – Triggered by an event (e.g., when an email arrives in Outlook).

- **Instant Flows** – Manually triggered by the user (e.g., clicking a button in Power Automate).

- **Scheduled Flows** – Run at specific times or intervals (e.g., a flow that runs every morning to send a report).

Automated Flows

Automated flows trigger when a specific event occurs in a connected service. These flows are commonly used to **automate repetitive tasks** such as:

- Sending an email notification when a new file is uploaded to a SharePoint folder.
- Creating a task in Microsoft Planner when an email is flagged in Outlook.
- Storing form responses from Microsoft Forms in an Excel file.

Instant Flows

Instant flows require **manual initiation** by the user. These flows are triggered by clicking a button in **Power Automate, Power Apps, or Microsoft Teams**. Examples include:

- Sending an approval request to a manager with a single click.
- Manually copying files between OneDrive and Google Drive.
- Sending pre-written responses in Teams or Outlook.

Scheduled Flows

Scheduled flows execute at predefined times or intervals, making them useful for **routine automation** such as:

- Sending a daily summary email of new sales orders.
- Backing up a SharePoint list to an Excel file every week.
- Running a database cleanup process every night.

1.2 How to Create a Cloud Flow

1. Go to **Power Automate (https://make.powerautomate.com/)**.

2. Click on **"Create"** and choose the desired type of cloud flow.

3. Select a **trigger** (e.g., "When an email arrives in Outlook").

4. Add **actions** (e.g., "Send an email to a manager").

5. Configure **conditions**, loops, or approvals as needed.

6. Save and **test** the flow.

2. Desktop Flows (RPA Flows)

Desktop Flows are designed for **Robotic Process Automation (RPA)**, allowing users to automate manual tasks on their local machines. Unlike Cloud Flows, which work with online services, Desktop Flows interact with **Windows applications, legacy systems, and web pages**.

When to Use Desktop Flows

Desktop flows are ideal for:

- Automating repetitive data entry tasks.

- Extracting data from PDF files or websites.

- Interacting with legacy applications that lack API support.

Creating a Desktop Flow

To create a Desktop Flow, you need to install **Power Automate Desktop**:

1. **Download and Install Power Automate Desktop**

   o Go to **Power Automate > Install Power Automate Desktop**.

   o Follow the installation instructions.

2. **Record Actions**

   o Click **"New Flow"** and open the flow editor.

   o Select **"Record Desktop Actions"** and interact with your applications.

3. **Add Steps and Logic**

   o Insert conditions, loops, and error handling.

4. **Test and Deploy**

   o Run the flow and refine as needed.

Example Use Case for Desktop Flows

- A user needs to extract invoice data from PDFs and input it into an Excel spreadsheet. A Desktop Flow can open each PDF, copy relevant data, and paste it into Excel automatically.

---

3. Business Process Flows (BPFs)

Business Process Flows (BPFs) guide users through structured multi-step processes to ensure consistency in business workflows. Unlike Cloud or Desktop Flows, BPFs provide a visual roadmap for completing tasks in applications like Microsoft Dynamics 365 and Power Apps.

Key Features of Business Process Flows

- Define **stages** (e.g., "Lead Qualification" in a sales pipeline).

- Include **required steps** to ensure compliance.

- Track progress and enforce **business rules**.

Example Use Cases for Business Process Flows

1. **Employee Onboarding Process**

    o Step 1: HR verifies new employee details.

    o Step 2: IT creates necessary accounts.

    o Step 3: Manager assigns training sessions.

2. **Customer Service Ticket Resolution**

    o Step 1: Receive a new ticket.

    o Step 2: Assign to an agent.

    o Step 3: Resolve the issue and close the ticket.

How to Create a Business Process Flow

1. Open **Power Automate** and go to **Business Process Flows**.

2. Click **"Create New"** and define the process **stages**.

3. Add **steps, conditions, and branching logic**.

4. Publish the flow and integrate it with Dynamics 365.

Summary

Understanding the different types of flows in Power Automate is key to choosing the right automation approach.

- **Cloud Flows** handle integrations with online services and can be automated, instant, or scheduled.

- **Desktop Flows** use RPA to automate tasks on local machines.

- **Business Process Flows** provide structured guidance for complex business processes.

By leveraging these different flow types, businesses and individuals can streamline operations, eliminate repetitive tasks, and improve efficiency.

2.2.2 Components of a Flow: Triggers, Actions, and Conditions

In Microsoft Power Automate, **flows** are built using three key components: **Triggers, Actions, and Conditions**. Understanding these components is essential for creating effective and automated workflows. Each component plays a crucial role in how a flow is initiated, executed, and controlled.

This section will guide you through the details of each component, explain their functionality, and provide practical examples to help you master the process of building workflows in Power Automate.

1. What are Triggers?

A **trigger** is an event that starts a flow. Every flow must begin with a trigger, which determines when and how the automation will be executed. Triggers can be categorized into three main types:

1.1 Types of Triggers

Instant Triggers (Manual Triggers)

These triggers require user intervention to start the flow. The user manually initiates the flow by clicking a button in Power Automate or another integrated platform like Microsoft Teams or Power Apps.

✅ *Example:*

- A flow triggered by a button in Power Automate to send an email to a predefined recipient.

- A mobile push notification that is manually triggered to send a reminder.

Automated Triggers (Event-Based Triggers)

These triggers are activated when a specific event occurs in a connected app or service. They continuously monitor for changes and execute the flow when the predefined event takes place.

✅*Example:*

- When a new email arrives in Outlook, a flow is triggered to save its attachments to OneDrive.

- When a new row is added to a SharePoint list, the flow updates a related Microsoft Excel file.

Scheduled Triggers

These triggers allow you to set up flows that run at predefined times or intervals. They are ideal for automating repetitive tasks that must be executed at specific times.

✅*Example:*

- A flow that runs every morning at 9:00 AM to generate a daily sales report.

- A flow that deletes temporary files from a folder every week to free up storage.

1.2 Commonly Used Triggers

Power Automate provides a wide variety of triggers that connect with Microsoft and third-party applications. Here are some frequently used triggers:

Trigger Type	Example Use Case
When an email arrives (Outlook, Gmail)	Automatically save attachments to OneDrive.
When a new row is added (Excel, SharePoint, SQL Database)	Send a notification to a team channel.
When a file is created or modified (OneDrive, Dropbox, Google Drive)	Back up the file to another location.
When a form response is submitted (Microsoft Forms, Google Forms)	Save the data to an Excel file and notify a team.

2. What are Actions?

An **action** is a step within a flow that performs a specific task. Actions are executed after a trigger is activated, allowing the flow to interact with different applications, manipulate data, or send notifications.

2.1 Types of Actions

Data Retrieval and Storage Actions

These actions involve retrieving, updating, or storing data in various platforms such as SharePoint, Excel, or databases.

✅*Example:*

- Retrieve a list of new tasks from Microsoft Planner and store them in an Excel sheet.

- Save email attachments from Outlook to Google Drive.

Messaging and Notification Actions

These actions send messages, alerts, or notifications through email, chat applications, or push notifications.

✅*Example:*

- Send an email alert when a new customer fills out a contact form.

- Post a message in a Microsoft Teams channel when a new order is placed.

File Management Actions

These actions allow you to create, modify, delete, or move files between cloud storage providers like OneDrive, SharePoint, or Dropbox.

✅*Example:*

- Rename and move newly uploaded files to a categorized folder.

- Convert Word documents to PDFs automatically and email them.

2.2 Commonly Used Actions

Action Type	Example Use Case
Send an email (Outlook, Gmail)	Notify a team when a new task is assigned.
Create a file (OneDrive, SharePoint, Google Drive)	Automatically save meeting notes.
Post a message (Teams, Slack, Twitter)	Send social media updates from an RSS feed.
Update a record (Excel, SQL, SharePoint List)	Modify a task status when marked as completed.

3. What are Conditions?

A **condition** is a decision-making component in Power Automate that controls the flow based on specific criteria. Conditions help direct a flow's path depending on whether certain conditions are met.

Types of Conditions

If-Else Conditions

These conditions allow you to define different actions based on whether a specified condition is true or false.

✓ *Example:*

- **If** an invoice amount is greater than $5000, send it for managerial approval.

- **Else**, process the invoice automatically.

Switch Conditions

A **Switch** condition evaluates a single variable and executes different actions depending on the value. It is useful when there are multiple possible outcomes.

✓ *Example:*

- If a customer selects "Billing Issue" in a support form, assign the case to the billing team.

- If the customer selects "Technical Issue," assign it to the IT team.

Loop Conditions (Apply to Each & Do Until)

These conditions repeat actions multiple times based on a defined criterion.

✅*Example:*

- Loop through a list of email addresses and send personalized messages to each recipient.

- Process each row in an Excel spreadsheet and update a database.

Common Use Cases for Conditions

Condition Type	Example Use Case
If-Else Condition	Check if an invoice amount exceeds $5000 before requiring approval.
Switch Condition	Assign a helpdesk request based on selected issue type.
Loop Condition	Iterate through all unread emails and move them to a folder.

4. Putting It All Together: Example Flow

Let's build a real-world example using Triggers, Actions, and Conditions:

Scenario:

A company wants to automate the process of responding to customer inquiries submitted via Microsoft Forms.

Flow Steps:

1. **Trigger:** "When a new response is submitted" in Microsoft Forms.

2. **Action:** Retrieve the response details.

3. **Condition:**

   - **If** the response is about "Billing," assign it to the Finance team.

   - **Else if** the response is about "Technical Support," assign it to the IT team.

   - **Else,** assign it to Customer Service.

4. **Action:** Send an automated email confirming receipt of the inquiry.

This flow ensures that inquiries are categorized and assigned automatically, saving time and improving efficiency.

5. Conclusion

Understanding **Triggers, Actions, and Conditions** is fundamental to building effective flows in Power Automate. By mastering these components, you can create powerful automations that save time, reduce manual work, and increase efficiency.

In the next section, we will explore **how to create your first flow from scratch**, guiding you through step-by-step instructions to build and execute a real-world automation.

2.2.3 Flow Structure and Execution

Microsoft Power Automate is built around **flows**, which are automated sequences of actions triggered by specific events. Understanding the structure of a flow and how it executes is crucial to designing efficient automation processes. This section will guide you through the core components of a flow's structure and how the execution process works.

1. Understanding Flow Structure

Every Power Automate flow follows a structured approach consisting of three main components:

1.1 Triggers

A **trigger** is the event that starts a flow. Triggers determine when and how a flow is executed. There are three main types of triggers:

- **Automated Triggers** – These run when a specific event occurs, such as receiving an email in Outlook or a new file being added to OneDrive.

- **Instant Triggers** – These require manual execution, such as pressing a button in a mobile app or selecting a command in Power Automate.

- **Scheduled Triggers** – These run at predefined intervals, such as every day at 8 AM or every Monday at noon.

Examples of Triggers in Action

- A flow triggered by a new email arriving in Outlook.

- A flow that starts when a new row is added to an Excel spreadsheet.

- A flow that runs every day at 7 AM to generate and send a report.

1.2 Actions

Actions are the steps executed after a trigger occurs. These steps define what the flow does with the triggered data. Common actions include:

- **Sending an email** (e.g., notifying a manager when a task is completed).

- **Updating a database** (e.g., adding a new row in SharePoint when a form is submitted).

- **Copying files** (e.g., moving a file from OneDrive to Google Drive).

Each action follows a structured execution, with the ability to reference dynamic content (data from the trigger or previous actions).

1.3 Conditions and Control Logic

Power Automate allows you to implement conditional logic to control the execution of a flow. This includes:

- **If-Else Conditions** – Executes different actions based on conditions.

- **Loops** – Runs a set of actions multiple times (e.g., processing a list of items).

- **Parallel Branching** – Executes multiple actions simultaneously to improve efficiency.

These logic-based controls help tailor flows to specific automation needs.

2. Flow Execution Process

Once a flow is triggered, it follows a sequential execution process, executing each step as per its structure. Here's a detailed breakdown of how a flow executes:

2.1 Flow Execution Lifecycle

Step 1: Trigger Activation

When the specified event occurs, the flow is activated. For example:

- If an **automated trigger** is used (e.g., receiving an email), the flow listens for incoming data and starts execution when the condition is met.

- If an **instant trigger** is used, the flow begins execution immediately upon user action.

- If a **scheduled trigger** is used, the flow starts at the predefined time.

Step 2: Data Collection and Processing

Once triggered, the flow captures data from the source. This data can be used dynamically in later steps. For example:

- A flow triggered by a **new email** will capture the sender, subject, and message body.

- A flow triggered by a **SharePoint list update** will collect the modified record's details.

Power Automate stores this data as **dynamic content**, which can be referenced in subsequent actions.

Step 3: Execution of Actions

After capturing data, Power Automate executes the sequence of actions. The execution order follows the flow's structure:

1. Actions are executed **sequentially** unless parallel branching is used.

2. If an action depends on dynamic content, it waits for data before execution.

3. If an action fails, error handling is triggered (if configured).

Example: A flow that sends a notification when a new file is uploaded to OneDrive follows this sequence:

1. Trigger: **New file added to OneDrive**.

2. Action: **Retrieve file details**.

3. Action: **Send an email notification with file details**.

Step 4: Conditional and Loop Execution

- If a **condition** is used, Power Automate checks the specified criteria before continuing.

- If a **loop** is used, actions within it are repeated until the condition is met.

- If **parallel branching** is used, multiple actions are executed simultaneously.

Example: A flow that processes new form submissions:

1. Trigger: **New Microsoft Forms submission received**.

2. Condition: **Check if submission includes an attachment**.

   - **If yes** → Save the attachment to OneDrive.

   - **If no** → Send an email requesting additional information.

3. Send a confirmation email to the user.

Step 5: Completion and Logging

Once all actions are executed, the flow reaches completion. Power Automate provides **run history logs**, which store details about execution time, action status, and potential errors. Users can monitor these logs to debug and optimize flows.

3. Best Practices for Flow Execution

Optimizing Flow Performance

- **Reduce Unnecessary Steps** – Remove redundant actions to improve execution speed.

- **Use Parallel Branching** – Execute independent actions simultaneously instead of sequentially.

- **Optimize API Calls** – Limit API-based actions to avoid hitting service limits.

Error Handling and Troubleshooting

- **Add Error Conditions** – Use "Run After" settings to define fallback actions in case of failure.

- **Implement Notifications for Failures** – Configure alerts for failed executions.

- **Use Flow Checker** – Power Automate's built-in tool detects common errors.

Ensuring Data Security

- **Use Secure Connections** – Ensure authentication credentials are stored securely.

- **Limit Flow Permissions** – Restrict access to sensitive data in shared flows.

- **Monitor Execution Logs** – Regularly review flow execution history to detect unauthorized access.

4. Example: End-to-End Flow Execution

Let's walk through an example of a fully structured flow:

Scenario:

A company wants to automatically process leave requests submitted via Microsoft Forms. The process involves:

1. Capturing the form submission.

2. Checking if the request is within the allowable leave balance.

3. Sending an approval request to the manager.

4. Notifying the employee of approval or rejection.

Flow Steps:

1. **Trigger:** "When a new response is submitted" (Microsoft Forms).

2. **Action:** "Get response details" to extract form data.

3. **Condition:** Check if the requested leave days exceed available balance.

   o **If yes:** Send rejection email to employee.

   o **If no:** Continue to next step.

4. **Action:** "Start an approval process" to request manager review.

5. **Condition:** If approval is granted, update HR records and notify the employee.

6. **Completion:** Log details in SharePoint and send confirmation.

Conclusion

Understanding the structure and execution of flows in Power Automate is key to creating **efficient, reliable, and scalable** automation solutions. By leveraging triggers, actions, conditions, and loops effectively, users can automate complex business processes with ease.

In the next section, we will explore **how to create your first Power Automate flow**, guiding you through template selection, configuration, and execution testing.

2.3 Creating Your First Flow

2.3.1 Choosing a Template vs. Building from Scratch

Microsoft Power Automate offers two primary ways to create automated workflows: using pre-built templates or building a flow from scratch. Choosing the right approach depends on your familiarity with Power Automate, the complexity of the workflow, and how much customization you need. In this section, we'll explore both options, their advantages and limitations, and step-by-step instructions for getting started.

1. Understanding the Two Approaches

Using a Template

Microsoft Power Automate provides a library of pre-configured templates that automate common business tasks. These templates serve as ready-made workflows that you can modify to fit your needs.

✅ **Advantages of Using Templates:**

- **Faster Implementation:** Saves time by providing a pre-built structure.

- **Beginner-Friendly:** Requires little to no prior knowledge of Power Automate.

- **Best Practices Built-In:** Designed by Microsoft or the Power Automate community, ensuring efficiency.

- **Customizable:** You can modify and add additional steps to meet specific needs.

✖ **Limitations of Using Templates:**

- **Less Flexibility:** May not fully match unique workflow requirements.

- **Predefined Triggers and Actions:** You may need to remove or modify existing steps.

- **May Require Additional Configuration:** Some templates rely on specific permissions or integrations that need to be set up manually.

Building a Flow from Scratch

This method allows you to define every aspect of your automation, from selecting triggers to configuring actions. It offers full control over the workflow but requires a better understanding of Power Automate's capabilities.

✓ **Advantages of Building from Scratch:**

- **Fully Customizable:** You define every step based on your exact needs.

- **Scalability:** Can be extended and modified as your processes evolve.

- **No Unnecessary Steps:** Unlike templates, there are no pre-existing actions that may need removal.

✗ **Limitations of Building from Scratch:**

- **Requires More Time:** You need to create and configure everything manually.

- **Learning Curve:** Users unfamiliar with Power Automate may find it overwhelming.

2. Getting Started with Power Automate Templates

If you're new to Power Automate, templates are a great way to start automating tasks without having to build a flow from scratch. Let's go through the process step by step.

Step 1: Accessing the Template Library

1. **Log in to Power Automate:**

   o   Go to Power Automate and sign in with your Microsoft account.

2. **Navigate to Templates:**

   o   On the left navigation panel, click **Templates** to browse available options.

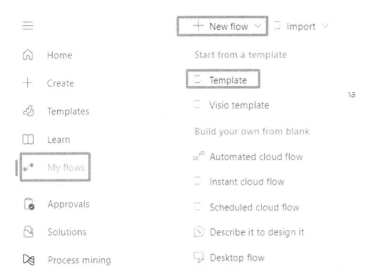

3. **Search for a Template:**

   o Use the search bar to find a template that matches your needs. For example,
   type **"Save email attachments to OneDrive"** if you want to automate file
   storage.

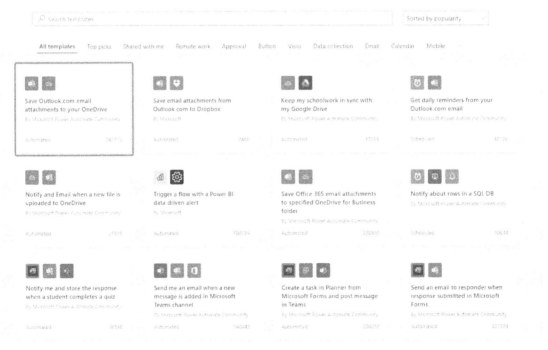

4. **Filter Templates by Category:**

   o   Power Automate organizes templates into categories such as Productivity, Notifications, Approvals, and Data Collection.

Step 2: Selecting and Configuring a Template

1. **Choose a Template:**

   o   Click on a template to view its details, including the apps it connects to and the workflow steps.

2. **Connect Required Services:**

   o   If the template requires access to apps like Outlook, SharePoint, or OneDrive, you'll need to grant permissions. Click **Continue** to proceed.

3. **Modify the Flow (If Needed):**

   o   You can customize the steps to fit your specific workflow by clicking on any action or trigger and adjusting its parameters.

Step 3: Saving and Testing the Template-Based Flow

1. **Save the Flow:**

  o Click **Save** to store your new automation.

2. **Test the Flow:**

  o Click **Test** (top-right corner) to ensure it works as expected. Follow the prompts to manually trigger the workflow or wait for the specified event.

3. **Monitor Flow Runs:**

  o Navigate to **My Flows** and select your flow to review run history and troubleshoot issues.

✦ **Example:** If you selected the "Save email attachments to OneDrive" template, Power Automate will automatically monitor incoming emails in Outlook and move attachments to a designated OneDrive folder.

3. Building a Flow from Scratch

For more advanced automation needs, building a flow from scratch gives you full control over triggers, actions, and workflow logic. Let's go through the step-by-step process.

Step 1: Creating a New Flow

1. **Navigate to My Flows:**

  o On the Power Automate dashboard, click **My Flows** in the left menu.

2. **Click on "New Flow":**

  o Select **+ New Flow** and choose the appropriate type:

    ▪ **Instant Flow:** Triggered manually by a button.

    ▪ **Automated Flow:** Runs when a specific event occurs.

    ▪ **Scheduled Flow:** Runs on a predefined schedule.

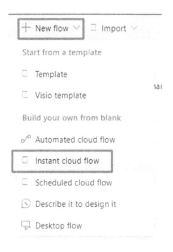

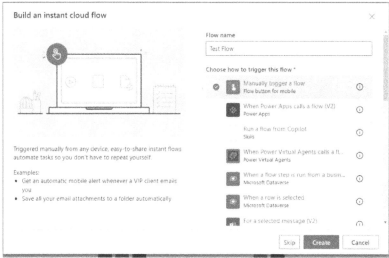

Step 2: Choosing a Trigger

Every flow starts with a trigger—an event that initiates the workflow.

1. **Select a Trigger Source:**

    o   Click **Choose a Trigger** and search for an app (e.g., Outlook, SharePoint, Forms).

2. **Define Trigger Conditions:**

    o Specify when the flow should start. For example:

        ▪ "When a new email arrives in Outlook"

        ▪ "When a file is added to OneDrive"

Step 3: Adding Actions to the Flow

After setting the trigger, define what the flow should do.

1. **Click on "+ New Step"**

   o Search for an action, such as:

      ▪ Sending an email

      ▪ Moving a file to OneDrive

      ▪ Posting a message in Microsoft Teams

2. **Configure Action Parameters:**

   o Specify details like recipient email addresses, file locations, or message content.

Step 4: Adding Conditions and Loops (Optional)

To create more advanced workflows, you can add conditions, loops, or approvals.

- **Conditions:** If/Then logic (e.g., "If email contains 'urgent,' then send a Teams notification").

- **Loops:** Run an action multiple times (e.g., "For each file in a folder, move to a new location").

Step 5: Saving and Testing the Flow

1. **Click "Save"** to store the flow.

2. **Test the Flow:** Click **Test** and follow the instructions to validate its behavior.

3. **Check Flow History:** Go to **My Flows → Run History** to troubleshoot any failures.

★ **Example:** If you create a flow from scratch that triggers when a new form response is submitted in Microsoft Forms, you can automatically save the response to an Excel file and send an email confirmation to the user.

4. When to Use Templates vs. Build from Scratch?

Factor	Use a Template	Build from Scratch
Ease of Use	Beginner-friendly	Requires familiarity with Power Automate
Customization	Limited customization	Fully customizable workflows
Time Required	Quick setup	Requires more setup time
Scalability	May not scale well	Easily scalable and expandable
Best For	Simple, common automations	Complex, unique workflows

Conclusion

Choosing between a template and building a flow from scratch depends on your specific needs. If you're just getting started, templates offer a quick and easy way to automate tasks. However, for more advanced, custom workflows, building from scratch provides greater flexibility and control.

Now that you understand these approaches, let's move on to **Configuring a Simple Flow** in the next section! 🚀

2.3.2 Configuring a Simple Flow

Now that you understand the basics of flows, it's time to configure your first simple flow in Microsoft Power Automate. This section will take you through the step-by-step process of creating, configuring, and customizing a basic automated workflow.

By the end of this section, you will have a working flow that automatically saves email attachments from Outlook to OneDrive. This example is one of the most commonly used Power Automate workflows, demonstrating how automation can streamline repetitive tasks.

1. Understanding the Structure of a Simple Flow

Before diving into the configuration, let's review the basic components of a flow:

- **Trigger:** The event that starts the flow (e.g., receiving an email with an attachment).

- **Action(s):** The steps that the flow performs after the trigger (e.g., saving the attachment to OneDrive).

- **Conditions (Optional):** Rules that determine how the flow should proceed under different circumstances.

For our example flow:

- **Trigger:** A new email with an attachment arrives in Outlook.

- **Action:** Save the email attachment to a designated OneDrive folder.

2. Setting Up a Flow from a Template vs. From Scratch

Power Automate allows you to create flows in two ways:

1. **Using a Pre-Built Template:** This is the fastest way to create a flow. Microsoft provides ready-made templates for common automation tasks.

2. **Building from Scratch:** This allows for more customization, letting you define each step yourself.

In this guide, we will **build a simple flow from scratch** to better understand how each component works.

3. Step-by-Step Guide to Configuring Your First Flow

Step 1: Access Power Automate

1. Open your web browser and go to Power Automate.

2. Sign in with your **Microsoft 365 account**.

3. Click on **Create** in the left sidebar to start a new flow.

Step 2: Choose a Trigger

1. Click **Automated Cloud Flow** (since we want the flow to trigger automatically when an email arrives).

2. Enter a name for your flow, such as **"Save Email Attachments to OneDrive"**.

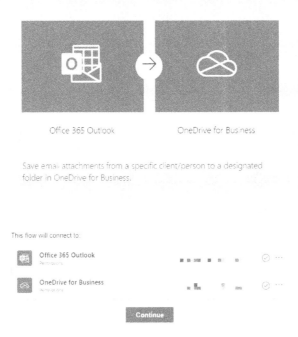

3. In the "Choose your flow's trigger" search bar, type **"When a new email arrives"** and select the **Outlook trigger**.

4. Click **Create** to proceed.

Step 3: Configure the Trigger

1. **Choose Your Email Account**: If prompted, sign in to your Outlook account and grant Power Automate the necessary permissions.

2. **Set Up Trigger Conditions:**

   - *Folder*: Select **Inbox** (or another folder if you prefer).

   - *Include Attachments*: Select **Yes** (since we only want emails with attachments).

   - *From*: (Optional) You can specify a sender if you only want attachments from a particular person.

   - *Subject Filter*: (Optional) You can specify a keyword to filter emails.

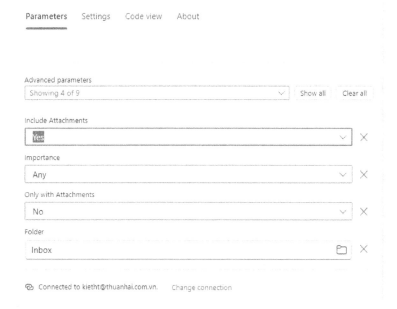

Click **Next Step** to proceed.

Step 4: Add an Action (Save Attachments to OneDrive)

1. Click **+ New Step** and search for "OneDrive for Business".

2. Select **"Create file"** (this action will save the email attachments to OneDrive).

3. Configure the action:

   o **Folder Path:** Choose or create a folder in OneDrive (e.g., "/Email Attachments").

   o **File Name:** Click in the field and select **"Attachments Name"** from dynamic content.

   o **File Content:** Click in the field and select **"Attachments Content"** from dynamic content.

Your flow now has a trigger (email received) and an action (saving attachments to OneDrive).

Step 5: Testing the Flow

1. Click **Save** to store your flow configuration.

2. Click **Test** in the top right corner.

3. Select **Manually trigger a test** and click **Test**.

4. Send yourself an email with an attachment.

5. Check OneDrive to see if the attachment appears in the specified folder.

4. Enhancing the Flow with Additional Features

Once your basic flow is working, you can improve it by adding:

Adding Conditions to Filter Attachments

You may not want to save every email attachment. To filter attachments:

1. Click **+ New Step** and search for **Condition**.

2. Set the condition:

   o In the first box, choose **Attachment Name**.

   o Select **"ends with"** from the dropdown.

   o Enter **".pdf"** (this will only save PDF files).

3. Under **If yes**, leave the OneDrive action as is.

4. Under **If no**, add a step to send yourself a notification about the skipped file.

Adding a Notification for Successful File Uploads

To receive a Teams or email notification when an attachment is saved:

1. Click **+ New Step** and search for "Send a message".

2. Choose **Microsoft Teams - Post a message** or **Outlook - Send an email**.

3. Enter your message, such as:
   "A new attachment from [Email Sender] has been saved to OneDrive."

Automatically Organizing Attachments by Date

Instead of saving all files in one folder, create subfolders by date:

1. Modify the **Folder Path** field in the OneDrive action.

2. Use **dynamic content** to add the date, e.g.:
   "/Email Attachments/" + formatDateTime(utcNow(), 'yyyy-MM-dd')

3. This ensures attachments are saved in separate folders by date.

5. Troubleshooting Common Issues

Issue 1: The Flow Does Not Trigger

- Ensure your Outlook account is correctly connected.

- Check the **Inbox** folder settings in the trigger.

- Verify that the test email meets the filter conditions.

Issue 2: Attachments Are Not Saving in OneDrive

- Ensure the OneDrive folder exists.

- Check that the **Attachment Content** field is mapped correctly.

- Verify that the file is not too large (Power Automate has size limits).

Issue 3: Flow is Running Slowly

- Reduce unnecessary steps and conditions.

- Optimize the trigger settings to avoid processing too many emails.

- Upgrade to a higher Power Automate plan if performance remains an issue.

6. Summary and Next Steps

In this section, you learned how to:

✓ Configure a simple Power Automate flow from scratch.

✓ Use triggers and actions to automate email attachment management.

✓ Enhance your flow with conditions and notifications.

✓ Troubleshoot common issues to ensure smooth execution.

Now that you have successfully built and tested your first automated flow, you are ready to explore more advanced features in Power Automate. In the next sections, we will dive deeper into **workflow logic, error handling, and integration with third-party applications.**

2.3.3 Testing and Running a Flow

After building your first Power Automate flow, the next crucial step is to test and run it. Testing ensures that your flow functions as expected, while running it allows it to execute automatically when triggered. This section will guide you through the step-by-step process of testing and running a flow, identifying potential issues, troubleshooting errors, and optimizing your flow for reliable performance.

1. Understanding Flow Execution

Before testing a flow, it's important to understand how Power Automate executes flows:

- **Trigger Activation:** The flow starts executing when the trigger conditions are met.

- **Action Processing:** Each action in the flow is processed sequentially or conditionally, depending on the logic.

- **Data Input & Output:** Data passes through different actions, where it can be modified, stored, or sent to external applications.

- **Completion or Failure:** The flow either completes successfully or encounters an error, requiring troubleshooting.

2. Running a Flow Manually

One of the simplest ways to test a flow is to run it manually before automating it fully.

2.1 Steps to Run a Flow Manually

1. **Navigate to Power Automate**

   o Sign in to Power Automate.

   o Click on **My flows** in the left menu.

   o Locate the flow you want to test.

2. **Start the Flow Manually**

   o Click on the flow to open its details.

   o Click **Run** or **Test** (depending on whether it has been saved and edited).

   o If your flow has a manual trigger (such as a button press), follow the instructions to provide the necessary input.

3. **Monitor Execution**

   o Power Automate will display the execution steps in real time.

   o If the flow runs successfully, you will see a **green checkmark** for each step.

   o If the flow fails, Power Automate will highlight the failed step and provide an error message.

3. Testing a Flow in Power Automate

Power Automate offers different ways to test a flow before full deployment.

Using the Test Feature in Power Automate

Power Automate provides a built-in **Test** option to simulate real-world execution.

Steps to Test a Flow

1. **Open Your Flow**

   o Navigate to **My flows** and select the flow you want to test.

2. **Click the Test Button**

   o Inside the flow editor, click **Test** (top-right corner).

3. **Choose a Test Method**

   o **Manually Triggered Flows**: Run the flow manually and provide sample data if required.

   o **Automatically Triggered Flows**: Select a previous successful run to test with existing data.

4. **Review Test Results**

   o Each step will be marked as **Successful (✓)** or **Failed (✗)**.

   o If an error occurs, click on the failed step to view detailed logs and suggestions.

---

4. Debugging and Troubleshooting Flow Errors

Testing may reveal issues that need to be addressed before full automation. Here's how to troubleshoot common problems.

Common Flow Errors and How to Fix Them

Error Type	Cause	Solution
Trigger Not Firing	Incorrect configuration or missing input	Verify trigger conditions and required data
Action Fails	API or service error	Check authentication, permissions, and service availability

Error Type	Cause	Solution
Data Not Passed Correctly	Missing dynamic content	Ensure correct variable usage and data mapping
Flow Runs But Does Not Perform Expected Actions	Logic errors or incorrect conditions	Use **Conditions**, **Scopes**, and **Parallel Branching** for control
Too Many Flow Runs	Infinite loop or frequent triggering	Add rate limits or configure trigger filters

5. Reviewing Flow Run History

To analyze how your flow performs over time, Power Automate stores execution history.

How to View Flow Run History

1. **Go to My Flows**

    o   Select the flow you want to review.

2. **Click on Run History**

    o   The **Run History** section displays all executions.

    o   Successful runs are marked **green**, while failed ones are **red**.

3. **Check Execution Details**

    o   Click on any execution to see step-by-step logs, data processed, and any errors encountered.

6. Optimizing Your Flow for Better Performance

Once your flow is tested and running, you can optimize it for better efficiency.

Best Practices for Running Flows Efficiently

- **Reduce Unnecessary Actions**: Remove redundant steps to improve performance.

- **Use Parallel Processing**: Run independent tasks simultaneously where possible.

- **Minimize API Calls**: Reduce the number of calls to external services.

- **Add Error Handling**: Use **Try-Catch** logic to handle failures gracefully.

- **Use Environment Variables**: Store settings centrally instead of hardcoding them in the flow.

7. Automating the Flow Execution

Once testing is successful, you can set your flow to run automatically:

- **For Automated Flows**: Ensure that the trigger is correctly set up (e.g., new email, file upload, etc.).

- **For Scheduled Flows**: Define execution intervals (e.g., every hour, daily, weekly).

- **For Button-Triggered Flows**: Share the flow with users who need to execute it manually.

8. Conclusion

Testing and running a flow in Power Automate is a crucial step in ensuring reliable automation. By following the steps outlined in this section, you can confidently execute your flow, troubleshoot potential issues, and optimize performance for real-world use.

Now that you understand how to test and run flows, you are ready to explore more advanced automation techniques in the next sections of this book!

PART III
Understanding Triggers and Actions

3.1 What are Triggers?

In Microsoft Power Automate, **triggers** are the foundation of any automated workflow. A trigger is an event that starts a flow, determining when and how the automation process begins. Every flow in Power Automate must have a trigger, which listens for specific conditions and initiates actions accordingly.

Triggers can come from various sources, such as emails, databases, cloud storage services, or even user interactions. Microsoft Power Automate provides three main types of triggers:

1. **Instant Triggers** – Manually triggered by a user.

2. **Automated Triggers** – Activated by an external event (e.g., receiving an email).

3. **Scheduled Triggers** – Run at predefined times or intervals.

Understanding how triggers work is crucial for designing effective automation workflows. In this section, we will explore **instant triggers**, which allow users to manually start flows when needed.

3.1.1 Instant Triggers

What are Instant Triggers?

Instant triggers, also known as **manual triggers**, allow users to start a flow **on demand**. Unlike automated triggers, which rely on external events, instant triggers require a user action—such as clicking a button in Power Automate, Power Apps, or Microsoft Teams—to begin the workflow.

Instant triggers are useful when users need to execute tasks as needed rather than relying on an event occurring in the background. Some common scenarios include:

- Sending an approval request when a user clicks a button.
- Manually transferring files between systems.
- Running a report whenever needed.
- Posting a message to a Microsoft Teams channel.

Power Automate provides several built-in instant triggers that users can configure in different environments.

Types of Instant Triggers in Power Automate

Power Automate offers a variety of instant triggers, each designed to suit different user needs. Below are some of the most commonly used instant triggers:

1. Manually Trigger a Flow

The **"Manually trigger a flow"** trigger allows users to start a flow by clicking a button inside Power Automate. This is one of the most flexible and widely used instant triggers.

📌 **Example Use Case**:

- A salesperson needs to generate a sales report on demand. Instead of waiting for a scheduled report, they can click a button in Power Automate to run the flow and receive the report instantly.

📌 **How to Set It Up**:

1. Open **Power Automate** and click **Create → Instant cloud flow**.
2. Select **Manually trigger a flow** as the trigger.
3. Click **Create**, and add actions as needed.

2. Power Apps Button Trigger

The **Power Apps trigger** allows users to start a flow from within a **Power Apps application**. This is useful when integrating automation into a business application.

📌 **Example Use Case**:

- A company's HR team uses a Power Apps form for employee leave requests. When an employee submits the form, they click a button that triggers a Power Automate flow to process the request.

📌 **How to Set It Up**:

1. In **Power Automate**, create an **Instant cloud flow**.

2. Select **Power Apps (V2)** as the trigger.

3. Define the actions the flow should execute.

4. Link the flow to a button inside a Power Apps form.

3. Microsoft Teams Button Trigger

Users can start a Power Automate flow **directly from Microsoft Teams** using a button. This is useful for automating tasks within a team collaboration environment.

📌 **Example Use Case**:

- A manager needs to send a team announcement quickly. Instead of composing a message every time, they can click a button in Microsoft Teams that triggers a pre-configured flow to send the announcement.

📌 **How to Set It Up**:

1. Open **Power Automate** and create a new **Instant cloud flow**.

2. Choose **For a selected message (Microsoft Teams)** as the trigger.

3. Define the flow actions (e.g., sending a reply or forwarding a message).

4. Deploy the flow for use within Teams.

Building an Instant Trigger Flow: Step-by-Step Example

To demonstrate how to use instant triggers, let's walk through a **real-world example** of setting up a flow that allows a user to manually trigger an email notification.

Scenario:

Imagine you work in a **customer support team**, and you need to **send an urgent email notification** to a manager when an important issue arises. Instead of writing a manual email every time, you create a **Power Automate flow** that sends a pre-written email when you click a button.

Steps to Create the Flow

1. **Open Power Automate**

   o Navigate to Power Automate.

   o Click **Create** → **Instant cloud flow**.

2. **Select the Trigger**

   o Choose **Manually trigger a flow** as the trigger.

   o Click **Create** to continue.

3. **Add Input Fields (Optional)**

   o If you want the user to provide input (e.g., a custom message), click **Add an input**.

   o Choose **Text** and name it **Issue Description**.

4. **Add an Action (Send an Email)**

   o Click **New step** → Search for "Send an email (V2)".

   o Choose **Office 365 Outlook** → **Send an email (V2)**.

   o Configure the email fields:

      ▪ **To**: Enter the manager's email.

      ▪ **Subject**: "Urgent Customer Issue"

      ▪ **Body**: Include **Issue Description** (the user input).

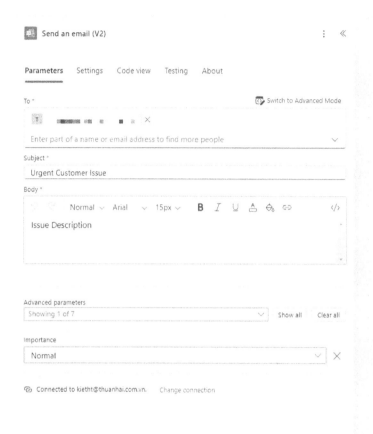

5. **Save and Test the Flow**

   ○   Click **Save** and then **Test**.

   ○   Click the **Run Flow** button and enter test data.

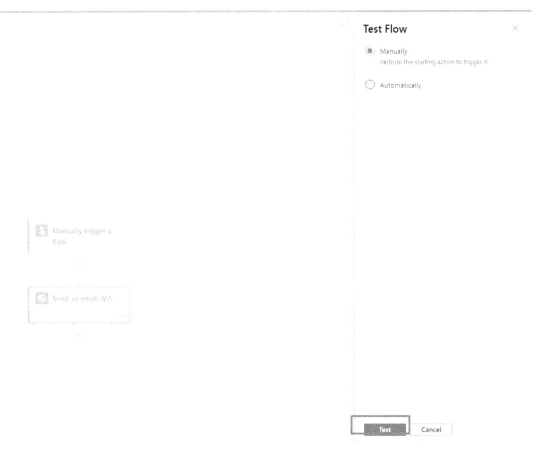

Run flow   ×

Your flow run successfully started. To monitor it,
go to the Flow Runs Page.

Done

6. **Deploy and Use**

- Users can now access the flow in **Power Automate** and trigger it manually whenever needed.

Best Practices for Using Instant Triggers

To ensure efficient and reliable workflows, follow these best practices when using instant triggers:

✓ **Keep Flows Simple**: Avoid overly complex instant-triggered flows. Keep them straightforward to ensure quick execution.

✓ **Use User Input Wisely**: If the flow requires user input, keep the fields minimal and relevant.

✓ **Optimize for Mobile Users**: Instant flows should be mobile-friendly for quick execution via the **Power Automate mobile app**.

✓ **Secure Sensitive Data**: If triggering workflows involving sensitive data, use **role-based access control** (RBAC) and **data protection policies**.

☑ **Monitor Flow Usage**: Regularly check **flow analytics** in Power Automate to optimize execution and troubleshoot any issues.

Conclusion

Instant triggers provide **on-demand** automation capabilities, making workflows more flexible and user-driven. Whether starting a flow from Power Automate, Power Apps, or Microsoft Teams, instant triggers help streamline repetitive tasks and improve efficiency.

By mastering **instant triggers**, users can take full control of their automation needs, reducing manual work and enabling fast, reliable workflows in everyday tasks.

Next, we'll explore **automated triggers**, which allow Power Automate to execute flows automatically when specific conditions are met.

3.1.2 Automated Triggers

Introduction to Automated Triggers

Automated triggers are one of the most powerful features in Microsoft Power Automate. Unlike **instant triggers**, which require a manual initiation, or **scheduled triggers**, which execute at a fixed time, automated triggers activate **automatically** based on specific events occurring in connected apps or services.

For example, an automated trigger can fire when:

- A new email arrives in Outlook.

- A new file is uploaded to OneDrive.

- A form response is submitted in Microsoft Forms.

- A new record is created in SharePoint, Dataverse, or a CRM system.

These triggers allow workflows to respond in real-time, eliminating the need for users to monitor systems manually.

How Automated Triggers Work

1. Event-Driven Execution

Automated triggers rely on event-based monitoring. Power Automate continuously listens for changes in specified data sources. When a matching event occurs, the trigger is activated, and the associated flow executes.

2. Connection to External Services

Power Automate supports a wide variety of external applications and cloud services through **connectors**. Each connector has predefined triggers that respond to specific changes in data. Some popular services include:

- **Microsoft 365 Apps** (Outlook, SharePoint, OneDrive, Teams)
- **Third-Party Services** (Google Drive, Dropbox, Twitter, Slack)
- **Business Applications** (Salesforce, Dynamics 365, SAP)

3. Types of Automated Triggers

Automated triggers can be broadly categorized into three types:

1. **Data Change Triggers** – Activated when data is added, updated, or deleted.
2. **New Item Triggers** – Activated when a new item or record is created.
3. **System Event Triggers** – Activated by external system notifications or API calls.

Examples of Common Automated Triggers

Power Automate provides numerous automated triggers across different services. Let's explore some of the most commonly used ones.

1. Email-Based Triggers

Trigger: "When a new email arrives" (Outlook or Gmail)

This trigger activates when a new email is received in the specified inbox. It can be customized with filters such as:

- **Sender Address** – Only trigger when emails come from a specific sender.
- **Subject Line** – Only trigger if the email contains specific words.
- **Attachments** – Only trigger if the email includes an attachment.

💡 **Use Case:**

- Automatically save email attachments to **OneDrive** or **SharePoint**.

- Send a **Teams notification** when a critical email arrives.

- Forward specific emails to another department.

Trigger: "When an email is flagged" (Outlook)

This trigger activates when you manually flag an email in Outlook.

💡 **Use Case:**

- Convert flagged emails into **tasks in Microsoft Planner**.

- Automatically create a **follow-up reminder in Microsoft To Do**.

2. File-Based Triggers

Trigger: "When a file is created" (OneDrive, SharePoint, Google Drive, Dropbox)

This trigger runs when a new file is added to a designated folder.

💡 **Use Case:**

- Automatically back up new files from OneDrive to a **secondary cloud storage**.

- Notify a **team channel in Microsoft Teams** when a document is uploaded.

- Move **PDF files to a "Processed" folder** once they are reviewed.

Trigger: "When a file is modified" (OneDrive, SharePoint)

💡 **Use Case:**

- Send a notification when a **contract or report is updated**.

- Maintain a **version history log in Excel**.

3. Form-Based Triggers

Trigger: "When a new response is submitted" (Microsoft Forms, Google Forms)

This trigger activates when someone submits a form response.

💡 **Use Case:**

- Save form responses to a **SharePoint list or Excel sheet**.
- Automatically send a **confirmation email to the respondent**.
- Create a **follow-up task in Planner**.

---

4. Database and Record-Based Triggers

Trigger: "When an item is created or modified" (SharePoint, Dataverse, SQL Server)

💡 **Use Case:**

- Update a **Power BI dashboard when new data is added**.
- Notify the sales team when a **new lead is created in Dynamics 365**.

Trigger: "When a record is deleted" (Dataverse, Salesforce)

💡 **Use Case:**

- Log deletions for compliance purposes.
- Send a **deletion confirmation to the administrator**.

---

5. Social Media and External App Triggers

Trigger: "When a new tweet is posted" (Twitter)

💡 **Use Case:**

- Automatically **save tweets mentioning your brand** to an Excel sheet.
- Notify the marketing team when a **negative tweet is detected**.

Trigger: "When a message is posted in a Slack channel"

💡 **Use Case:**

- Forward important Slack messages to an **email inbox**.

Configuring an Automated Trigger in Power Automate

Step 1: Create a New Flow

1. Open **Power Automate**.

2. Click **Create** > **Automated cloud flow**.

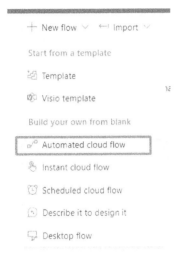

Step 2: Choose a Trigger

1. Search for a trigger (e.g., **"When a new email arrives"**).

2. Select the correct service (Outlook, Gmail, etc.).

3. Click **Create**.

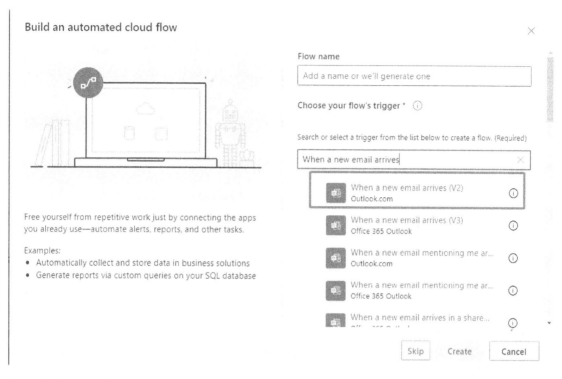

Build an automated cloud flow

Free yourself from repetitive work just by connecting the apps you already use—automate alerts, reports, and other tasks.

Examples:
- Automatically collect and store data in business solutions
- Generate reports via custom queries on your SQL database

Flow name

Add a name or we'll generate one

Choose your flow's trigger * ⓘ

Search or select a trigger from the list below to create a flow. (Required)

When a new email arrives

When a new email arrives (V2)
Outlook.com

When a new email arrives (V3)
Office 365 Outlook

When a new email mentioning me ar...
Outlook.com

When a new email mentioning me ar...
Office 365 Outlook

When a new email arrives in a share...

Skip   Create   Cancel

Step 3: Customize Trigger Settings

1. Define conditions (e.g., filter emails by subject or sender).

2. Set **folder locations** for file-based triggers.

3. Specify **event parameters** for database triggers.

Step 4: Add Actions to Process the Trigger Event

- Choose an action (e.g., send an email, save to SharePoint).

- Configure the action settings.

Step 5: Save and Test the Flow

- Click **Save** and run a test to verify the trigger behavior.

Best Practices for Using Automated Triggers

1. Minimize Unnecessary Trigger Activations

- Use filters to ensure the flow **only triggers when necessary**.

- Avoid selecting **"All Emails"** for email triggers—target specific folders.

2. Monitor and Optimize Flow Performance

- Check the **Flow Run History** to analyze performance.

- Use **delay actions** if the system processes too fast.

3. Handle Errors and Exceptions

- Use **"Try-Catch" error handling** to manage failures.

- Enable **retry policies** for unstable external services.

Conclusion

Automated triggers in Power Automate allow workflows to run **seamlessly in response to real-time events**. By leveraging different triggers—such as emails, file uploads, database updates, and social media activities—you can build **smart, time-saving automations** that enhance productivity.

Whether you're automating **email processing**, **document management**, or **customer interactions**, automated triggers provide the foundation for a **fully connected and efficient workflow system**.

3.1.3 Scheduled Triggers

Introduction to Scheduled Triggers

Scheduled triggers in Microsoft Power Automate allow users to automate workflows at predefined times or recurring intervals. Unlike instant triggers (which require manual activation) or automated triggers (which respond to external events), scheduled triggers execute based on a set schedule, making them ideal for repetitive, time-sensitive tasks.

For example, you can use scheduled triggers to:

- Run daily, weekly, or monthly reports.

- Perform routine data synchronization between systems.

- Send automated reminders or notifications.

- Archive emails or documents at the end of each business day.

- Generate and distribute status reports at a fixed time.

This section will explore how scheduled triggers work, how to configure them, and best practices for ensuring efficient and error-free automation.

How Scheduled Triggers Work

A scheduled trigger in Power Automate is a **time-based execution mechanism**. When you create a flow with a scheduled trigger, Power Automate runs it at the specified intervals without requiring user input or external system events.

Scheduled triggers rely on the **Recurrence** trigger, which defines the frequency and specific conditions under which the flow should execute. The Recurrence trigger is flexible and allows customization in terms of:

- **Frequency** – The time interval at which the flow runs (e.g., every minute, hour, day, week, or month).

- **Start Time** – The specific time when the flow should begin execution.

- **Time Zone** – Ensuring the flow runs in the correct time zone.

- **Advanced Scheduling Options** – Defining complex scheduling patterns such as running a flow on specific weekdays or the last day of the month.

Configuring a Scheduled Trigger in Power Automate

Step 1: Creating a Flow with a Scheduled Trigger

1. **Open Power Automate** – Log in to Power Automate using your Microsoft account.

2. **Click on "Create"** – This will present different flow types.

3. **Select "Scheduled cloud flow"** – This will open a configuration window for the scheduled trigger.

4. **Enter Flow Name** – Provide a meaningful name (e.g., "Daily Data Backup").

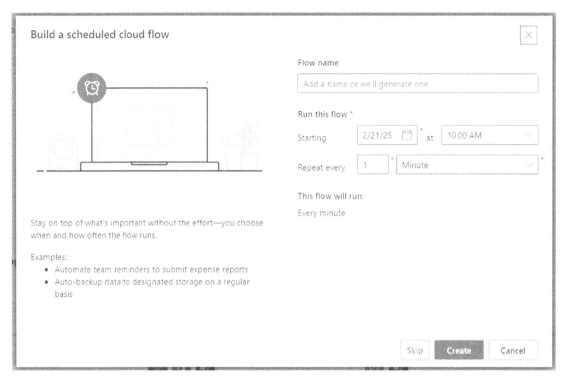

Step 2: Setting Up the Recurrence Trigger

Once inside the flow editor, you will need to configure the Recurrence trigger:

- **Choose Frequency** – Select how often the flow should run (Minute, Hour, Day, Week, Month).

- **Set Interval** – Define the interval between each execution (e.g., every 1 hour or every 7 days).

- **Select Start Time** – If required, specify the exact time when the flow should begin execution.

- **Set Time Zone** – Ensures the execution time aligns with your desired timezone.

Example: Running a Flow Every Day at 6 AM

- Frequency: **Day**

- Interval: **1** (Every day)

- Start Time: **06:00 AM**

- Time Zone: **Pacific Standard Time (PST)**

Step 3: Configuring Additional Scheduling Options

Power Automate offers more control over execution times using advanced scheduling features.

- **Running on Specific Days of the Week**

  o Example: Run only on Mondays, Wednesdays, and Fridays.

  o Configuration:

    - Frequency: **Week**

    - Interval: **1**

    - Days: **Monday, Wednesday, Friday**

- **Running on the Last Day of the Month**

  o Example: Generate and send a financial report on the last day of every month.

  o Configuration:

    - Frequency: **Month**

    - Interval: **1**

    - Days: **Last Day of Month**

- **Skipping Weekends**

- o Example: Run a report only on weekdays.

- o Configuration:

  - Use the "Condition" action inside the flow to check if the current day is a weekend.

Step 4: Adding Actions to the Flow

Once the trigger is set, you need to define **actions** that should be executed. Some common use cases include:

- **Sending automated reports** – Generate a summary and email it.

- **Updating a SharePoint list** – Append data from a database to a SharePoint list.

- **Archiving old emails** – Move emails to a different folder or export them to OneDrive.

- **Triggering approval workflows** – Start an approval process at the start of each business week.

Example: Sending a Daily Email Summary

1. **Add a new action**: Select "Send an email (Outlook)"

2. **Set recipient**: Enter an email address.

3. **Define email subject**: Example: "Daily Sales Report"

4. **Set email body**: Use dynamic content to pull data from a database or an Excel file.

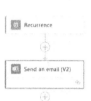

Step 5: Testing and Running the Flow

Before deploying the flow, it's essential to test it:

- **Run a manual test** – Execute the flow once to check for issues.

- **Monitor execution history** – View past runs in the Power Automate dashboard.

- **Check for errors** – Use logs to identify and fix issues.

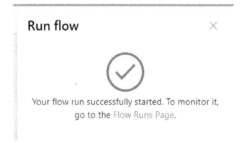

Best Practices for Using Scheduled Triggers

1. Optimize Flow Performance

- Avoid running flows too frequently to prevent unnecessary API calls.

- Use filters to limit execution scope.

2. Consider API and Service Limits

- Many services have rate limits; excessive requests can result in throttling.
- Group similar tasks to reduce the number of calls.

3. Implement Error Handling

- Add a "Retry Policy" to handle transient errors.
- Use "Scope" actions to isolate and manage failures.

4. Manage Time Zones Correctly

- Ensure your flow operates in the correct time zone, especially for international workflows.
- Use dynamic expressions to adjust times if necessary.

5. Secure Sensitive Data

- Avoid hardcoding credentials.
- Use environment variables to store sensitive information.

Real-World Use Cases for Scheduled Triggers

Use Case 1: Automating Weekly Reports

A sales team needs to generate and send a report every Monday at 9 AM. A Power Automate flow can:

1. Extract data from an Excel file stored in OneDrive.
2. Format the data into a table.
3. Send the report via email to stakeholders.

Use Case 2: Archiving Emails at the End of Each Month

A company wants to automatically archive emails older than 30 days into a SharePoint folder.

1. The flow runs on the last day of every month.

2. It searches Outlook for emails older than 30 days.

3. It moves selected emails to an "Archived Emails" folder in SharePoint.

Use Case 3: Daily Database Cleanup

A system administrator wants to clear temporary database entries every night at midnight.

1. The flow runs daily at 12:00 AM.

2. It deletes entries older than 24 hours.

3. It logs actions into a tracking sheet.

Conclusion

Scheduled triggers are one of the most powerful automation tools in Power Automate. By leveraging **time-based execution**, users can eliminate manual work, improve efficiency, and ensure critical tasks run reliably without human intervention.

In the next section, we will explore **common triggers** used in Power Automate, such as email-based triggers, SharePoint triggers, and external app triggers, to further expand your automation capabilities.

3.2 Commonly Used Triggers

3.2.1 Email-Based Triggers (Outlook, Gmail)

Email is one of the most common communication tools used in businesses and personal workflows. Microsoft Power Automate allows users to automate email-related tasks using triggers from email services like Outlook and Gmail. These triggers help streamline repetitive processes, ensuring that actions occur automatically when specific email conditions are met.

In this section, we will explore:

- How email-based triggers work

- The different types of email triggers available in Power Automate

- How to set up email triggers for Outlook and Gmail

- Common use cases for email automation

- Best practices for handling email triggers

Understanding Email-Based Triggers

An email-based trigger in Power Automate is an event that activates a flow when an email-related action occurs. For example, you can configure a trigger to start a flow when:

- You receive a new email in your inbox

- An email is received from a specific sender

- A new email contains an attachment

- A flagged email is detected

- A specific keyword appears in the email subject

Power Automate supports triggers for multiple email providers, with Microsoft Outlook and Gmail being the most commonly used services. The flexibility of these triggers allows users to create custom workflows based on their business or personal needs.

Types of Email-Based Triggers in Power Automate

Power Automate provides different types of email-based triggers for both Outlook and Gmail. These triggers fall into three main categories:

1. New Email Received

This is one of the most commonly used triggers in Power Automate. It activates a flow whenever a new email arrives in a specific inbox or folder.

- **Trigger name:** *When a new email arrives (V3)*

- **Available for:** Outlook, Gmail

- **Configuration options:**

    o   Specify the folder where the email should arrive (Inbox, Custom Folder)

    o   Define whether the email should be unread or read

    o   Filter based on importance (High, Normal, Low)

    o   Set conditions for attachments (Include or exclude)

Example Use Case: A business receives hundreds of customer support emails daily. With this trigger, a Power Automate flow can scan incoming emails for specific keywords (e.g., "urgent") and automatically assign them to a support agent in Microsoft Teams.

2. New Email from a Specific Sender

This trigger activates when a new email arrives from a defined sender or email address.

- **Trigger name:** *When a new email arrives from a specific sender*

- **Available for:** Outlook, Gmail

- **Configuration options:**

    o   Specify one or multiple sender email addresses

    o   Choose the destination folder

    o   Apply additional filters like importance or subject keywords

Example Use Case: A sales team wants to track emails from key customers. Using this trigger, a flow can log every new email from a high-value client into a SharePoint list for record-keeping.

3. New Email with Attachments

This trigger starts a flow whenever a new email arrives that includes an attachment.

- **Trigger name:** *When a new email arrives with an attachment*

- **Available for:** Outlook, Gmail

- **Configuration options:**

    o   Define file types to filter (PDF, Excel, Word, etc.)

    o   Set a minimum file size condition

    o   Choose a folder for the email filter

Example Use Case: A finance department receives invoices via email. This trigger can automatically save attachments (PDF invoices) to a designated OneDrive folder and notify the accounting team in Microsoft Teams.

4. New Email with Specific Keywords

This trigger activates when a new email contains specific words or phrases in the subject or body.

- **Trigger name:** *When an email with a specific subject arrives*

- **Available for:** Outlook, Gmail

- **Configuration options:**

    o   Define keywords or phrases to look for

    o   Apply conditions to check for multiple words

    o   Choose a destination folder

Example Use Case: A recruitment team wants to track job applications. This trigger can scan for subject lines containing "Job Application" and forward them to the HR database automatically.

5. Flagged Email Detection

This trigger activates when a user marks an email as "Flagged" in their inbox.

- **Trigger name:** *When an email is flagged*

- **Available for:** Outlook

- **Configuration options:**

  o Define flag categories

  o Choose specific folders to monitor

Example Use Case: A project manager flags important emails for follow-up. This trigger can automatically create a task in Microsoft Planner whenever a flagged email is detected.

Setting Up an Email-Based Trigger in Power Automate

Now, let's go through a step-by-step guide to creating an email-triggered flow in Power Automate.

Step 1: Open Power Automate

1. Navigate to Power Automate.

2. Sign in with your Microsoft or Gmail account.

Step 2: Create a New Flow

1. Click **Create** on the left panel.

2. Choose **Automated Cloud Flow** (since email-based triggers are automatic).

Step 3: Choose an Email Trigger

1. In the "Choose a flow's trigger" search bar, type "email."

2. Select the appropriate trigger, e.g., "When a new email arrives (V3)" for Outlook.

3. Click **Create** to proceed.

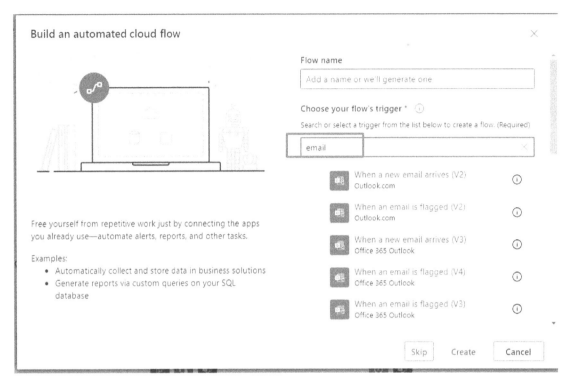

Step 4: Configure the Trigger Settings

1. Select your email provider (Outlook or Gmail).

2. Define the folder (Inbox, Custom Folder).

3. Apply filters (Sender, Subject, Attachments).

4. Click **Save** to finalize the trigger settings.

Step 5: Add an Action

1. Click **New Step** and choose an action.

2. Some common actions include:

    o **Save attachments to OneDrive**

    o **Forward email to another person**

    o **Send a Teams notification**

3. Configure the action settings and click **Save**.

Step 6: Test and Activate the Flow

1. Click **Test** in the top-right corner.

2. Send a test email that meets your trigger conditions.

3. Check if the flow executes correctly.

4. If successful, click **Turn On** to activate the flow.

Best Practices for Using Email Triggers

- **Avoid Overloading Your Inbox:** Use filters to target specific emails rather than triggering flows for every new email.

- **Limit API Calls:** Gmail and Outlook have API usage limits. Be mindful of excessive triggers.

- **Use Error Handling:** Set up conditions to manage unexpected email formats.

- **Secure Sensitive Data:** If handling confidential emails, ensure proper security measures are in place.

- **Monitor Flow Performance:** Regularly check the flow history to troubleshoot failed runs.

Conclusion

Email-based triggers in Power Automate are powerful tools for automating email-related tasks, reducing manual effort, and improving productivity. Whether you're tracking important emails, saving attachments, or flagging critical messages, Power Automate makes the process seamless. By following best practices and properly configuring your triggers, you can create efficient and reliable email automation workflows.

Next, we will explore **"3.2.2 SharePoint and OneDrive Triggers,"** where we discuss how Power Automate can help manage document-based workflows efficiently.

3.2.2 SharePoint and OneDrive Triggers

Introduction to SharePoint and OneDrive Triggers

Microsoft Power Automate provides seamless integration with SharePoint and OneDrive, allowing users to automate various file and document management tasks. These triggers help streamline business processes by automatically responding to changes in document libraries, lists, and files stored in these Microsoft services.

This section will cover:

- The different types of SharePoint and OneDrive triggers

- How to configure and use them

- Real-world automation scenarios

- Best practices for optimizing workflows

By the end of this section, you will have a solid understanding of how to leverage these triggers to automate document management, approvals, and notifications effectively.

1. Understanding SharePoint and OneDrive Triggers

What Are SharePoint and OneDrive Triggers?

Triggers in Power Automate serve as the starting point for a flow. SharePoint and OneDrive triggers activate when an event occurs, such as:

- A new file is created

- A file is modified

- A file is deleted

- A new item is added to a SharePoint list

- A file is shared

Key Differences Between SharePoint and OneDrive Triggers

While SharePoint and OneDrive both deal with file storage, they have different use cases:

- **SharePoint** is used primarily for collaborative document management, team-based content organization, and structured data storage using lists and libraries.

- **OneDrive** is designed for personal and small-scale file storage but still supports automation for managing documents and syncing data.

Power Automate provides separate triggers for each service, and understanding these differences will help in choosing the right trigger for your workflow.

2. Common SharePoint Triggers and How to Use Them

2.1 When a File is Created (SharePoint)

Overview

This trigger starts a flow when a new file is uploaded to a specified SharePoint document library.

Use Case

- Automatically send a notification when a new document is uploaded.

- Move files to a different folder based on naming conventions.

- Start an approval process when a document is added.

How to Configure

1. Create a new **Automated Cloud Flow** in Power Automate.

2. Select **When a file is created (SharePoint)** as the trigger.

3. Specify the **Site Address** and **Library Name** where the trigger should monitor for new files.

4. Add subsequent actions, such as sending an email notification.

Example Flow

- **Trigger:** A file is uploaded to the "Contracts" document library.

- **Action:** Send an email to the legal team with a link to the new document.

2.2 When a File is Modified (SharePoint)

Overview

This trigger activates when an existing file in a SharePoint library is modified.

Use Case

- Track document changes for compliance.
- Notify team members when a file is updated.
- Sync updated files to another location.

How to Configure

1. Choose **When a file is modified (SharePoint)** as the trigger.
2. Select the **SharePoint site** and **library** to monitor.
3. Define additional actions, such as logging changes in an Excel file.

Example Flow

- **Trigger:** A project plan document is modified in the "Project Docs" library.
- **Action:** Log the modification date in an Excel file stored in OneDrive.

2.3 When an Item is Created or Modified (SharePoint List)

Overview

This trigger fires when a new item is added to a SharePoint list or when an existing item is updated.

Use Case

- Automate task assignments when a new item is added to a SharePoint list.
- Send approval requests for list updates.

Example Flow

- **Trigger:** A new item is added to the "Employee Requests" SharePoint list.
- **Action:** Send an approval request to the HR manager.

3. Common OneDrive Triggers and How to Use Them

3.1 When a File is Created (OneDrive)

Overview

This trigger starts a flow when a new file is added to a specified OneDrive folder.

Use Case

- Automatically copy new files to a SharePoint document library.

- Convert newly uploaded Word documents into PDFs.

Example Flow

- **Trigger:** A file is added to the "Invoices" folder in OneDrive.

- **Action:** Convert the file to PDF and move it to a "Final Invoices" folder.

3.2 When a File is Modified (OneDrive)

Overview

Triggers a flow when an existing file in OneDrive is changed.

Use Case

- Backup updated files to another cloud storage.

- Notify a manager when a document is edited.

Example Flow

- **Trigger:** A report is modified in OneDrive.

- **Action:** Send a Teams notification to the finance department.

3.3 When a File is Deleted (OneDrive)

Overview

This trigger activates when a file is deleted from OneDrive.

Use Case

- Maintain a log of deleted files.

- Prevent accidental data loss by backing up deleted files.

Example Flow

- **Trigger:** A file is deleted from a OneDrive folder.

- **Action:** Restore the file from a backup location.

---

4. Real-World Automation Scenarios

Automating Document Approvals

- **Scenario:** A company requires manager approval for all purchase orders uploaded to SharePoint.

- **Solution:**

    1. Use the **"When a file is created"** trigger.

    2. Send an approval request to the manager.

    3. If approved, move the document to a "Processed Orders" folder.

    4. If rejected, notify the requester.

Managing File Organization

- **Scenario:** A team wants to categorize files uploaded to OneDrive based on file type.

- **Solution:**

    1. Use the **"When a file is created"** trigger.

    2. Identify the file extension.

    3. Move PDFs to a "Reports" folder, images to "Graphics," and Word documents to "Drafts."

Keeping Teams Notified About File Changes

- **Scenario:** A sales team needs real-time alerts when client contracts are updated in SharePoint.

- **Solution:**

    1. Use the **"When a file is modified"** trigger.

2. Send a message in a Teams channel with details of the update.

5. Best Practices for Using SharePoint and OneDrive Triggers

1. **Limit Scope to Necessary Folders or Lists** – Avoid monitoring an entire site or OneDrive to reduce unnecessary trigger activations.

2. **Use Filters to Optimize Flow Execution** – Use dynamic conditions to ensure only relevant changes trigger a flow.

3. **Prevent Infinite Loops** – Ensure your flow doesn't modify a file in a way that retriggers itself.

4. **Monitor Flow Runs for Errors** – Regularly check the Power Automate run history to troubleshoot failed flows.

5. **Implement Security Best Practices** – Restrict access to sensitive flows and ensure proper permission settings.

Conclusion

By leveraging SharePoint and OneDrive triggers, organizations can streamline document management, improve collaboration, and automate repetitive tasks. Whether you need real-time notifications, automated approvals, or enhanced data organization, Power Automate provides a powerful set of tools to optimize your workflow.

Now that you understand how these triggers work, you can start building your own automated flows to enhance efficiency and productivity.

3.2.3 Social Media and External App Triggers

Introduction

Social media and external applications play a significant role in modern business operations. From marketing campaigns and customer interactions to project management and collaboration, organizations rely on various platforms to streamline workflows.

Microsoft Power Automate enables users to connect with these platforms and automate routine tasks, ensuring efficiency and consistency.

This section explores how to use social media and external app triggers in Power Automate, including common use cases, step-by-step guides for setting up automation, and best practices for optimizing workflows.

1. What Are Social Media and External App Triggers?

Triggers in Power Automate are events that initiate an automated workflow. Social media and external app triggers specifically detect activities occurring on platforms such as Twitter, Facebook, LinkedIn, Trello, Slack, and more. These triggers allow users to automate processes based on real-time interactions without manual intervention.

Power Automate provides pre-built connectors for many external applications, enabling seamless integration with minimal configuration. Users can also create custom connectors for apps that are not natively supported.

2. Common Social Media Triggers and Their Use Cases

2.1 Twitter Triggers

Power Automate offers several Twitter-based triggers that allow automation based on user activity and engagement.

Available Twitter Triggers:

- When a new tweet is posted (by a specific user or containing a specific keyword)
- When a new direct message is received
- When a user is mentioned in a tweet

Use Cases:

- **Automated Customer Engagement:** Set up a workflow to send an email notification or Teams message when your brand is mentioned on Twitter.
- **Content Curation:** Collect and store tweets containing a specific hashtag in an Excel file or SharePoint list for marketing analysis.

- **Customer Support:** Automatically create a help desk ticket when a customer tweets about an issue related to your company.

Example: Creating a Flow to Save Tweets to Excel

1. Open Power Automate and create a new automated cloud flow.

2. Select **"When a new tweet is posted"** as the trigger.

3. Define the search parameters (e.g., tweets containing "#YourBrand").

4. Add an action **"Add a row to Excel"**, selecting an Excel file stored in OneDrive or SharePoint.

5. Map the tweet content to the appropriate Excel columns.

6. Save and test the flow to ensure it captures relevant tweets.

Facebook Triggers

Facebook automation with Power Automate primarily focuses on business pages and interactions.

Available Facebook Triggers:

- **When a new post is published on a page**

- **When a new comment is added to a post**

- **When a new message is received**

Use Cases:

- **Marketing Automation:** Send notifications to a marketing team whenever a new post is published on the company's Facebook page.

- **Sentiment Analysis:** Use AI Builder with Power Automate to analyze comments on a post and categorize them as positive or negative.

- **Lead Capture:** Save messages received via Facebook Messenger to a CRM system for follow-ups.

LinkedIn Triggers

LinkedIn is a key platform for professional networking and recruitment.

Available LinkedIn Triggers:

- When a new post is created on a LinkedIn company page

- When someone engages with a LinkedIn post (likes, comments, shares)

- When a new job application is received

Use Cases:

- **Recruitment Automation:** Store job applications in an Excel file or SharePoint for HR processing.

- **Engagement Tracking:** Notify the marketing team when a post receives high engagement to optimize content strategy.

- **Personal Branding:** Automatically share LinkedIn posts across other social media platforms.

3. Common External App Triggers and Their Use Cases

Trello Triggers

Trello is widely used for task and project management.

Available Trello Triggers:

- When a new card is created

- When a card is moved to a specific list

- When a due date is approaching

Use Cases:

- **Task Assignment Alerts:** Notify team members via Microsoft Teams when a card is moved to "In Progress."

- **Deadline Reminders:** Send automatic reminders via email when a task is due in 24 hours.

- **Project Status Updates:** Synchronize Trello board changes with SharePoint lists for reporting.

Slack Triggers

Slack is a popular communication tool used in many workplaces.

Available Slack Triggers:

- When a new message is posted in a channel
- When a specific keyword appears in a message
- When a user joins a channel

Use Cases:

- **Automated Notifications:** Alert the sales team when a client sends a message in a Slack channel.
- **Keyword Monitoring:** Track messages mentioning certain topics and log them into a SharePoint file.
- **Onboarding Automation:** Send a welcome message and resources to new channel members.

Custom API and Webhook Triggers

For applications without built-in Power Automate connectors, webhooks and APIs can be used.

How to Use Webhook Triggers:

1. Choose **"When an HTTP request is received"** as a trigger in Power Automate.
2. Configure the webhook URL in the external application.
3. Define the data structure expected from the request.
4. Add actions based on the received data, such as storing it in a database or sending notifications.

Use Cases:

- **Synchronizing Custom CRM Systems:** Capture customer data from a proprietary CRM and log it into SharePoint.

- **Real-Time Event Logging:** Send event notifications from an external app to Microsoft Teams.

4. Best Practices for Using Social Media and External App Triggers

Avoiding Spam and Over-Automation

- Implement **filters** to prevent unnecessary triggers.
- Use **delays and batching** to control workflow execution.
- Monitor API limits to avoid excessive requests.

Ensuring Data Security and Compliance

- Use **secure authentication** for social media integrations.
- Follow **GDPR and data privacy regulations** when handling user data.
- Regularly review **permissions and access controls**.

Optimizing Workflow Efficiency

- Use **conditional logic** to refine automation triggers.
- Combine multiple triggers into a **single multi-step workflow**.
- Monitor and debug **flow performance** using Power Automate analytics.

Conclusion

Social media and external app triggers in Power Automate enable businesses and individuals to automate repetitive tasks, enhance engagement, and improve workflow efficiency. Whether it's tracking social media mentions, integrating collaboration tools, or leveraging APIs for custom applications, these triggers open endless possibilities for automation. By following best practices, users can ensure secure, efficient, and meaningful automation processes tailored to their needs.

3.3 What are Actions?

In Power Automate, **actions** are the fundamental building blocks of workflows. While **triggers** initiate a flow, **actions** define what happens next. Actions allow users to process data, retrieve information, store records, and automate various operations across multiple applications.

Each flow consists of one or more actions that execute in a sequence based on predefined conditions and logic. These actions can be as simple as sending an email or as complex as processing data from an API and storing it in a database.

Power Automate provides a vast library of **predefined actions** that interact with different applications, services, and databases. Additionally, users can create **custom actions** using APIs and connectors to enhance automation capabilities.

In this section, we will focus on one of the most essential categories of actions: **Data Retrieval and Storage Actions**.

3.3.1 Data Retrieval and Storage Actions

Data retrieval and storage actions in Power Automate allow users to extract, manipulate, and store data from various sources. These actions enable automation of repetitive tasks such as fetching emails, retrieving SharePoint records, updating databases, or storing files in cloud storage.

1. Overview of Data Retrieval and Storage Actions

Data retrieval and storage actions can be categorized into:

- **Retrieving Data**: Extracting information from databases, cloud storage, web services, and applications.

- **Storing Data**: Saving or updating records in cloud databases, SharePoint, OneDrive, and other platforms.

- **Transforming Data**: Manipulating and structuring data before storage.

Power Automate supports multiple services and platforms for handling data, including:
✓ **Microsoft Excel and Google Sheets** – For spreadsheet-based data storage.

✅ **SharePoint Lists and Libraries** – For structured data storage within SharePoint.

✅ **Dataverse** – Microsoft's data platform for relational database storage.

✅ **SQL Server and Other Databases** – For storing and retrieving structured data.

✅ **OneDrive, Dropbox, and Google Drive** – For cloud-based file storage.

✅ **APIs and Web Services** – For retrieving data from online sources.

2. Retrieving Data in Power Automate

Retrieving data is an essential part of automation, allowing users to access information dynamically from different sources. Power Automate provides multiple connectors for data extraction from various platforms.

2.1 Retrieving Data from Excel and Google Sheets

Power Automate allows users to fetch data from Excel Online, Google Sheets, and other spreadsheet applications. Some common actions include:

- **"List rows present in a table"** (Excel Online) – Retrieves all rows from a specific table in an Excel file.

- **"Get a row"** – Retrieves a specific row from an Excel table based on a key value.

- **"List rows" (Google Sheets)** – Retrieves data from a Google Sheet.

Example: Retrieving Customer Data from an Excel Sheet
📌 **Use Case**: A company wants to retrieve customer information from an Excel file and send an automated email.
💡 **Steps**:

1. Create a flow with a trigger (e.g., "When a new row is added to an Excel table").

2. Use the **"List rows present in a table"** action to fetch customer records.

3. Apply a condition to filter specific customer data.

4. Use the **"Send an email"** action to notify the relevant department.

2.2 Retrieving Data from SharePoint Lists

SharePoint is widely used for data storage in organizations. Power Automate provides multiple actions to fetch SharePoint data:

- **"Get items"** – Retrieves all items from a SharePoint list.

- **"Get item"** – Retrieves a single item based on ID.

Example: Retrieving Pending Tasks from a SharePoint List

📌 **Use Case**: A manager wants to retrieve all pending tasks from a SharePoint list and send reminders.

💡 **Steps**:

1. Trigger the flow using **"Recurrence"** (e.g., run every morning).

2. Use **"Get items"** to fetch all tasks from the SharePoint list.

3. Filter tasks where the status is "Pending."

4. Use the **"Send an email"** action to notify the assigned users.

2.3 Retrieving Data from Databases (SQL, Dataverse, etc.)

For advanced data handling, Power Automate supports **SQL Server, Dataverse, and other databases**:

- **"Execute a SQL query"** – Runs a custom SQL query to fetch records.

- **"Get row by ID"** – Retrieves a specific database record.

- **"List records" (Dataverse)** – Fetches multiple records from a Dataverse table.

Example: Fetching Customer Orders from SQL Server

📌 **Use Case**: A business wants to retrieve customer orders from a SQL Server database.

💡 **Steps**:

1. Trigger the flow with **"When an HTTP request is received"** (for API-based queries).

2. Use **"Execute a SQL query"** to retrieve customer order data.

3. Store the retrieved data in a structured format (e.g., JSON).

4. Return the data as an API response.

---

3. Storing Data in Power Automate

Once data is retrieved, it often needs to be stored or updated in a structured location. Power Automate supports multiple destinations for storing data.

3.1 Storing Data in SharePoint

Power Automate allows users to create and update SharePoint records:

- **"Create item"** – Adds a new item to a SharePoint list.

- **"Update item"** – Modifies an existing SharePoint record.

Example: Saving Employee Feedback in SharePoint
📌 **Use Case**: A company collects employee feedback via Microsoft Forms and stores it in SharePoint.
💡 **Steps**:

1. Use **"When a new response is submitted"** (Forms trigger).

2. Retrieve responses using **"Get response details"**.

3. Store feedback in SharePoint using **"Create item"**.

3.2 Storing Data in OneDrive, Dropbox, or Google Drive

File storage actions allow users to save documents, images, and reports:

- **"Create file"** – Uploads a new file to cloud storage.

- **"Update file"** – Modifies an existing file.

Example: Saving Email Attachments in OneDrive
📌 **Use Case**: Automatically save email attachments to OneDrive.
💡 **Steps**:

1. Use **"When a new email arrives"** (Outlook trigger).

2. Extract attachments using **"Get attachments"**.

3. Save files to OneDrive using **"Create file"**.

3.3 Storing Data in Dataverse and SQL Databases

For structured data, Power Automate supports:

- **"Add a new record" (Dataverse)** – Saves a new entry in a Dataverse table.

- **"Insert row" (SQL Server)** – Adds a record to an SQL database.

Example: Logging Sales Transactions in SQL Database

📌 **Use Case**: A company logs sales transactions in an SQL database.

💡 **Steps**:

1. Use **"When a new sale is made"** as the trigger.

2. Capture sales details.

3. Store the transaction using **"Insert row" (SQL Server)**.

---

4. Best Practices for Data Retrieval and Storage

✅ Optimize queries to avoid performance issues.

✅ Use filtering and conditions to retrieve only necessary data.

✅ Ensure data security when storing confidential information.

✅ Leverage Dataverse for structured enterprise data.

3.3.2 Conditional and Loop Actions

Introduction to Conditional and Loop Actions

When building automated workflows in **Microsoft Power Automate**, it's often necessary to introduce decision-making logic and repeat certain actions based on specific conditions. This is where **conditional actions** and **loop actions** come into play.

- **Conditional actions** allow flows to make decisions based on predefined rules (e.g., "If an email contains 'urgent,' then send a notification").

- **Loop actions** repeat tasks multiple times, either a fixed number of times or dynamically based on available data (e.g., "For each row in an Excel table, send an email").

These actions enhance the flexibility and intelligence of your workflows, making them more dynamic and adaptive to various scenarios. In this section, we'll explore how these actions work, their common use cases, and best practices for implementing them effectively.

1. Understanding Conditional Actions in Power Automate

1.1 What Are Conditional Actions?

Conditional actions in Power Automate allow flows to **branch** based on specific conditions. This means that different actions can be executed depending on whether a condition evaluates to **true or false**.

The most commonly used conditional action in Power Automate is the **"Condition"** control, which operates similarly to an "IF-THEN-ELSE" statement in traditional programming.

1.2 How to Use the "Condition" Action

The **"Condition"** action allows you to set up logical conditions that dictate the flow's behavior. Here's how you can configure a condition:

Step 1: Add a "Condition" Action

1. Open **Power Automate** and create or edit a flow.

2. Click on **"+ New Step"** and search for **"Condition"** in the action list.

3. Select the **Condition** control.

Step 2: Define the Condition

1. In the condition box, select a dynamic value (e.g., "Email Subject").

2. Choose a comparison operator (e.g., "contains," "equals," "greater than").

3. Enter a comparison value (e.g., "Urgent").

Step 3: Configure the "If Yes" and "If No" Branches

- Under **"If Yes,"** add actions that should execute when the condition is met.

- Under **"If No,"** add actions that should execute when the condition is not met.

Example Use Case: Filtering Urgent Emails

- **Trigger:** When an email arrives in Outlook.

- **Condition:** If the email subject contains the word **"Urgent."**

- **If Yes:** Send a **Teams notification** and move the email to the "High Priority" folder.

- **If No:** Move the email to a "General" folder.

1.3 Nested Conditions

Power Automate allows **nested conditions**, meaning you can have conditions inside conditions. This is useful for scenarios with multiple decision points.

Example Use Case: Employee Leave Approval

- **Condition 1:** If the employee has more than 10 days of leave balance:

  - **Condition 2 (inside Condition 1):** If the leave request is for less than 5 days → **Approve Automatically**

  - **Else:** Send for **Manager Approval**

- **Else:** Reject the request automatically.

1.4 Advanced Conditional Logic with Expressions

Power Automate supports expressions in conditions using **Power Automate Expressions (based on Azure Logic Apps language)**. Some useful functions include:

- equals(variables('var1'), variables('var2')) → Checks if two values are equal.

- contains(outputs('Email_Subject'), 'Urgent') → Checks if a string contains another string.

- if(variables('var1') > 10, 'Approved', 'Rejected') → A simple IF-ELSE expression.

---

2. Understanding Loop Actions in Power Automate

2.1 What Are Loop Actions?

Loop actions allow Power Automate to repeat a sequence of steps multiple times. This is useful for scenarios such as:

- Processing all rows in an Excel spreadsheet.

- Sending an email to multiple recipients.

- Looping through a list of SharePoint files.

Power Automate provides two types of loop actions:

1. **"Apply to Each"** – Executes actions for each item in a collection.

2. **"Do Until"** – Repeats actions until a specified condition is met.

2.2 Using the "Apply to Each" Loop

The **"Apply to Each"** loop is used when you need to process multiple items dynamically.

Step 1: Add an "Apply to Each" Action

1. Add an action that returns multiple results (e.g., "Get Items" from SharePoint).

2. Click **"+ New Step"** and search for **"Apply to Each"** in the action list.

3. Select the **"Apply to Each"** control.

Step 2: Configure the Loop

1. In the **"Select an Output"** field, choose the dynamic content that contains multiple items (e.g., "Value" from SharePoint list).

2. Inside the loop, add actions that should execute for each item.

Example Use Case: Sending Personalized Emails

- **Trigger:** When a new Excel file is uploaded.

- **Loop through each row:**

  o Retrieve the **email address** and **name** of each user.

  o Send a **personalized email** to each user.

2.3 Using the "Do Until" Loop

The **"Do Until"** loop repeats a set of actions **until** a condition is met.

Step 1: Add a "Do Until" Action

1. Click **"+ New Step"** and search for **"Do Until"** in the action list.

2. Select the **"Do Until"** control.

Step 2: Define the Exit Condition

- Specify the condition that will **stop** the loop.

- Example: Run until Status = "Approved".

Example Use Case: Waiting for Approval

- **Trigger:** A leave request is submitted.

- **Do Until Condition:** Loop until **"Approval Status" = "Approved"**.

- **Inside the Loop:** Check approval status and send reminders.

3. Best Practices for Using Conditional and Loop Actions

- **Avoid Infinite Loops:** Ensure that loops have an exit condition.

- **Minimize API Calls:** Excessive loops can lead to API throttling, especially with large datasets.

- **Optimize Performance:** Use filters before loops to reduce unnecessary iterations.

- **Use Variables:** Store intermediate values to reduce unnecessary lookups.

Conclusion

Conditional and loop actions are essential for building intelligent and dynamic workflows in Power Automate. By leveraging "Condition," "Apply to Each," and "Do Until", you can create powerful automations that adapt to different scenarios, optimize business processes, and save time.

In the next section, we'll explore advanced workflow features, including error handling, parallel branching, and debugging techniques to enhance the efficiency and reliability of your flows.

3.3.3 Approval and Notification Actions

In Microsoft Power Automate, **Approval and Notification Actions** are essential for automating decision-making processes and keeping users informed. Whether you need to streamline approval workflows for documents, requests, or business processes, or you want to send notifications for important events, Power Automate provides powerful tools to automate these tasks efficiently.

This section will cover:

- What approval actions are and how they work

- How to configure an approval flow

- Types of approval processes in Power Automate

- What notification actions are and how they are used

- Configuring notifications via email, Teams, SMS, and push notifications

- Best practices for using approvals and notifications in workflows

1. Understanding Approval Actions in Power Automate

Approval actions in Power Automate allow users to automate decision-making processes by sending approval requests to individuals or groups. These actions ensure that a specific step in a workflow does not proceed until an approval is granted.

Common use cases for approvals include:

- Document and expense approvals

- Leave and time-off requests

- Contract and purchase order approvals

- Customer service escalations

- IT and security access requests

1.1 How Approval Actions Work

An approval action in Power Automate follows a structured process:

1. **Triggering the Approval**

   o A flow starts when a trigger condition is met (e.g., a new document is uploaded to SharePoint, an email is received, or a form is submitted).

2. **Sending the Approval Request**

   o Power Automate sends an approval request to one or more users via email, Teams, or the Power Automate mobile app.

3. **Receiving a Response**

   o   Approvers receive a notification and can approve or reject the request.

4. **Handling the Response**

   o   The flow proceeds based on the response: If approved, the next step is executed; if rejected, an alternative action is taken.

1.2 Types of Approvals in Power Automate

Power Automate supports several types of approvals:

Single Approver Approval

- A request is sent to one person, who either approves or rejects it.

- Example: An employee submits a leave request that goes to their manager for approval.

Sequential Approval (Multi-Step Approval)

- Approvals occur in stages, where one approval must be completed before moving to the next approver.

- Example: A purchase request first goes to the department head, then to finance, and finally to the CEO.

Parallel Approval

- Multiple approvers receive the request simultaneously, and approval can be based on different conditions (e.g., majority approval or all must approve).

- Example: A new software license request needs approval from both IT and the finance department.

First to Respond Approval

- The request is sent to multiple people, but only the first response is considered.

- Example: A customer support escalation goes to a team, and the first person to approve or reject handles the request.

2. Creating an Approval Workflow in Power Automate

To create an approval workflow, follow these steps:

Step 1: Choose a Trigger

- Common triggers include:

    - A new item is created in SharePoint

    - A new email arrives in Outlook with specific conditions

    - A new response is submitted in Microsoft Forms

Step 2: Add an Approval Action

- Use the **"Start and wait for an approval"** action in Power Automate.

- Configure the approval type (single, sequential, parallel, or first response).

- Define the approvers (individual users or Office 365 groups).

- Add a title, description, and relevant details.

Step 3: Handle the Response

- Add a condition to check if the approval was granted.

- If approved, continue to the next action (e.g., send a confirmation email, update a SharePoint list).

- If rejected, trigger a different action (e.g., notify the requester, log the rejection).

Step 4: Test and Deploy the Flow

- Test the approval workflow with sample data.

- Monitor run history and fix any errors.

- Deploy the workflow to production.

---

3. Understanding Notification Actions in Power Automate

Notification actions are used to send alerts or messages based on specific events. Power Automate supports multiple types of notifications, including:

- **Email notifications** (via Outlook, Gmail)

- **Microsoft Teams notifications**
- **SMS notifications** (via Twilio or other services)
- **Push notifications** (via the Power Automate mobile app)

Configuring Email Notifications

Email notifications are commonly used to inform users about important events. To send an email notification:

1. Add the **"Send an email (V2)"** action.

2. Specify the recipient's email address.

3. Enter a subject and body text.

4. Optionally, attach files or include dynamic content.

Configuring Microsoft Teams Notifications

For team collaboration, Power Automate can send notifications to Microsoft Teams:

1. Add the **"Post a message in a chat or channel"** action.

2. Choose whether to send a direct message or post in a channel.

3. Enter the message text and include dynamic content if needed.

4. Test the notification to ensure delivery.

Configuring SMS Notifications

To send SMS notifications, use services like Twilio:

1. Add the **"Twilio – Send SMS"** action.

2. Enter the recipient's phone number.

3. Compose the SMS message.

4. Test the workflow.

Configuring Push Notifications

Push notifications can alert users on their mobile devices via the Power Automate app:

1. Add the **"Send me a mobile notification"** action.

2. Define the notification text.

3. Test the flow on a mobile device.

4. Best Practices for Approval and Notification Actions

Best Practices for Approval Actions

✓ Use structured approval processes to avoid confusion.
✓ Notify users when an approval request is pending.
✓ Set deadlines for approvals to ensure timely decisions.
✓ Use approval history logs for tracking and auditing.

Best Practices for Notification Actions

✓ Avoid excessive notifications to prevent alert fatigue.
✓ Use clear, concise message content.
✓ Test notifications to ensure they reach the intended recipients.
✓ Integrate notifications with other automation steps for better workflow efficiency.

5. Conclusion

Approval and Notification Actions in Power Automate enhance business processes by automating decision-making and keeping users informed. By configuring structured approval workflows and effective notification systems, organizations can improve efficiency, reduce manual work, and streamline communication.

By implementing the steps and best practices outlined in this section, you can leverage Power Automate to create automated workflows that simplify approvals and ensure timely notifications, making your day-to-day tasks more efficient.

PART IV
Building Automated Workflows

4.1 Understanding Workflow Logic

4.1.1 Conditions and Branching

When building automated workflows in Microsoft Power Automate, understanding **conditions and branching** is essential. These elements allow you to create dynamic workflows that respond differently based on specific conditions, making your automations more intelligent and efficient.

This section will cover:

- What conditions and branching are

- How to use conditions to control workflow logic

- Different types of conditions in Power Automate

- Using branching to create multiple workflow paths

- Practical examples of conditions and branching in real-world scenarios

What Are Conditions and Branching?

In Power Automate, conditions and branching define how a flow behaves based on **specific criteria**. Instead of having a static, linear automation, you can introduce logic that allows the flow to **evaluate data, make decisions, and take different actions** based on predefined conditions.

- **Conditions**: These are rules that check whether a certain condition is met (e.g., "If an email contains an attachment, then save it to OneDrive; otherwise, ignore it").

- **Branching**: This refers to the ability of a workflow to split into **multiple paths** based on different conditions. Each branch can execute different actions depending on the condition met.

Why Are Conditions and Branching Important?

- **Enhanced Decision-Making**: Flows can **process data dynamically** and execute different actions based on user input or external events.

- **More Efficient Workflows**: Instead of creating separate flows for different scenarios, you can **consolidate multiple outcomes into one automated process**.

- **Better Error Handling**: You can **define fallback actions** in case something goes wrong in a workflow.

How to Use Conditions in Power Automate

1. Adding a Condition to a Flow

In Power Automate, conditions work similarly to "If-Else" statements in programming. You can add a condition by following these steps:

1. **Create a new flow** or open an existing one.

2. **Add a trigger** (e.g., "When a new email arrives in Outlook").

3. Click on **"+ New step"** and select **"Condition"** from the list of actions.

4. Define the condition using a field from the trigger (e.g., "If the email contains an attachment").

5. Specify what should happen in the **"If yes"** and **"If no"** paths.

6. Save and test the flow.

2. Example of a Simple Condition

Scenario: Automatically saving email attachments to OneDrive

- **Trigger**: When an email arrives in Outlook

- **Condition**: Check if the email contains an attachment

- **Actions**:

  - **If Yes** → Save the attachment to OneDrive

  - **If No** → Send a notification saying no attachment was found

Step-by-Step Guide

1. **Trigger**: Select **"When a new email arrives"** in Outlook.

2. **Condition**: Add a "Condition" action and set it to check:

   - "Has Attachments" is **equal to** true.

3. **If Yes**:

   - Use "Create File" action in OneDrive.

   - Save the attachment in a designated folder.

4. **If No**:

   - Use "Send an email" action to notify the user that no attachments were found.

Types of Conditions in Power Automate

Power Automate provides different types of conditions to control workflow logic:

1. Basic Conditions

- **Equals** (=): Checks if a value is equal to another value.

- **Not Equals** (!=): Checks if a value is NOT equal to another value.

- **Greater Than / Less Than** (>, <): Used for numerical values, dates, or strings.

- **Contains**: Checks if a text field contains a specific word or phrase.

- **Does Not Contain**: Checks if a text field **does not** contain a specific value.

Example: If a customer's feedback rating is **greater than 4**, send a thank-you email; otherwise, escalate the issue to support.

2. Multiple Conditions (AND / OR Logic)

- **AND Condition**: All conditions must be **true** for the action to run.

- **OR Condition**: At least **one** condition must be **true** for the action to run.

Example:

- **AND Condition**: If an email is from "example@domain.com" **AND** contains the word "urgent", forward it to the manager.

- **OR Condition**: If an email is from "example@domain.com" **OR** contains the word "urgent", forward it to the manager.

Using Branching in Power Automate

What is Branching?

Branching allows workflows to take **different paths** based on **multiple conditions**. Instead of a simple "Yes or No" decision, **branching allows multiple outcomes**.

1. Parallel Branching

Parallel branching allows a workflow to execute **multiple actions simultaneously**.

Example: Processing Multiple Tasks at Once

- **Scenario**: When an order is received,
  - Send an email confirmation to the customer **(Path 1)**
  - Notify the warehouse team **(Path 2)**
  - Log the order in a SharePoint list **(Path 3)**

2. Switch Case Branching

A **Switch case** action allows different outcomes based on a variable's value.

Example: Assigning Support Tickets Based on Priority

- If the **priority level** of a support ticket is:
  - "High" → Assign to **Senior Support**

- o "Medium" → Assign to **Standard Support**

- o "Low" → Assign to **Junior Support**

Steps to Create a Switch Case in Power Automate:

1. Add a **Switch** action.

2. Use the **priority field** as the switch value.

3. Define multiple cases (e.g., High, Medium, Low).

4. Set the corresponding actions for each case.

3. Nested Conditions (If-Else Within If-Else)

Nested conditions allow you to create **complex decision trees**.

Example: Handling Different Email Responses

- If an email contains **"invoice"**

  - o If it is from <u>accounting@company.com</u>, forward it to **finance**

  - o If it is from **an unknown sender**, flag it as spam

Real-World Examples of Conditions and Branching

1. Automating Expense Approvals

- If the **expense amount** is **below $500**, approve automatically.

- If the **expense amount** is **above $500**, send for manager approval.

2. Handling Customer Support Requests

- If the request **contains "urgent"**, mark as **high priority**.

- If the request **contains "billing"**, assign to **finance team**.

- If the request **contains "technical"**, assign to **IT team**.

3. Processing Job Applications

- If the applicant has a **Bachelor's degree**, move them to **next round**.

- If the applicant has a **Master's degree**, assign to a **priority queue**.

- If the applicant **does not meet requirements**, send a **rejection email**.

Conclusion

Understanding **conditions and branching** in Power Automate is key to building powerful workflows that **adapt to different scenarios**. By implementing conditions, parallel branching, and switch cases, you can create **dynamic, efficient, and intelligent automation workflows** that enhance productivity.

In the next section, we will explore **Loops and Iterations**, which allow flows to **process multiple items in a structured way**.

4.1.2 Loops and Iterations

In Microsoft Power Automate, loops and iterations are essential for automating repetitive tasks efficiently. Whether you need to process multiple emails, update multiple records, or cycle through a dataset, loops allow your flows to execute actions multiple times without manual intervention. Understanding how to implement loops correctly can help streamline processes, improve efficiency, and reduce the likelihood of errors.

This section explores the different types of loops available in Power Automate, how they work, common use cases, best practices, and troubleshooting techniques.

1. What Are Loops in Power Automate?

A loop is a control mechanism that repeatedly executes a block of actions until a specified condition is met. This is useful when working with lists, tables, arrays, or sets of records that require processing one by one.

Loops allow automation of:

- Processing multiple email attachments

- Iterating over items in a SharePoint list

- Sending notifications to multiple recipients

- Extracting and storing data from multiple rows in Excel

Power Automate offers two main types of loops:

1. **Apply to Each** – Used to iterate over a collection of items

2. **Do Until** – Repeats an action until a specific condition is met

2. Apply to Each Loop

2.1 Understanding Apply to Each

The **Apply to Each** loop executes an action for each item in an array or collection. This loop is commonly used when dealing with data sources that return multiple values, such as:

- SharePoint lists

- Excel tables

- Email attachments

- API responses containing arrays

Whenever Power Automate detects that an action outputs an array (a list of items), it automatically suggests using an **Apply to Each** loop.

2.2 How to Use Apply to Each

Step 1: Define the Collection

Before using an **Apply to Each** loop, you need a collection to iterate through. This could be an array of values from:

- A SharePoint List

- An Excel table

- Email attachments

- API responses

Step 2: Add an Apply to Each Action

1. In Power Automate, open a new or existing flow.

2. Add a trigger (e.g., "When an email arrives").

3. Insert an **Apply to Each** action.

4. Select the dynamic content that represents the array (e.g., "Attachments" from an email).

Step 3: Define Actions Inside the Loop

- Add actions inside the **Apply to Each** loop to process each item in the collection.

- Example: If iterating over email attachments, add a "Save file" action to store each attachment in OneDrive.

Step 4: Run and Monitor the Flow

- Test the flow with sample data to ensure it processes each item correctly.

- Use the **Flow Run History** to verify that all iterations execute as expected.

3. Do Until Loop

3.1 Understanding Do Until

The **Do Until** loop repeats actions until a specified condition is met. Unlike **Apply to Each**, which iterates through a defined collection, **Do Until** continues running until a logical condition becomes true.

Common use cases include:

- Waiting for an approval response

- Checking system status until a certain condition is met

- Retrying an API call until a successful response is received

3.2 How to Use Do Until

Step 1: Add a Do Until Action

1. In Power Automate, create a flow and add a trigger (e.g., "Manually trigger a flow").

2. Insert a **Do Until** control action.

3. Define the condition that determines when the loop should stop.

Step 2: Add Actions Inside the Loop

- Define actions that should repeat until the condition is met.

- Example: Sending a reminder email every 24 hours until a SharePoint list item is updated.

Step 3: Set a Timeout or Maximum Iterations (Optional)

- **Timeout:** Prevents the loop from running indefinitely.

- **Max Iterations:** Limits the number of times the loop executes to avoid performance issues.

---

4. Best Practices for Using Loops in Power Automate

1. **Minimize the Number of Iterations**

   o Avoid excessive looping to improve flow performance.

   o Filter data before processing to reduce the number of iterations.

2. **Use Parallel Processing When Possible**

   o Instead of sequential loops, explore parallel processing to handle multiple tasks simultaneously.

3. **Limit API Calls and Avoid Infinite Loops**

   o Excessive looping can cause throttling or API limitations.

   o Ensure **Do Until** loops have exit conditions to prevent infinite loops.

4. **Monitor and Debug Flows**

   o Use the **Run History** in Power Automate to track loop executions.

   o Add logging steps (e.g., sending loop iteration numbers to a log file).

---

5. Common Troubleshooting Issues

Loop Not Executing All Items

Issue: The loop does not process all items in a collection.
Solution:

- Check if the array being passed to the **Apply to Each** is complete.

- Ensure pagination is enabled for large datasets.

Do Until Loop Running Indefinitely

Issue: The **Do Until** condition is never met, causing an infinite loop.
Solution:

- Ensure the condition is reachable.

- Set a timeout or maximum iteration count.

Performance Issues Due to Large Loops

Issue: A large loop slows down or fails due to too many iterations.
Solution:

- Use **filtering** to reduce the dataset size before looping.

- Optimize loop logic by avoiding unnecessary actions.

6. Real-World Examples

Example 1: Processing Multiple Email Attachments

Scenario: A user receives daily reports via email and needs to save attachments to OneDrive.
Solution:

1. Use **"When an email arrives"** trigger.

2. Apply an **Apply to Each** loop to process each attachment.

3. Save each attachment to OneDrive using **"Create file"** action.

Example 2: Automating Approval Reminders

Scenario: A manager wants to send reminder emails every 24 hours until an approval request is completed.
Solution:

1. Use a **Do Until** loop with a condition checking the approval status.

2. Inside the loop, send an email reminder.

3. Add a **"Delay"** action (e.g., 24 hours) before the next iteration.

---

7. Summary

Loops and iterations are powerful tools in Power Automate for handling repetitive tasks efficiently. The **Apply to Each** loop is ideal for processing collections, while the **Do Until** loop allows for condition-based automation. By following best practices and troubleshooting potential issues, users can optimize their workflows for performance and reliability.

Now that you understand loops in Power Automate, the next section will explore **Advanced Workflow Features**, including error handling, parallel branching, and debugging techniques.

4.1.3 Variables and Expressions

In Power Automate, **variables** and **expressions** are essential components for building dynamic, flexible, and powerful workflows. Variables store and manipulate data throughout a flow, while expressions allow users to perform calculations, format text, and extract information dynamically. Understanding how to use these features effectively will help you create more advanced and efficient workflows.

---

1. Understanding Variables in Power Automate

A **variable** in Power Automate is a container used to store data temporarily during a flow's execution. Variables allow you to manipulate and reuse data within different steps of a flow.

Why Use Variables?

Variables are useful for:

- Storing and modifying data dynamically

- Passing data between different steps in a flow

- Counting occurrences (e.g., keeping track of loop iterations)

- Holding temporary data that needs to be used multiple times

Types of Variables in Power Automate

Power Automate supports different types of variables based on the data they store:

Variable Type	Description	Example
String	Stores text values	"Hello, Power Automate!"
Integer	Stores whole numbers	100
Float	Stores decimal numbers	3.14
Boolean	Stores true/false values	true
Array	Stores a collection of values	["Item1", "Item2", "Item3"]
Object	Stores structured data	{"name": "John", "age": 30}

Declaring and Using Variables

Initializing a Variable

To create a variable in Power Automate:

1. Add a **"Initialize variable"** action.

2. Provide a **name** for the variable.

3. Select the **type** (String, Integer, Boolean, etc.).

4. Set an **initial value** (optional).

Setting and Modifying Variables

After initialization, you can change a variable's value using:

- **"Set variable"**: Assigns a new value to a variable.

- **"Increment variable"**: Increases a numeric variable by a specific amount.

- **"Append to array variable"**: Adds new items to an array.

Using Variables in a Flow

1. **Store User Input:** Capture user input from a form and store it in a variable.

2. **Count Loop Iterations:** Keep track of the number of times a loop runs.

3. **Store API Response Data:** Store and manipulate data retrieved from an API.

2. Understanding Expressions in Power Automate

Expressions in Power Automate allow users to perform calculations, format data, and manipulate variables dynamically. They use the **Workflow Definition Language (WDL)** and are written using **Power Automate Functions**.

Why Use Expressions?

Expressions are used for:

- Performing calculations (add(5, 3) → 8)

- Formatting text (concat("Hello ", "World") → "Hello World")

- Extracting data from JSON (outputs('GetData')?['name'] → "John")

- Date and time manipulations (utcNow() → "2024-02-21T12:00:00Z")

Common Expression Functions

Power Automate provides various functions for manipulating data.

String Functions

Function	Description	Example	Output
concat()	Joins multiple strings	concat("Hello", " ", "World")	"Hello World"
substring()	Extracts part of a string	substring("Power Automate", 0, 5)	"Power"

Function	Description	Example	Output
replace()	Replaces part of a string	replace("Hello World", "World", "Power Automate")	"Hello Power Automate"
toUpper()	Converts text to uppercase	toUpper("hello")	"HELLO"
toLower()	Converts text to lowercase	toLower("HELLO")	"hello"

Numeric Functions

Function	Description	Example	Output
add()	Adds two numbers	add(10, 5)	15
sub()	Subtracts numbers	sub(10, 5)	5
mul()	Multiplies numbers	mul(10, 2)	20
div()	Divides numbers	div(10, 2)	5

Date and Time Functions

Function	Description	Example	Output
utcNow()	Gets the current date/time	utcNow()	"2024-02-21T12:00:00Z"
addDays()	Adds days to a date	addDays(utcNow(), 5, 'yyyy-MM-dd')	"2024-02-26"
formatDateTime()	Formats date/time	formatDateTime(utcNow(), 'yyyy-MM-dd')	"2024-02-21"

3. Using Variables and Expressions in Real Scenarios

Example 1: Dynamic Email Greeting

Scenario: Send a personalized email greeting based on the recipient's name.

Flow Steps:

1. **Trigger:** When a new email arrives in Outlook.

2. **Action:** Extract the sender's name using substring() and split().

3. **Action:** Store the name in a variable.

4. **Action:** Use concat() to format the greeting dynamically.

5. **Action:** Send an email reply with the personalized greeting.

Expression Used:

concat("Hello ", variables('SenderName'), ", welcome to our service!")

Example 2: Calculate Due Dates Automatically

Scenario: Add 7 days to an invoice issue date to determine the due date.

Flow Steps:

1. **Trigger:** When a new invoice is added to a SharePoint list.

2. **Action:** Extract the invoice issue date.

3. **Action:** Use addDays() to calculate the due date.

4. **Action:** Store the due date in a variable.

5. **Action:** Update the SharePoint list with the due date.

Expression Used:

addDays(variables('InvoiceDate'), 7, 'yyyy-MM-dd')

Example 3: Loop Counter for Approval Requests

Scenario: Track the number of times an approval request is sent.

Flow Steps:

1. **Trigger:** When an approval process starts.

2. **Action:** Initialize a variable Counter with value 0.

3. **Action:** Inside a loop, increment Counter each time an approval is sent.

4. **Action:** Store the final count for reporting.

Expression Used:

increment(variables('Counter'), 1)

Conclusion

Variables and expressions are essential for creating dynamic and efficient workflows in Power Automate. By mastering these concepts, you can automate complex processes, manipulate data effectively, and improve productivity in your workflows.

4.2 Advanced Workflow Features

4.2.1 Error Handling in Workflows

Automation is a powerful tool for increasing efficiency and reducing repetitive tasks, but no system is perfect. Errors can occur due to incorrect configurations, unexpected data inputs, or service outages. **Proper error handling in Power Automate** is essential to ensure that workflows continue to function smoothly and provide users with the necessary feedback when issues arise. This section will cover the fundamentals of error handling, common failure points, and strategies to build resilient workflows.

1. Understanding Errors in Power Automate Workflows

What Causes Errors in Power Automate?

Errors in Power Automate can originate from several sources, including:

- **Invalid Data Inputs**: When a flow expects a specific format (e.g., a date field) but receives an incorrect value.

- **Missing Required Fields**: If a flow depends on required information that is not provided, it may fail.

- **Service Outages or API Failures**: If an external service like SharePoint or Outlook is down, flows that rely on them will fail.

- **Incorrect Logic or Conditions**: Flows with misconfigured conditions, expressions, or loops can produce unexpected results or errors.

- **Authentication and Permissions Issues**: If a user does not have the correct permissions, flows may not execute successfully.

Understanding these failure points is the first step in designing workflows that can handle errors efficiently.

2. Strategies for Error Handling in Power Automate

Using the "Configure Run After" Feature

Power Automate allows you to define how an action should behave if a previous step fails. The **"Configure run after"** feature provides different conditions:

- **Success**: The step runs only if the previous action is successful.

- **Failed**: The step runs only if the previous action fails.

- **Timed Out**: The step runs if the previous action does not complete within a given time.

- **Skipped**: The step runs if the previous action was skipped (often due to conditions).

How to Use "Configure Run After" for Error Handling

1. Click on an action within your flow.

2. Select the three-dot menu (**...**) and choose **"Configure run after"**.

3. Select one or more failure conditions (e.g., "Failed" or "Timed Out").

4. Add an alternative action, such as sending an email alert or retrying the step.

Example: If an email cannot be sent, you can configure an alternative step to log the error in a SharePoint list for later review.

Implementing Try-Catch Logic in Power Automate

Similar to programming, Power Automate allows you to implement **"Try-Catch"** error handling using Scope actions.

Steps to Create Try-Catch Logic

1. **Create a "Try" Scope**:

    o Add a "Scope" action and name it "Try".

    o Place all the main workflow actions inside this scope.

2. **Create a "Catch" Scope**:

    o Add a second "Scope" action and name it "Catch".

    o Configure its "Run After" settings to execute only if "Try" fails.

     o Add actions to log the error, send notifications, or execute alternative processes.

3. **Create a "Finally" Scope (Optional)**:

     o This scope runs regardless of whether "Try" succeeds or fails.

     o Useful for cleanup tasks such as closing connections or finalizing logs.

Example Use Case: If a flow tries to retrieve data from SharePoint and fails, the "Catch" scope can notify the user and provide troubleshooting steps.

Adding Error Notifications

When an error occurs, users should be notified promptly. Power Automate supports various notification methods:

- **Email Alerts**: Send an email notification to administrators or users when an error occurs.

- **Microsoft Teams Messages**: Post a message in a Teams channel to inform support teams.

- **Logging Errors in SharePoint or Dataverse**: Maintain a record of failed executions for tracking and auditing.

How to Add Error Notifications

1. Create an action that sends an email or a Teams message.

2. Use **dynamic content** to include details of the error.

3. Configure the action to run only if the previous step fails (using "Configure Run After").

Example: If a document upload fails, the flow can automatically notify the IT team via Microsoft Teams.

3. Handling Specific Types of Errors

Managing Data Validation Errors

To prevent errors caused by invalid data inputs:

- Use **Condition** actions to verify data before processing.

- Implement **Data Operations – Parse JSON** to ensure correct data formatting.

- Use **Expressions** to check for null or incorrect values before proceeding.

Example: Before saving a phone number in a database, ensure it contains only numbers and has the correct length.

Handling Service Outages and API Failures

If an external service (e.g., SharePoint, Outlook, or an API) is temporarily down, your flow may fail. To mitigate this:

- **Enable retries**: Many actions allow you to configure retry policies.

- **Use delay and retry loops**: Implement a **Do Until** loop that retries a request after a short delay.

- **Provide fallback mechanisms**: If SharePoint is unavailable, store data in an alternative location like OneDrive.

Example: If an API request fails, the flow can retry three times before notifying the user.

Handling Authentication and Permissions Issues

If a flow fails due to authentication issues (e.g., expired credentials or insufficient permissions):

- Use **Service Accounts** instead of personal accounts to avoid permission-based failures.

- Periodically check and refresh authentication credentials.

- Implement **Fallback Mechanisms**, such as using an alternative API key or notifying an admin to update permissions.

Example: If a flow fails due to lack of access to a SharePoint site, the system can alert an administrator to resolve the issue.

4. Best Practices for Error Handling in Power Automate

- **Test Flows in Different Scenarios**: Simulate failures to verify how your error-handling logic works.

- **Use Logging and Monitoring**: Maintain logs of failed flows for debugging and auditing.

- **Minimize Dependencies on External Services**: Reduce reliance on unstable APIs or services.

- **Optimize Flow Performance**: Avoid unnecessary actions that may lead to timeouts.

- **Document Error Handling Procedures**: Ensure team members understand how errors are managed and resolved.

5. Conclusion

Error handling is a crucial part of building reliable and efficient workflows in Power Automate. By using **"Configure Run After"**, **Try-Catch logic**, **error notifications**, and **fallback mechanisms**, you can create resilient automation that minimizes disruptions and improves user experience.

The next section will explore **"Using Parallel Branching"**, an advanced feature that enables workflows to run multiple processes simultaneously for greater efficiency.

4.2.2 Using Parallel Branching

Introduction to Parallel Branching

Parallel branching in Power Automate is a powerful feature that allows users to execute multiple actions simultaneously rather than sequentially. This capability significantly improves workflow efficiency by enabling concurrent operations, reducing processing time, and optimizing resource usage.

Parallel branches are particularly useful when dealing with tasks that are independent of each other, such as:

- Sending multiple notifications to different users at the same time

- Running different data processing tasks in parallel

- Retrieving data from multiple sources simultaneously

- Executing separate approval processes that do not depend on one another

By leveraging parallel branching, you can create workflows that handle multiple operations in an optimized and scalable manner.

How Parallel Branching Works in Power Automate

In a typical sequential workflow, actions execute one after another, meaning that each step must be completed before the next one begins. However, with parallel branching, multiple actions can run simultaneously, which speeds up workflow execution.

Key Characteristics of Parallel Branching:

- **Independent Execution:** Each branch runs its actions independently.

- **Concurrency:** Actions in parallel branches start at the same time.

- **Synchronization at the End:** After the parallel branches finish executing, the workflow continues to the next step.

Power Automate allows you to create parallel branches easily using the graphical user interface (GUI) without needing to write any code.

Setting Up Parallel Branching in Power Automate

To implement parallel branching in Power Automate, follow these steps:

Step 1: Create a New Flow

1. Open **Power Automate** and log in to your Microsoft account.

2. Click on **Create** and choose **Automated cloud flow** or **Instant cloud flow** based on your requirements.

3. Select a trigger (e.g., **When an email arrives in Outlook** or **When an item is created in SharePoint**).

4. Click **Create** to proceed.

Step 2: Add a Parallel Branch

1. After adding the first action in your flow, click the **+ (Add an action)** button.

2. Select **Add a parallel branch** instead of adding a regular action.

3. A new panel appears, allowing you to define two separate actions that will run in parallel.

4. Configure each branch with its own set of actions.

Step 3: Define Actions in Each Branch

Each branch can perform different operations based on your workflow requirements. Here are a few examples:

- **Example 1: Sending Notifications in Parallel**

  o One branch sends an email notification to the manager.

  o Another branch sends a Microsoft Teams message to the project team.

- **Example 2: Retrieving Data from Multiple Sources**

  o One branch retrieves customer information from a SharePoint list.

  o Another branch pulls sales data from an Excel file.

- **Example 3: Running Parallel Approval Processes**

  o One branch sends an approval request to the HR department.

  o Another branch sends an approval request to the finance team.

Step 4: Execute and Monitor the Flow

1. Click **Save** to store your flow.

2. Click **Test** and select **Manually** to trigger the flow.

3. Monitor the execution by navigating to **Run History** in Power Automate.

4. Check if both parallel branches execute correctly and complete simultaneously.

Use Cases of Parallel Branching

1. Multi-Channel Notifications

A common use case for parallel branching is sending notifications through multiple channels simultaneously. For instance, when a critical issue is detected in an IT system, a parallel branch can:

- Send an email to the IT support team

- Send an SMS alert to on-call engineers

- Post an urgent message on Microsoft Teams

This ensures that all relevant parties receive alerts without delay.

2. Data Processing from Multiple Sources

When working with large datasets, retrieving information from different sources can be time-consuming if done sequentially. With parallel branching, you can:

- Retrieve customer records from a **SQL database**

- Fetch order history from an **Excel spreadsheet**

- Get recent interactions from **Microsoft Dynamics 365**

Each operation runs simultaneously, significantly reducing wait times.

3. Parallel Approval Workflows

Parallel branching is particularly useful for approval workflows where multiple departments need to approve a request independently. For example, in an **employee promotion request**, parallel branches can:

- Send an approval request to **HR**

- Send an approval request to **Finance**

- Send an approval request to **Department Head**

Each branch executes independently, ensuring a faster and more efficient approval process.

4. Simultaneous Document Generation and Storage

A document processing workflow might need to:

- Generate a PDF version of a contract

- Upload the PDF to **SharePoint**

- Send the contract via **email to stakeholders**

With parallel branching, all these steps can happen concurrently instead of sequentially, improving efficiency.

Best Practices for Using Parallel Branching

1. Keep Parallel Branches Independent

Ensure that each branch runs independently without dependencies on other branches. If branches require shared data, retrieve the data before initiating the parallel process.

2. Avoid Overloading the Flow

Running too many parallel branches simultaneously can cause performance issues. Microsoft Power Automate has limits on concurrent executions, so keep the number of branches reasonable.

3. Use Parallel Branching for Time-Consuming Tasks

Leverage parallel branching when dealing with tasks that usually take a long time, such as:

- Fetching data from multiple APIs

- Sending bulk notifications

- Processing approval requests

4. Handle Errors Gracefully

Each branch should include error-handling mechanisms to prevent failures from affecting the entire workflow. Use the **Configure Run After** settings to specify actions for failed branches.

5. Monitor and Optimize Performance

Regularly check the **Run History** in Power Automate to analyze execution times. If a particular branch takes significantly longer than others, consider optimizing the actions within that branch.

Troubleshooting Common Issues

1. One Branch Finishes Before the Other

Issue: A branch completes faster while others are still processing, causing unexpected behavior.
Solution: Use the **Delay** action to synchronize execution times or restructure the workflow to ensure proper sequencing.

2. Parallel Actions Not Executing Simultaneously

Issue: Some branches appear to run sequentially instead of concurrently.
Solution: Ensure that actions within each branch are not dependent on external factors causing delays.

3. Flow Fails Due to API Limits

Issue: Running too many parallel actions can exceed API limits for certain services.
Solution: Reduce the number of parallel branches or implement **rate limiting** strategies.

Conclusion

Parallel branching in Power Automate is an essential feature for optimizing workflows by executing multiple actions simultaneously. Whether you're automating notifications, processing approvals, or retrieving data from different sources, parallel branches help enhance efficiency and scalability.

By following best practices and troubleshooting common issues, you can ensure that your parallel workflows run smoothly, improving productivity and automation reliability.

Now that you understand parallel branching, the next step is to explore **monitoring and debugging flows**, which will help you analyze and optimize your automation processes further.

4.2.3 Monitoring and Debugging Flows

Microsoft Power Automate provides powerful tools to monitor and debug your flows, ensuring that automation runs smoothly and efficiently. By keeping track of flow execution, troubleshooting errors, and optimizing performance, you can maintain high reliability in your automated workflows. This section will guide you through the key aspects of monitoring and debugging flows in Power Automate, covering built-in monitoring tools, troubleshooting techniques, and best practices.

1. Understanding the Importance of Monitoring and Debugging

Automated workflows are designed to eliminate manual tasks and improve efficiency, but they can encounter failures due to issues such as misconfigured actions, missing data, or connection problems. Monitoring helps:

- Detect and resolve errors quickly.

- Improve workflow performance and reliability.

- Ensure data integrity across connected apps and services.

- Provide insights into how flows operate over time.

Power Automate offers several built-in monitoring and debugging tools that allow you to track flow performance, identify failures, and optimize execution.

2. Built-In Monitoring Tools in Power Automate

Power Automate provides several ways to monitor the execution of flows. These include:

2.1 Flow Run History

The **Flow Run History** is a fundamental tool for tracking execution details. Every time a flow runs, Power Automate logs information about its status, duration, and any encountered errors.

How to Access Flow Run History:

1. Open **Power Automate** (https://flow.microsoft.com).

2. Click on **My Flows** in the left navigation pane.

3. Select the flow you want to monitor.

4. Click **Runs** to see a list of past executions.

Key Features of Flow Run History:

- **Success and Failure Indicators** – Each run is marked as **Succeeded, Failed, or Canceled**.

- **Timestamp Information** – Shows when the flow was triggered and how long it took to complete.

- **Detailed Run Logs** – Provides insights into each step of the flow, including inputs, outputs, and any errors.

- **Resubmitting Flows** – Allows you to retry failed runs after making necessary corrections.

2.2 Run Details and Step-by-Step Logs

Power Automate logs details about each step of a flow, which is helpful for debugging. You can view:

- **Trigger Details** – See what data triggered the flow.

- **Action Inputs and Outputs** – Understand what data was passed between actions.

- **Error Messages** – Identify the root cause of failed actions.

How to View Detailed Run Logs:

1. Open the **Flow Run History** (as described in section 2.1).

2. Click on a specific run to open its details.

3. Expand each step to see input and output data, as well as any error messages.

2.3 Notifications and Alerts for Flow Failures

To avoid manually checking flow statuses, Power Automate can send **email notifications** or **Teams alerts** when a flow fails.

How to Enable Failure Notifications:

1. Open your flow in Power Automate.

2. Click on **Edit** to modify the flow.

3. Add a new action at the end of the flow:

   o Select **"Send an email notification"** (or use Microsoft Teams for alerts).

   o Configure the recipient and message content.

4. Save the flow.

Now, whenever a failure occurs, you will receive an instant notification with details about the error.

---

3. Common Errors and Debugging Techniques

Power Automate flows can fail due to various reasons. Below are some common errors and strategies to debug them.

Connection and Authentication Issues

Problem:

- Actions fail due to missing or expired connections to services (e.g., SharePoint, Outlook, Excel).

- You receive an error like **"Connection not found"** or **"Authentication required"**.

Solution:

1. Open **Power Automate** and navigate to **Data → Connections**.

2. Find the affected connection and **re-authenticate** if needed.

3. If necessary, delete and recreate the connection.

Missing or Incorrect Data

Problem:

- Flows fail because required data is missing or in an unexpected format.

- Errors like **"Invalid JSON format"** or **"Required field is missing"** appear.

Solution:

1. Use the **"Compose" action** to inspect input data before passing it to other actions.

2. Add **"Condition" actions** to check for missing values before executing dependent steps.

3. Test flows with different sample inputs to ensure they handle variations correctly.

Loops and Infinite Recursion

Problem:

- Flows with loops (e.g., **Apply to Each** or **Do Until**) fail or run indefinitely.

- Flow run history shows excessive executions without completing.

Solution:

1. Ensure loop conditions have an **exit condition** to prevent infinite execution.

2. Use **timeout settings** in actions to limit execution time.

3. Check for unexpected data duplication causing redundant iterations.

API Rate Limits and Throttling

Problem:

- Microsoft or third-party APIs enforce rate limits, causing flow actions to fail.

- You receive an error like **"429 Too Many Requests"**.

Solution:

1. **Add "Delay" actions** between API calls to reduce request frequency.

2. Use **pagination** and **batch processing** to handle large data sets more efficiently.

3. Monitor API usage and consider upgrading to a premium plan if limits are frequently exceeded.

4. Optimizing Flows for Better Performance

Beyond debugging, optimizing your flows improves efficiency and reduces failures.

Reducing Unnecessary Actions

- Remove redundant steps that don't contribute to the flow's outcome.

- Combine multiple conditions into a **single expression** where possible.

Using Parallel Branching

- Instead of executing steps sequentially, split independent tasks into **parallel branches** to speed up execution.

Caching Data to Reduce API Calls

- Store frequently used data in **variables** or **SharePoint lists** instead of retrieving it repeatedly from external services.

Monitoring Flow Performance Over Time

- Use **Power BI dashboards** to track flow execution trends and detect performance bottlenecks.

- Regularly review and update flows to align with evolving business needs.

5. Conclusion

Monitoring and debugging are critical for maintaining reliable Power Automate workflows. By leveraging the **Flow Run History**, **detailed logs**, and **error handling mechanisms**, users can identify and resolve issues efficiently. Additionally, implementing **best practices** such as reducing unnecessary actions, optimizing loops, and handling API rate limits can significantly enhance workflow performance.

By mastering these techniques, you will ensure that your automated processes run smoothly, ultimately saving time and improving business efficiency.

Next Steps:

- Try monitoring your existing flows using the **Flow Run History**.

- Set up **failure notifications** to receive real-time alerts.

- Experiment with **debugging techniques** for different error scenarios.

4.3 Connecting Power Automate with Other Apps

4.3.1 Integrating with Microsoft 365 Apps (Excel, Teams, SharePoint)

Microsoft Power Automate seamlessly integrates with Microsoft 365 applications, allowing users to automate repetitive tasks, improve efficiency, and connect various services without the need for complex coding. Among the most commonly used integrations are **Excel, Microsoft Teams, and SharePoint**, which are essential tools for collaboration and data management.

This section will guide you through the integration of Power Automate with these three Microsoft 365 apps, providing practical use cases and step-by-step instructions to help you build effective automated workflows.

1. Integrating Power Automate with Excel

Microsoft Excel is widely used for data storage, analysis, and reporting. Power Automate enables users to automate Excel-related processes, such as **data entry, updates, and notifications** when changes occur in a spreadsheet.

Understanding Power Automate and Excel Integration

Power Automate connects with Excel using **Excel Online (Business)** and requires the spreadsheet to be stored in OneDrive or SharePoint. This allows cloud-based automation, eliminating the need for manual updates.

Some common use cases include:

- Automatically adding new rows to an Excel table when data is submitted through a form.

- Sending email notifications when a specific value in a spreadsheet changes.

- Exporting data from an Excel file to another system, such as SharePoint or a database.

Setting Up Power Automate with Excel

To use Power Automate with Excel, follow these steps:

Step 1: Prepare Your Excel File

1. Ensure your Excel file is stored in **OneDrive or SharePoint** (local files are not supported).

2. Convert your data into a **table** (Power Automate only works with structured tables in Excel).

   o Open Excel, select your data, and click **"Format as Table"** under the **Home** tab.

   o Assign a **table name** (e.g., SalesData).

Step 2: Create a Flow in Power Automate

1. Open **Power Automate** and click **Create → Automated Cloud Flow**.

2. Choose a **trigger**, such as **"When a row is added, modified, or deleted"** from the Excel connector.

3. Select your **Excel file** and **table name** from OneDrive or SharePoint.

4. Add an **action**, such as **sending an email notification** or **copying the data to another system**.

5. Click **Save and Test** to ensure the automation works correctly.

Example: Sending an Email When a Value Exceeds a Threshold

Scenario: You have an Excel sheet tracking sales, and you want to receive an email when a sales value exceeds $5000.

1. **Trigger**: "When a row is modified in Excel"

2. **Condition**: If the "Sales Amount" column is greater than $5000

3. **Action**: Send an email notification with the sales details

This flow ensures that managers are alerted whenever a high-value sale occurs.

---

2. Integrating Power Automate with Microsoft Teams

Microsoft Teams is the central hub for collaboration in Microsoft 365. Integrating Power Automate with Teams allows users to automate notifications, approvals, and data-sharing processes, making teamwork more efficient.

Common Use Cases for Power Automate and Teams

- Sending automated messages when a new task is assigned in a project.

- Notifying team members about critical updates from SharePoint or Excel.

- Creating approval workflows for requests submitted via Teams.

- Scheduling Teams meetings automatically based on triggers from other apps.

Setting Up Power Automate with Teams

Follow these steps to integrate Power Automate with Microsoft Teams:

Step 1: Create a New Flow

1. Open **Power Automate** and click **Create → Automated Cloud Flow**.

2. Select a **trigger**, such as **"When a new message is posted in a channel"** (Teams connector).

3. Choose the specific **Team and Channel** where the message will be monitored.

Step 2: Define the Action

1. Choose an **action**, such as **"Post a message in Teams"**.

2. Customize the message with dynamic content from the trigger.

Example: Notifying a Team When a Document is Uploaded

Scenario: You want to send an automated Teams notification when a document is uploaded to a SharePoint folder.

1. **Trigger**: "When a file is created in a SharePoint folder"

2. **Action**: "Post a message in Teams" with the file name and link

This flow ensures that team members are instantly informed about new files.

---

3. Integrating Power Automate with SharePoint

SharePoint is a powerful document management and collaboration platform. By integrating Power Automate, users can automate workflows such as document approvals, data synchronization, and notifications.

Common Use Cases for Power Automate and SharePoint

- Automatically copying files from one SharePoint site to another.

- Sending approval requests for newly uploaded documents.

- Syncing SharePoint lists with external applications such as Excel, Outlook, or Teams.

- Notifying users when a document is modified or approved.

Setting Up Power Automate with SharePoint

To integrate Power Automate with SharePoint, follow these steps:

Step 1: Choose a SharePoint Trigger

1. Open **Power Automate** and click **Create → Automated Cloud Flow**.

2. Select a **trigger**, such as **"When a file is created or modified in a SharePoint library"**.

3. Select the specific **SharePoint site and document library**.

Step 2: Add an Action Based on the Trigger

1. Choose an action, such as **sending an approval request** or **copying the document to another folder**.

2. Configure the action to include relevant details (e.g., file name, approver email).

Example: Automating a Document Approval Process

Scenario: You need an approval workflow where a manager reviews and approves new files uploaded to a SharePoint folder.

1. **Trigger**: "When a file is created in a SharePoint library"

2. **Action 1**: "Start an approval process" (assign to manager)

3. **Action 2**: "Send an email notification" with the approval status

This flow streamlines document approval, ensuring quick responses without manual tracking.

Conclusion

Integrating Power Automate with **Excel, Teams, and SharePoint** unlocks powerful automation capabilities, reducing manual effort and improving collaboration. By following the steps and examples provided, users can create custom workflows that fit their specific business needs.

Key Takeaways:

- **Excel integration** is useful for data updates, notifications, and tracking changes.

- **Teams integration** helps automate messaging, task management, and approvals.

- **SharePoint integration** enables document automation, approval workflows, and data synchronization.

By mastering these integrations, you can transform your Microsoft 365 experience and significantly enhance productivity.

4.3.2 Working with Third-Party Connectors (Trello, Slack, Twitter)

Introduction to Third-Party Connectors

Microsoft Power Automate offers a vast range of connectors that allow users to integrate their workflows with third-party applications. These connectors enable seamless automation between Power Automate and external services, eliminating the need for manual data transfers and repetitive tasks.

Some of the most commonly used third-party connectors include:

- **Trello** – A popular project management tool that helps teams organize tasks and projects.

- **Slack** – A widely used communication platform for team collaboration.

- **Twitter** – A social media platform used for marketing, customer engagement, and brand awareness.

This section will guide you through the process of integrating Power Automate with these three third-party applications.

1. Connecting Trello with Power Automate

Overview of Trello Integration

Trello is a project management tool that allows users to create boards, lists, and cards to organize tasks efficiently. With Power Automate, you can automate actions such as:

- Creating new Trello cards from emails or form submissions.
- Sending notifications when a card is updated.
- Moving Trello cards based on specific triggers.

Setting Up Trello in Power Automate

Step 1: Connecting Trello to Power Automate

1. Open Power Automate and sign in to your Microsoft account.
2. Click on **"Connectors"** from the left panel.
3. Search for **Trello** in the connector search bar.
4. Click on the **Trello** connector and select **"Sign in"**.
5. Authorize Power Automate to access your Trello account.

Step 2: Creating a Flow with Trello

Example: **Automatically Create a Trello Card from an Email**

1. Click **"Create"** and select **"Automated Cloud Flow"**.
2. Choose **Outlook – When a new email arrives** as the trigger.
3. Click **"New step"**, search for **Trello**, and select **"Create a card"** action.
4. Choose the Trello **board** and **list** where the card should be created.

5. Map the email subject and body to the Trello card's title and description fields.

6. Click **"Save"** and test the flow.

Advanced Trello Automation

- Move Trello cards when an approval is granted.

- Assign tasks in Trello when a new form submission is received.

- Archive completed Trello cards automatically.

2. Connecting Slack with Power Automate

Overview of Slack Integration

Slack is a messaging platform widely used for team communication. With Power Automate, you can automate various Slack interactions, such as:

- Sending automated messages to a Slack channel.

- Notifying a user when an important event occurs.

- Posting messages based on emails or SharePoint updates.

Setting Up Slack in Power Automate

Step 1: Connecting Slack to Power Automate

1. Open Power Automate and go to the **Connectors** section.

2. Search for **Slack** and click on it.

3. Click **"Sign in"** and authorize Power Automate to access Slack.

Step 2: Creating a Flow with Slack

Example: **Send a Slack Notification When a SharePoint File is Updated**

1. Click **"Create"** and choose **"Automated Cloud Flow"**.

2. Select **"When a file is created or modified"** (SharePoint) as the trigger.

3. Click **"New Step"**, search for **Slack**, and choose **"Post a message"** action.

4. Select the Slack **channel** where the message should be sent.

5. Customize the message, including file name and link.

6. Click **"Save"** and test the flow.

Advanced Slack Automation

- Notify a team when a new Trello card is created.

- Send a direct message when a specific keyword is mentioned in an email.

- Archive Slack messages after a project is completed.

---

3. Connecting Twitter with Power Automate

Overview of Twitter Integration

Twitter is a popular social media platform used for marketing, customer service, and brand engagement. With Power Automate, you can:

- Post tweets automatically.

- Monitor Twitter for specific keywords.

- Respond to tweets based on predefined conditions.

Setting Up Twitter in Power Automate

Step 1: Connecting Twitter to Power Automate

1. Open Power Automate and navigate to **Connectors**.

2. Search for **Twitter** and click on it.

3. Click **"Sign in"** and authorize Power Automate to access your Twitter account.

Step 2: Creating a Flow with Twitter

Example: **Automatically Post a Tweet When a Blog is Published**

1. Click **"Create"** and choose **"Automated Cloud Flow"**.

2. Select **RSS – When a new feed item is published** as the trigger.

3. Click **"New Step"**, search for **Twitter**, and select **"Post a Tweet"** action.

4. Enter the **Tweet text**, including the blog title and link.

5. Click **"Save"** and test the flow.

Advanced Twitter Automation

- Send a notification when your brand is mentioned on Twitter.

- Auto-reply to tweets with predefined responses.

- Retweet posts that contain a specific hashtag.

4. Best Practices for Using Third-Party Connectors

Security Considerations

- Limit permissions for third-party apps to protect sensitive data.

- Regularly review API access and revoke unnecessary connections.

Managing API Limits

- Some services have API call limits—optimize your flows to avoid hitting these limits.

- Use scheduled triggers instead of instant triggers where possible.

Monitoring and Troubleshooting Flows

- Regularly check Power Automate **run history** to identify failures.

- Use **error handling** techniques to manage API call failures gracefully.

Conclusion

Integrating Power Automate with third-party services like Trello, Slack, and Twitter enables businesses to enhance efficiency and streamline workflows. By automating routine tasks such as task management, notifications, and social media engagement, users can focus on more strategic activities.

With the right configuration, security measures, and API management, Power Automate becomes a powerful tool for connecting different platforms, making automation a seamless part of daily work.

4.3.3 Custom Connectors and APIs

Introduction to Custom Connectors and APIs

Power Automate provides a vast library of built-in connectors that allow users to integrate different applications and services seamlessly. However, there may be scenarios where the built-in connectors do not support the specific needs of your business or application. In such cases, **custom connectors** and **APIs** come into play, allowing users to extend Power Automate's functionality and integrate with almost any service that has an API.

This section will explore how custom connectors work, how to create and configure them, and how to use APIs within Power Automate to create powerful automation workflows.

---

1. What is a Custom Connector in Power Automate?

A **custom connector** is a user-defined connector that allows Power Automate to communicate with external services using APIs. Custom connectors act as a bridge between Power Automate and an API that is not natively supported by Microsoft's built-in connectors.

Custom connectors can be used for:

- Connecting to **internal company applications** that do not have public connectors.

- Integrating with **third-party services** that provide APIs but do not have a built-in Power Automate connector.

- Adding **custom authentication methods** that are required by certain services.

- Extending the functionality of Power Automate beyond the default connectors.

---

2. Understanding APIs in Power Automate

Before diving into custom connectors, it's essential to understand **APIs (Application Programming Interfaces)** and how they interact with Power Automate.

What is an API?

An API is a set of rules that allows applications to communicate with each other. APIs use **HTTP requests** to send and receive data between systems.

APIs typically support the following request methods:

- **GET** – Retrieve data from an external service.

- **POST** – Send data to an external service.

- **PUT** – Update existing data in an external service.

- **DELETE** – Remove data from an external service.

Types of APIs Supported in Power Automate

Power Automate supports APIs that follow the **REST (Representational State Transfer)** standard, as well as **SOAP (Simple Object Access Protocol)** in some cases. Most modern APIs use REST, which works well with Power Automate's HTTP-based actions.

When working with APIs in Power Automate, you often need to interact with **JSON (JavaScript Object Notation)**, which is the standard data format used by most APIs. Understanding JSON structure is crucial when handling API responses and requests in Power Automate.

3. Creating a Custom Connector in Power Automate

Prerequisites

Before you create a custom connector, you need:

- A Power Automate or Power Apps environment

- An API with a valid OpenAPI definition (Swagger), Postman collection, or HTTP endpoint

- Authentication details (if the API requires authentication)

Steps to Create a Custom Connector

Step 1: Accessing the Custom Connector Portal

1. Log in to **Power Automate** (https://flow.microsoft.com).

2. Click on **"Data"** in the left navigation panel.

3. Select **"Custom Connectors"** from the dropdown menu.

4. Click **"New custom connector"**, then choose from the following options:

- o **Create from blank** (Manually define API endpoints)

- o **Import an OpenAPI file** (Use an API definition in OpenAPI format)

- o **Import from Postman collection** (Use a collection of API calls from Postman)

Step 2: Defining General Connector Information

- Provide a **name** for your connector.

- Upload an **icon** and provide a **description**.

- Define the **host URL** of the API you are connecting to.

Step 3: Configuring Authentication

Depending on the API, you may need to configure authentication, such as:

- **No authentication** (Public APIs)

- **API Key** authentication

- **OAuth 2.0** authentication

- **Basic authentication** (Username and Password)

Step 4: Defining API Endpoints

- Click **"Definition"** and add a new action.

- Define the **request method (GET, POST, PUT, DELETE, etc.)**.

- Specify the **API URL endpoint**.

- Configure **query parameters**, **headers**, and **body schema**.

- Test the request to ensure it works correctly.

Step 5: Testing and Deploying the Connector

- Click **"Test"** and provide the required credentials.

- Send a sample request to verify that the API is responding correctly.

- Save and deploy the custom connector.

4. Using a Custom Connector in Power Automate

Once the custom connector is created, you can use it in Power Automate workflows:

Adding the Custom Connector to a Flow

1. Create a new flow in Power Automate.

2. Select a **trigger** (e.g., "When an email arrives").

3. Click **"New step"** and search for the custom connector.

4. Select the **custom connector action** you created.

5. Configure the action by specifying required parameters.

Example: Using a Custom API to Fetch Data

Let's say you have a **CRM system API** that provides customer details. You can create a flow that:

1. **Triggers** when a new email arrives.

2. **Calls the custom connector** to fetch customer details from the CRM API.

3. **Sends an automated email** with customer details to a sales team.

5. Best Practices for Custom Connectors and APIs in Power Automate

Security Best Practices

- **Use OAuth 2.0 authentication** when possible to ensure security.

- **Do not expose API keys in flows**—store them securely in environment variables.

- **Restrict API access** to authorized users only.

Performance Optimization

- Use **pagination** for APIs that return large datasets.

- Minimize API calls by **caching responses** when appropriate.

- Handle **error responses** properly to prevent flow failures.

Documentation and Maintenance

- Maintain **detailed documentation** for each custom connector.

- Regularly **test and update** API definitions to prevent broken integrations.

- Monitor API usage and **set rate limits** to avoid exceeding API quotas.

6. Troubleshooting Custom Connectors and APIs

Common Issues and Fixes

Issue	Solution
Authentication errors	Verify API keys, OAuth tokens, and permissions.
API response issues	Check the API endpoint and parameters.
Power Automate flow failures	Debug using flow history and API response logs.

Debugging API Requests in Power Automate

- Use **"Test" mode** in the custom connector editor.

- Inspect API response logs in **Power Automate run history**.

- Utilize tools like **Postman** to verify API endpoints.

Conclusion

Custom connectors and APIs allow you to extend Power Automate's capabilities beyond built-in connectors, enabling deeper integrations and powerful automation workflows. By following best practices for security, performance, and maintenance, you can build reliable custom connectors that integrate seamlessly with your business applications.

PART V
Power Automate Desktop: Automating Local Tasks

5.1 What is Power Automate Desktop?

Introduction

In today's digital world, automation is a key component in improving efficiency and reducing manual tasks. While cloud-based automation is powerful, many business processes still involve local files, legacy applications, and desktop interactions. **Microsoft Power Automate Desktop (PAD)** extends the capabilities of Power Automate by allowing users to automate processes that involve their local computers.

Power Automate Desktop is a **Robotic Process Automation (RPA)** tool that enables users to create **desktop flows** that interact with local applications, files, and web browsers. With PAD, users can record their actions, such as mouse clicks and keystrokes, and then replay them as automated workflows.

In this chapter, we will explore the **features, benefits, and components of Power Automate Desktop**, giving you a solid foundation to start automating your local tasks effectively.

Understanding Power Automate Desktop

Power Automate Desktop is an **RPA solution** designed to automate repetitive tasks on a local machine. Unlike **cloud flows**, which primarily automate web-based tasks using cloud services, **desktop flows** interact directly with applications and files stored on a user's computer.

Key Differences Between Power Automate Desktop and Cloud Flows

Feature	Power Automate Desktop	Power Automate Cloud Flows
Execution	Runs on a local machine	Runs in the cloud
Automation Scope	Automates desktop applications, files, and legacy systems	Automates cloud-based applications and services
Recording	Can record mouse movements, keyboard inputs, and UI interactions	Does not support recording local interactions
Connectivity	Works with on-premises systems	Works with cloud-based applications and services
User Interaction	Can simulate human interaction with desktop apps	Mainly handles backend automation without UI interaction

Who Can Benefit from Power Automate Desktop?

Power Automate Desktop is useful for:

- **Business users** who want to automate repetitive tasks, such as data entry and report generation.

- **IT teams** looking to automate system administration tasks and integrate legacy applications.

- **Finance professionals** who need to extract, transform, and process large amounts of data.

- **Customer service teams** aiming to improve efficiency by automating common interactions.

Features of Power Automate Desktop

Microsoft Power Automate Desktop offers **powerful automation capabilities**, including:

1. Recording and Playback

- Users can **record their actions**, such as clicking buttons, typing text, and navigating applications.

- The recorded steps can be **replayed** automatically to execute the same task without user intervention.

2. UI Automation

- PAD can interact with **graphical user interfaces (GUIs)** to control desktop applications.

- It can detect and manipulate elements like **buttons, menus, text fields, and checkboxes**.

3. File and Folder Management

- Users can automate operations such as **copying, moving, deleting, and renaming files**.

- It supports **reading and writing data from text files, CSV files, and Excel spreadsheets**.

4. Web Automation

- PAD can automate interactions with **web applications and browsers**.

- It supports automating form submissions, data extraction, and login processes.

5. Data Extraction and Processing

- Users can extract data from **web pages, PDFs, and emails** and process it using built-in actions.

- It integrates with **Microsoft Excel, SQL databases, and other data sources**.

6. Error Handling and Exception Management

- Users can define **error-handling rules** to manage unexpected failures.

- It supports **conditional logic** to handle different scenarios dynamically.

7. Integration with Power Automate Cloud

- Desktop flows can be **triggered by cloud flows**, allowing hybrid automation.

- Users can **combine RPA with cloud-based services** like SharePoint, Outlook, and Teams.

How Power Automate Desktop Works

1. Recording Actions

- Users can start a recording session where PAD tracks **mouse clicks, keyboard inputs, and UI interactions**.

- Recorded actions are converted into **steps in a workflow**.

2. Creating Automation Workflows

- Users can design workflows by **dragging and dropping predefined actions** in the PAD interface.

- Workflows can include **conditional logic, loops, and data manipulation**.

3. Running Desktop Flows

- Desktop flows can be **executed manually or scheduled** to run at specific times.

- They can also be **triggered by cloud flows** for seamless automation across different environments.

4. Monitoring and Debugging

- PAD provides **logs and debugging tools** to track workflow execution.

- Users can identify and fix errors by **reviewing execution steps and error messages**.

Benefits of Power Automate Desktop

Power Automate Desktop **offers several advantages**, making it an essential tool for modern automation:

1. Increased Productivity

- Automating repetitive tasks **reduces manual workload**, allowing employees to focus on higher-value activities.

2. Cost Savings

- Automating routine processes **reduces human errors and operational costs**, leading to **significant savings over time**.

3. Improved Accuracy

- Unlike humans, automation ensures **consistent and error-free execution of tasks**.

4. Scalability

- Organizations can **scale automation** across multiple departments, improving overall efficiency.

5. Hybrid Automation

- Power Automate Desktop **integrates seamlessly with cloud-based automation**, creating **end-to-end workflows** that handle both **desktop and online tasks**.

Real-World Use Cases of Power Automate Desktop

1. Automating Data Entry in Excel

- PAD can extract data from emails and **automatically populate Excel spreadsheets**.
- It can also **apply formulas, generate reports, and save the files** in designated folders.

2. Processing Invoices and Financial Documents

- PAD can read invoices from PDFs, extract key information, and enter it into **accounting software**.
- It can also **send notifications** when invoices are processed successfully.

3. Automating Customer Support Tasks

- PAD can **log customer complaints**, update CRM records, and send email confirmations.
- It can also **automate chat responses** by integrating with AI services.

4. Automating File Management

- Automatically **sort and organize files** based on predefined rules.
- Send **file update notifications** to relevant team members.

5. Running Legacy Applications

- Automate interactions with **old applications** that do not support modern APIs.

- Enable **smooth data transfer** between legacy systems and cloud applications.

Conclusion

Power Automate Desktop is a powerful RPA tool that allows users to automate local tasks, reducing manual effort and improving efficiency. Unlike cloud-based flows, desktop flows interact with applications and files directly on a user's computer, making them ideal for repetitive tasks, data processing, and system integration.

By leveraging UI automation, data extraction, and workflow management, Power Automate Desktop enables businesses to scale automation and streamline operations. In the next sections, we will explore how to install and configure Power Automate Desktop, create desktop flows, and integrate them with cloud automation to build seamless workflows.

5.2 Installing and Setting Up Power Automate Desktop

Microsoft Power Automate Desktop (PAD) is a powerful automation tool that enables users to automate repetitive tasks on their local machines. Unlike cloud-based Power Automate, which primarily automates workflows across online services, Power Automate Desktop allows you to interact with local applications, files, and even simulate human actions such as mouse clicks and keystrokes.

Before you can start creating and running desktop flows, you need to properly install and configure Power Automate Desktop. This section will guide you through the process of installing the software, setting up your environment, and ensuring everything is correctly configured for optimal performance.

System Requirements for Power Automate Desktop

Before installing Power Automate Desktop, you should verify that your system meets the minimum requirements to ensure smooth operation.

Minimum System Requirements

- **Operating System**: Windows 10 (Pro, Enterprise, or Education) or Windows 11

- **Processor**: 1.6 GHz or faster, 2-core CPU (Intel or AMD)

- **RAM**: At least 4 GB (8 GB recommended for better performance)

- **Storage**: Minimum 2 GB of available disk space

- **Internet Connection**: Required for installation and cloud-based functionalities

- **User Permissions**: Administrator rights are required for installation

Additional Requirements for Advanced Features

Some advanced functionalities, such as Optical Character Recognition (OCR) and AI-powered automation, may require additional system resources:

- .NET Framework 4.7.2 or later

- Microsoft Edge WebDriver for browser automation

- UI Automation dependencies for interacting with desktop applications

Downloading Power Automate Desktop

Microsoft provides Power Automate Desktop as a free application for Windows users. You can download the official version from Microsoft's website.

Steps to Download Power Automate Desktop

1. **Go to the Microsoft Power Automate website**:

   o Open a browser and visit: https://flow.microsoft.com

2. **Sign in with a Microsoft account**:

   o You need a Microsoft account to access the download section.

3. **Navigate to the "Downloads" section**:

   o Look for "Power Automate Desktop" and click on the download link.

4. **Download the installer**:

   o The setup file will be saved to your computer.

💡 *Tip: Always download Power Automate Desktop from the official Microsoft website to avoid security risks.*

Installing Power Automate Desktop

Once you have downloaded the setup file, you can proceed with the installation.

Step-by-Step Installation Guide

1. **Locate the Installer**

   o Open the folder where the Power Automate Desktop setup file was downloaded.

   o Double-click on the .exe file to start the installation.

2. **Begin the Installation Process**

        o   The installation wizard will launch. Click **Next** to continue.

3. **Accept the License Agreement**

        o   Read through the Microsoft Software License Terms and click **Accept** if you agree.

4. **Choose Installation Preferences**

        o   Select the installation location (default is C:\Program Files\Power Automate Desktop).

        o   Choose whether to install **Power Automate Desktop for all users or only the current user**.

5. **Install Required Components**

        o   The setup will install necessary dependencies, such as .NET Framework and UI automation components.

6. **Complete the Installation**

        o   Once the installation is complete, click **Finish** to close the installer.

💡 *Tip: Restart your computer after installation to ensure all components are properly initialized.*

Setting Up Power Automate Desktop

After installing Power Automate Desktop, you need to set up the application before creating your first flow.

Launching Power Automate Desktop

1. Click on the **Start Menu** and search for **Power Automate Desktop**.

2. Click on the application to launch it.

Signing in to Power Automate Desktop

1. You will be prompted to sign in with your **Microsoft account**.

2. If your organization uses **Microsoft Entra ID (formerly Azure Active Directory)**, sign in with your work credentials.

3. Once signed in, the **Power Automate Desktop console** will open.

Configuring Power Automate Desktop Settings

Before creating flows, it's important to configure some basic settings to enhance your experience.

Adjusting General Settings

To configure general settings:

1. Open **Power Automate Desktop**.

2. Click on the **Settings** icon (⚙▢) in the top-right corner.

3. Adjust the following options:

   o **Theme**: Light or Dark Mode

   o **Language**: Choose your preferred language

   o **Default Storage Location**: Where saved flows will be stored

Enabling UI Automation Mode

UI Automation allows Power Automate Desktop to interact with applications.

1. Go to **Settings > UI Automation**.

2. Ensure that **UI automation mode** is enabled.

Setting Up Browser Extensions

If you want to automate browser tasks, you need to install browser extensions.

1. Open Power Automate Desktop and navigate to **Browser Extensions**.

2. Click **Install Extension** for Chrome, Edge, or Firefox.

3. Follow the on-screen instructions to enable the extension.

💡 *Tip: If you are using Microsoft Edge, Power Automate Desktop may automatically suggest installing the extension.*

Verifying the Installation

After installation and configuration, it's a good idea to verify that everything is working correctly.

Checking the Version of Power Automate Desktop

1. Open **Power Automate Desktop**.

2. Click on **Help > About Power Automate Desktop**.

3. Ensure that you are using the latest version.

Running a Test Flow

To verify that Power Automate Desktop is working:

1. Click **New Flow** and name it "Test Flow".

2. Add a **"Display Message"** action.

3. Type "Power Automate Desktop is working!" as the message.

4. Click **Run**. If the message appears, your setup is successful!

Troubleshooting Common Installation Issues

If you encounter any issues during installation or setup, here are some common problems and solutions:

Issue	Solution
Installation fails due to missing .NET Framework	Install .NET 4.7.2 or later from the Microsoft website.
Cannot sign in	Ensure your internet connection is stable and check firewall settings.
UI Automation does not work	Make sure UI automation mode is enabled in settings.

Issue	Solution
Browser automation fails	Reinstall the Power Automate browser extension and restart your browser.

💡 *Tip: If problems persist, visit the* [Microsoft Power Automate Community](#) *for support.*

Conclusion

By following the steps outlined in this section, you have successfully installed and set up Power Automate Desktop. You are now ready to create desktop automation flows to streamline your daily tasks. In the next section, we will explore how to **create and run desktop flows** using Power Automate Desktop.

5.3 Creating and Running Desktop Flows

5.3.1 Recording Desktop Actions

Microsoft Power Automate Desktop allows users to automate repetitive tasks on their local machines by recording and replicating their actions. The **Recording Desktop Actions** feature enables users to capture their interactions with applications, websites, and system processes, which can then be replayed automatically as part of a **Desktop Flow**. This section will provide a detailed guide on how to effectively use this feature to automate routine tasks, improve productivity, and reduce manual workload.

Introduction to Recording Desktop Actions

Recording desktop actions is one of the easiest and most intuitive ways to create a Power Automate Desktop flow. Instead of manually configuring each step of the automation, users can simply perform the task once while Power Automate Desktop records their actions. These recorded actions are then converted into an editable flow, which can be enhanced with additional logic, conditions, and loops.

The **desktop recorder** captures various types of user interactions, such as:

- Mouse clicks (left-click, right-click, double-click)

- Keyboard inputs (typing, shortcuts, hotkeys)

- Window interactions (opening, closing, resizing)

- Data entry into forms and fields

- Navigation across applications and web browsers

By leveraging this feature, users can automate tasks such as:
✓☐ Filling out forms automatically
✓☐ Extracting and copying data between applications
✓☐ Automating report generation processes
✓☐ Performing bulk file operations

Step-by-Step Guide to Recording Desktop Actions

Step 1: Launching Power Automate Desktop

Before starting the recording process, ensure that Power Automate Desktop is installed and properly set up on your machine.

1. Open **Power Automate Desktop** from the Start Menu or by searching for it in Windows.

2. Click on **New Flow** to create a new automation project.

3. Give the flow a meaningful name (e.g., "Automate Data Entry") and click **Create**.

4. The flow editor interface will open, displaying a workspace where your recorded actions will be stored.

Step 2: Starting the Desktop Recorder

Once the flow is created, you can start recording actions using the built-in recorder tool.

1. In the **Power Automate Desktop** interface, click on the **Record** button located on the toolbar.

2. A small **Recording Control Panel** will appear on the screen, allowing you to start, pause, resume, and stop the recording.

3. Make sure all necessary applications and windows are open before you begin recording.

Step 3: Performing Actions to Be Recorded

As soon as you start recording, Power Automate Desktop will track and log your interactions. Follow these best practices to ensure a smooth and efficient recording process:

✓☐ Recording Mouse Clicks and Keyboard Inputs

- Click on buttons, menus, and fields exactly as you would in a real task.

- Type data into text fields, including usernames, passwords, and form entries.

- Use shortcut keys if necessary (e.g., Ctrl + C for copy, Ctrl + V for paste).

✓☐ Navigating Between Windows and Applications

- If your task involves switching between applications, ensure that each switch is clearly recorded.

- Resize and position windows properly to avoid confusion when the flow is replayed.

✓☐ Working with Forms and Data Entry

- If filling out a form, type carefully and confirm that each field is recognized by the recorder.

- For dropdown menus or list selections, make deliberate choices to ensure accuracy.

✓☐ Handling Pop-Ups and Dialog Boxes

- If a pop-up appears, interact with it as you normally would (click "OK," "Cancel," etc.).

- Ensure that error messages or notifications do not disrupt the recording process.

Step 4: Stopping and Reviewing the Recording

1. Once you have completed all the necessary actions, click the **Stop** button in the Recording Control Panel.

2. Power Automate Desktop will automatically convert the recorded actions into steps within your **Flow Editor**.

3. Review each step to ensure accuracy:

   - Check if mouse clicks and keystrokes were captured correctly.

   - Rename recorded steps for clarity (e.g., "Click Submit Button" instead of "Click UI Element").

   - Modify or delete unnecessary actions if needed.

Editing and Refining the Recorded Flow

After the recording is completed, you can refine and enhance the automation flow by adding logic and conditions.

1. Adding Delays Between Actions

Sometimes, applications take time to load or respond. You can add delays between actions to ensure the flow executes smoothly:

- Go to the **Actions Panel** on the left side of the Power Automate Desktop interface.

- Drag the **Delay** action into the flow and set the duration (e.g., 2 seconds).

- Place it between steps where extra time may be needed.

2. Adding Conditional Logic

If you want to automate tasks that require decision-making (e.g., clicking a different button based on input), use **If/Else** conditions:

- Drag the **If** action into the flow.

- Define the condition (e.g., "If text in field contains 'Error', click Retry").

- Add alternative actions for different scenarios.

3. Using Loops for Repetitive Tasks

For tasks that need to be repeated multiple times, such as processing multiple files or looping through spreadsheet rows, use the **Loop** action:

- Drag a **Loop** action into the flow.

- Set the repetition criteria (e.g., loop through each row in an Excel sheet).

- Insert actions that need to be performed within the loop.

4. Validating Data Entry and Error Handling

To prevent errors, add validation steps:

- Use the **Error Handling** feature to retry failed steps.

- Add a **Check Condition** action to verify if a field contains the expected data.

Running and Testing the Desktop Flow

1. Running the Flow

- Click the **Run** button to execute the recorded flow.

- Observe the automation in real-time to ensure all actions are performed correctly.

2. Debugging Issues

If the flow encounters an issue:

- Check the **Flow Log** for error messages.

- Modify any incorrect or missing steps.

- Re-run the flow after making adjustments.

Best Practices for Recording Desktop Actions

✓□ **Plan Before You Record** – Outline the steps you want to automate to avoid unnecessary actions.

✓□ **Use Clear and Consistent Naming** – Rename recorded steps to make the flow easier to understand.

✓□ **Test in a Safe Environment** – Before using automation on important data, test it on sample files or applications.

✓□ **Avoid Unnecessary Mouse Movements** – Keep actions simple and direct for efficiency.

✓□ **Regularly Save Your Flow** – Prevent data loss by saving your progress frequently.

Conclusion

Recording desktop actions is a fundamental feature of Power Automate Desktop that enables users to create powerful automation workflows without extensive coding. By following best practices and refining the recorded flow with additional logic, users can automate repetitive tasks efficiently, reduce human errors, and improve productivity.

In the next section (**5.3.2 Configuring UI Automation**), we will explore how to fine-tune automation for interacting with complex user interfaces, including dynamic elements and variable data inputs.

5.3.2 Configuring UI Automation

Introduction to UI Automation in Power Automate Desktop

User Interface (UI) automation is one of the most powerful features of **Power Automate Desktop (PAD)**, enabling users to interact with desktop applications and web-based interfaces without manual intervention. It allows businesses to automate repetitive, manual interactions with software, improving efficiency, reducing errors, and ensuring consistency across workflows.

In this section, we will explore how to configure **UI automation** effectively, covering the key components, best practices, and troubleshooting techniques to ensure smooth automation.

Understanding UI Automation in Power Automate Desktop

What is UI Automation?

UI automation refers to the process of interacting with on-screen elements of applications and websites using automation scripts. Power Automate Desktop achieves this by recognizing different UI components, such as buttons, text fields, dropdown menus, and checkboxes, and simulating user actions like clicking, typing, or selecting options.

UI automation is particularly useful when:

- Working with applications that do not have an API for integration.

- Automating tasks in legacy software that requires manual input.

- Processing web-based workflows that involve form filling or data extraction.

Configuring UI Automation in Power Automate Desktop

To configure UI automation in Power Automate Desktop, follow these key steps:

1. Identifying UI Elements

Before performing any UI automation, you must identify the elements of the interface that will be automated. Power Automate Desktop provides **UI element selectors**, which allow the software to recognize and interact with on-screen components.

How to Identify UI Elements:

1. **Open Power Automate Desktop** and create a new flow.

2. Add a **"Launch" action** to open the application you want to automate (e.g., Notepad, Excel, or a web browser).

3. Click on **"Add UI Element"** to capture a UI element within the target application.

4. Hover over the element you want to capture and click on it. Power Automate Desktop will store its properties.

5. Use the **UI elements pane** to view and manage captured elements.

2. Automating Basic UI Interactions

Once UI elements are captured, you can configure automation for common interactions such as clicking, typing, selecting, and extracting data.

Simulating Clicks and Navigation

- **Use the "Click UI Element" action** to simulate mouse clicks on buttons, links, or dropdown menus.

- Configure options like **single-click, double-click, or right-click** as needed.

- Example: Automating the login button click in a web application.

Typing into Input Fields

- Use the **"Populate Text Field" action** to enter text into text boxes, such as usernames and passwords.

- Choose between **"Simulated" and "Send Keys"** typing methods.

- Example: Automating data entry into an online form.

Selecting from Dropdown Menus

- Use **"Select from Dropdown"** to choose a value from a dropdown list.

- If the dropdown is not recognized, use keyboard navigation (arrow keys + Enter) for selection.

Extracting Text from UI Elements

- Use **"Get Text from UI Element"** to extract visible text from an application.

- Example: Retrieving an invoice number from a financial system.

3. Advanced UI Automation Techniques

As you progress, you may need to implement advanced UI automation techniques to handle dynamic or complex interfaces.

Handling Dynamic UI Elements

Some applications change element properties every time they are opened (e.g., changing IDs). To handle this:

- Use **"Anchor-based automation"** to locate elements based on nearby static elements.

- Enable **"Use OCR-based recognition"** to identify elements visually when selectors are unreliable.

- Implement **wildcards and regex** in element selectors to make them more flexible.

Working with Modal Dialogs and Pop-ups

Some applications display pop-ups or confirmation dialogs that require interaction:

- Use **"Wait for UI Element"** to ensure the pop-up is detected before interacting with it.

- Automate closing pop-ups with **"Click UI Element"** on the close button.

Scrolling and Navigating in Complex Interfaces

Some applications require scrolling to access elements:

- Use **"Send Keys" (Page Down, Arrow Keys, or Tab)** to navigate through lists.

- Automate scrolling using **"Mouse Scroll"** if necessary.

Automating Web UI Interactions

For web-based automation, Power Automate Desktop provides **Web Recorder**, which captures interactions within a browser.

- Use **"Launch New Browser"** to open a web application.

- Record interactions like **clicking, typing, and extracting data** using Web Recorder.

4. Best Practices for UI Automation

To ensure robust and reliable UI automation, follow these best practices:

Use Stable UI Selectors

- Avoid using element positions (e.g., absolute coordinates) as they may change.
- Prefer **text-based identifiers** (button labels, field names) when available.

Implement Error Handling

- Always use **"Try-Catch" blocks** to handle unexpected failures.
- Implement **timeouts and retries** for actions that depend on UI responses.

Optimize Performance

- Minimize unnecessary UI interactions (e.g., clicking only when needed).
- Use **background automation** for tasks that don't require UI interaction.

Maintain Flexibility

- Use **variables and dynamic selectors** to adapt to UI changes.
- Keep automation logic separate from hardcoded values.

5. Troubleshooting Common UI Automation Issues

UI Elements Not Recognized

- Ensure the target application is running with proper permissions.
- Try switching between **different UI frameworks** (e.g., Windows UI Automation, OCR).

UI Actions Failing Intermittently

- Use **"Wait for UI Element"** before performing actions to ensure elements are loaded.

- Add **delays** between steps if the application is slow to respond.

Text Extraction Not Working

- Switch between **native text extraction and OCR-based extraction** for better accuracy.

Conclusion

Configuring **UI automation** in **Power Automate Desktop** is a powerful way to streamline repetitive desktop tasks. By carefully selecting UI elements, implementing advanced techniques, and following best practices, you can build **robust, error-free automation** workflows that improve productivity and efficiency.

In the next section, we will explore **how to run desktop flows with cloud flows**, enabling seamless integration between Power Automate Desktop and cloud-based automation.

5.3.3 Running Desktop Flows with Cloud Flows

Microsoft Power Automate provides two primary automation environments: **Cloud Flows** and **Desktop Flows**. While **Cloud Flows** are ideal for automating tasks that involve cloud-based services (e.g., Microsoft 365, SharePoint, Outlook, or third-party web applications), **Desktop Flows** excel at automating tasks on a local machine (e.g., interacting with legacy applications, desktop software, or Windows-based processes).

However, in many business scenarios, automation requires both **Cloud Flows and Desktop Flows** to work together. This integration allows users to trigger Desktop Flows from a Cloud Flow, enabling a seamless workflow between web-based and on-premises processes.

This section explores how to connect Cloud Flows with Desktop Flows, set up and configure this integration, and leverage it for real-world automation use cases.

1. Understanding Cloud and Desktop Flow Integration

Before diving into the setup, it's essential to understand how **Cloud Flows** and **Desktop Flows** interact:

1. **Cloud Flow as the Trigger** – A Cloud Flow starts the automation. This could be triggered by an event, such as receiving an email, adding a new SharePoint file, or an automated schedule.

2. **Cloud Flow Calls a Desktop Flow** – The Cloud Flow then calls a **Desktop Flow**, which runs on a designated computer. The desktop flow can perform tasks such as interacting with a local application, filling out forms, extracting data from a PDF, or processing information in a legacy system.

3. **Desktop Flow Returns Data** – The **Desktop Flow** completes its task and can return data (if applicable) to the **Cloud Flow**, which can then continue with further actions (e.g., sending notifications, updating a database, or logging results).

Common Use Cases for Running Desktop Flows from Cloud Flows

- **Automating Data Entry:** A Cloud Flow retrieves customer order data from an online form and triggers a Desktop Flow to enter the data into a legacy ERP system.

- **Processing Invoices:** A Cloud Flow extracts an invoice from an email and triggers a Desktop Flow to enter the invoice details into an on-premises accounting software.

- **Generating Reports:** A Cloud Flow schedules a task that launches a Desktop Flow to extract data from multiple sources and generate a report in Excel.

2. Prerequisites for Running Desktop Flows with Cloud Flows

Before integrating **Cloud Flows** with **Desktop Flows**, ensure you meet the following prerequisites:

1. **Power Automate Installed** – Power Automate Desktop must be installed on the machine where the Desktop Flow will run.

2. **On-Premises Data Gateway** – If your Cloud Flow needs to communicate with a machine running a Desktop Flow, you must install and configure the **On-Premises Data Gateway**.

3. **User Permissions** – The user executing the Cloud Flow must have permission to run Desktop Flows and access the machine where the Desktop Flow is executed.

4. **Environment Setup** – Ensure that your **Power Automate environment** supports **attended or unattended RPA (Robotic Process Automation)**, depending on whether human intervention is required.

3. Setting Up Cloud Flow to Trigger a Desktop Flow

Step 1: Create a Desktop Flow

1. Open **Power Automate Desktop**.

2. Click **New Flow** and give it a meaningful name (e.g., *"Process Local Orders"*).

3. Design the Desktop Flow by adding **actions** such as:

   o Opening applications

   o Entering data

   o Extracting text

   o Clicking UI elements

4. Save and test the Desktop Flow to ensure it runs correctly.

Step 2: Create a Cloud Flow in Power Automate

1. Open **Power Automate (Cloud)** from flow.microsoft.com.

2. Click **Create** and select **Automated Cloud Flow**.

3. Choose a **trigger**, such as:

   o "When an email arrives" (to process email attachments).

   o "When a file is created in OneDrive" (to analyze documents).

   o "Manually trigger a flow" (to allow users to start the process manually).

4. Click **+ New Step** and search for **Run a flow built with Power Automate Desktop**.

5. Select the **Desktop Flow** you created earlier.

6. Specify the target **computer** and **authentication method** (Windows sign-in or API key).

Step 3: Passing Data Between Cloud Flow and Desktop Flow

- You can **send parameters** from the **Cloud Flow** to the **Desktop Flow**, such as:

    o   A file path for a document to be processed.

    o   A customer ID for a record lookup.

    o   A set of input values for form automation.

- After the **Desktop Flow** completes execution, it can return data to the **Cloud Flow**, enabling further actions (e.g., storing results in SharePoint, sending an email, or updating a CRM system).

4. Running and Monitoring the Flow

Executing the Flow

- Once the integration is set up, **trigger the Cloud Flow manually** or wait for an event to start it automatically.

- The Cloud Flow will send a request to Power Automate Desktop, executing the Desktop Flow on the target machine.

- The Desktop Flow will interact with the required desktop applications and return the results.

Monitoring and Troubleshooting

- **Flow History** – You can monitor execution logs in the Power Automate **Run History** section.

- **Error Handling** – Use **Try-Catch Blocks** in Desktop Flows to manage errors effectively.

- **On-Premises Gateway Issues** – If a Cloud Flow cannot reach the Desktop Flow, ensure the **On-Premises Data Gateway** is running and correctly configured.

5. Real-World Example: Processing Incoming Orders

Scenario:

A company receives **customer orders via email** as Excel attachments. The order processing system is a **legacy Windows application**, which does not support APIs. The goal is to **automate order processing** by:

1. A **Cloud Flow** monitoring incoming emails for attachments.

2. Extracting order details and sending them to a **Desktop Flow**.

3. The **Desktop Flow** opening the legacy system and entering order data.

4. Sending a confirmation email back to the customer.

Solution Implementation

1. **Cloud Flow:**

   o Trigger: "When a new email arrives in Outlook"

   o Extract order details from the attachment

   o Call the Desktop Flow with extracted data

2. **Desktop Flow:**

   o Open the legacy application

   o Enter customer details and order items

   o Submit the order and capture confirmation number

   o Return confirmation details to the Cloud Flow

3. **Cloud Flow Final Steps:**

   o Send a confirmation email to the customer

   o Log the transaction in SharePoint or a database

This integration eliminates **manual data entry**, reduces errors, and accelerates **order fulfillment**.

---

6. Best Practices for Running Desktop Flows with Cloud Flows

- **Use Variables and Parameters** – Pass dynamic data between Cloud and Desktop Flows.

- **Optimize UI Automation** – Avoid changes in UI structure that might break automation.

- **Monitor Flow Performance** – Track execution time and optimize slow steps.

- **Secure Credentials** – Use Power Automate's **secure credential storage** instead of hardcoding credentials in flows.

- **Implement Retry Mechanisms** – Set up **retry policies** in Cloud Flows for robustness.

7. Conclusion

Integrating **Cloud Flows with Desktop Flows** unlocks powerful automation possibilities, bridging **modern cloud-based applications** with **legacy desktop software**. By carefully designing these integrations, businesses can significantly improve efficiency, reduce manual effort, and enhance accuracy in process execution.

5.4 Common Use Cases for Power Automate Desktop

Power Automate Desktop (PAD) is a powerful tool that enables users to automate repetitive, manual tasks on their local machines. It allows businesses and individuals to save time, improve efficiency, and minimize human errors. Unlike cloud-based automation, PAD is designed specifically for desktop environments, providing automation capabilities for applications that don't have built-in APIs or cloud-based integrations.

This section explores common use cases for Power Automate Desktop across various industries and tasks. By understanding these applications, users can identify automation opportunities in their workflows and harness PAD's full potential.

Data Entry and Processing

Automating Data Extraction and Entry

Many businesses deal with large volumes of data, often requiring manual data entry from one system to another. Power Automate Desktop can automate:

- Copying data from PDFs, emails, or scanned documents into structured databases or spreadsheets.

- Extracting relevant information from invoices and entering it into financial software.

- Populating CRM systems with customer details collected from online forms or emails.

◆ **Example Use Case:** A company receives daily reports in Excel format and needs to input the data into an internal application. Instead of manually transferring the information, PAD can automate the extraction and insertion process, reducing errors and saving time.

Automating Data Validation

Businesses often need to validate data across multiple sources. PAD can:

- Compare and verify records in different databases or files.

- Flag inconsistencies and generate reports for review.

- Send notifications if data discrepancies are detected.

◆ **Example Use Case:** A retail company uses PAD to cross-check sales records from its e-commerce platform against its internal sales database, ensuring that all transactions are correctly logged.

File and Folder Management

Automating File Organization

Manually organizing files can be tedious, especially in environments with high data volumes. Power Automate Desktop can:

- Automatically rename files based on predefined rules.

- Move files to appropriate folders based on content or metadata.

- Archive old files or delete redundant data to maintain a clean file structure.

◆ **Example Use Case:** An HR department receives resumes via email. PAD can extract attachments, rename them based on candidate names, and move them into categorized folders (e.g., "Marketing Candidates," "Engineering Candidates").

Automating File Conversions

Many businesses need to convert files between different formats (e.g., Excel to CSV, Word to PDF). PAD can automate these tasks:

- Convert documents to standardized formats before uploading to a database.

- Merge multiple PDFs into a single file.

- Extract text from scanned images and save it as a text file.

◆ **Example Use Case:** A law firm processes multiple contracts daily. PAD can automatically convert Word documents into PDFs, rename them with case IDs, and store them in client-specific folders.

Web and Application Automation

Automating Web Scraping and Data Collection

Power Automate Desktop can interact with web browsers to collect information. This is useful for:

- Extracting competitor pricing data from e-commerce websites.

- Gathering financial data, such as exchange rates, from public websites.

- Scraping job listings or company data for market research.

◆ **Example Use Case:** A marketing team uses PAD to automatically gather social media analytics from multiple sources and consolidate them into a single report.

Automating Software Interactions

PAD can automate interactions with applications that don't support APIs by simulating human interactions, such as:

- Logging into legacy applications and retrieving data.

- Filling out forms in desktop applications.

- Navigating through software interfaces to complete repetitive tasks.

◆ **Example Use Case:** A finance team uses PAD to log into an old accounting system, extract monthly financial data, and import it into a modern ERP system.

Email and Communication Automation

Automating Email Processing

Businesses receive large volumes of emails daily. PAD can help manage them by:

- Automatically sorting emails based on keywords or sender information.

- Extracting attachments and saving them in designated folders.

- Sending automated replies based on predefined rules.

◆ **Example Use Case:** A customer service team uses PAD to scan incoming emails for refund requests, extract customer details, and forward them to the finance department.

Automating Report Distribution

PAD can generate and distribute reports automatically by:

- Gathering data from multiple sources and generating summaries.

- Converting reports into preferred formats (e.g., PDF, Excel).

- Sending reports via email to relevant stakeholders.

◆ **Example Use Case:** A sales team uses PAD to compile daily sales performance reports and email them to management every morning.

Integrating Power Automate Desktop with Cloud Flows

While Power Automate Desktop focuses on local automation, it can also work in tandem with cloud-based Power Automate flows to create seamless end-to-end automation.

Combining Desktop and Cloud Automation

- Cloud flows can trigger desktop flows when specific conditions are met.

- Desktop flows can send processed data to cloud applications like SharePoint, OneDrive, or Power BI.

◆ **Example Use Case:** A manufacturing company collects production data from factory machines (using Power Automate Desktop) and sends the data to a SharePoint list (using Power Automate Cloud).

Automating Hybrid Workflows

Power Automate Desktop can bridge gaps between systems that lack direct integrations by:

- Extracting data from legacy applications and sending it to cloud-based databases.

- Processing data locally before uploading it to cloud storage.

- Interacting with remote desktop sessions to execute cloud-triggered workflows.

◆ **Example Use Case:** A logistics company needs to sync delivery status updates from a local warehouse system to an online customer portal. PAD extracts and formats the data before sending it to the cloud system via Power Automate.

Enhancing Cybersecurity and Compliance

Automating Security Audits and Monitoring

PAD can improve security by:

- Monitoring system logs for suspicious activity.

- Automating user access audits by extracting login records.

- Checking compliance with internal security policies.

◆ **Example Use Case:** An IT department uses PAD to scan system logs daily and highlight unauthorized access attempts.

Automating Backup and Recovery Processes

Data security requires regular backups. PAD can:

- Automatically back up important files to external drives or cloud storage.

- Encrypt and archive sensitive documents.

- Ensure backup compliance with organizational policies.

◆ **Example Use Case:** A finance department uses PAD to copy monthly financial statements to a secure location and encrypt them for regulatory compliance.

Conclusion: The Power of Desktop Automation

Power Automate Desktop provides businesses and individuals with a robust solution for automating repetitive tasks, reducing errors, and improving efficiency. By leveraging PAD's capabilities, users can:

✓ Save time on manual data entry and processing.
✓ Improve accuracy in business operations.
✓ Automate tasks that were previously limited to human intervention.
✓ Integrate legacy and modern systems seamlessly.

Whether it's processing invoices, managing files, automating emails, or integrating with cloud solutions, Power Automate Desktop unlocks a world of possibilities. As businesses continue to embrace digital transformation, leveraging automation tools like PAD will be essential for staying competitive and efficient.

PART VI
Business Process Automation with Power Automate

6.1 Automating Approval Processes

In any business, approval processes play a critical role in ensuring smooth operations, compliance, and accountability. Whether it's approving expense reports, purchase requests, or project proposals, organizations need structured workflows to handle these tasks efficiently. Microsoft Power Automate simplifies and automates these processes, reducing manual effort, eliminating bottlenecks, and providing clear audit trails.

This section will explore how to set up approval workflows using Power Automate, including different types of approval processes, essential components, and best practices.

6.1.1 Setting Up Approval Workflows

Understanding Approval Workflows

An approval workflow is an automated process that routes a request to one or more approvers for review and action. Instead of manually sending emails or tracking approvals through spreadsheets, Power Automate provides a structured and automated way to manage approvals efficiently.

Approval workflows can range from simple one-step approvals to complex multi-tiered processes involving multiple stakeholders. Here are some common types of approval workflows:

- **Single Approver Workflow:** A request is sent to one person for approval.

- **Sequential Approval Workflow:** The request moves through multiple levels of approvers in a predefined order.

- **Parallel Approval Workflow:** Multiple approvers review the request at the same time, and a consensus is required before moving forward.

- **Custom Approval Workflow:** Approvals are based on conditions, such as department-specific routing or monetary thresholds.

By automating these workflows with Power Automate, businesses can ensure that approval requests are handled consistently and efficiently.

Step-by-Step Guide to Creating an Approval Workflow

Let's walk through the process of setting up a basic approval workflow using Power Automate. In this example, we will create an approval workflow for expense reports submitted via Microsoft Forms.

Step 1: Sign in to Power Automate

1. Go to Power Automate.

2. Sign in with your Microsoft account.

3. Click on **Create** from the left navigation panel.

Step 2: Choose a Flow Type

- Select **Automated cloud flow** (since we want the process to start when a form is submitted).

- Give the flow a name (e.g., "Expense Report Approval Process").

- Choose **When a new response is submitted (Microsoft Forms)** as the trigger.

- Click **Create** to proceed.

Step 3: Configure the Trigger (Microsoft Forms Submission)

1. Select your form from the dropdown list (e.g., "Expense Report Submission Form").

2. Click on **+ New Step** and search for **Get response details (Microsoft Forms)** to retrieve form responses.

Step 4: Add the Approval Action

1. Click **+ New Step** and search for **Start and wait for an approval** (from Microsoft Approvals).

2. Select the approval type:

    o **Approve/Reject – First to respond:** The first approver to respond determines the outcome.

    o **Approve/Reject – Everyone must approve:** All assigned approvers must approve.

    o **Custom Responses – Wait for one response:** Allows custom approval options.

3. Configure approval details:

    o **Title:** "Expense Report Approval Request"

    o **Assigned to:** Enter the email of the approver (e.g., Manager's email).

    o **Details:** Use dynamic content to include form responses (e.g., Employee Name, Expense Amount, Justification).

Step 5: Define Approval Outcomes

- Click **+ New Step** and search for **Condition** (from the Control category).

- Configure the condition: If **Approval Outcome is Approved**, proceed with the next action.

- Under the **If Yes** section:

    o Add **Send an email (Outlook)** to notify the requester of the approval.

- Under the **If No** section:

    o Add **Send an email (Outlook)** to notify the requester that their request was rejected.

Step 6: Test and Deploy the Flow

1. Click **Save** to store your workflow.

2. Click **Test** to run a manual test using sample data.

3. If everything works as expected, click **Turn on** to activate the flow.

Enhancing Approval Workflows with Advanced Features

Once the basic approval workflow is set up, you can enhance it with additional capabilities:

1. Multi-Step Approvals

If approvals require multiple levels (e.g., Manager → Finance → Director), you can use multiple **Start and wait for approval** actions in sequence. Each step should check the approval status before proceeding to the next level.

2. Conditional Approvals

Use **Condition** actions to implement business rules:

- If the expense is above $5000, send it to the Finance department.

- If the requester belongs to a specific department, route it to the appropriate manager.

3. Notifications and Reminders

Use **Delay** and **Send an email** actions to remind approvers if they haven't responded within a set time frame.

4. Integration with Power BI

You can track approval workflow performance by logging requests in **SharePoint** or **Dataverse**, then visualizing data in **Power BI**.

Best Practices for Approval Workflows

To ensure your approval workflows are efficient and scalable, consider the following best practices:

✅ **Keep it Simple:** Start with a basic workflow and expand as needed. Overcomplicated flows can be difficult to manage.

✅ **Use Dynamic Content:** Leverage Power Automate's ability to insert form responses, user details, and timestamps dynamically.

✅ **Error Handling:** Add **Scope** and **Try-Catch** mechanisms to handle failures gracefully.

✅ **Automate Notifications:** Use **Teams notifications** or **SMS alerts** to ensure timely responses from approvers.

✅ **Regularly Review and Optimize:** Monitor flow run history and optimize slow or failing workflows.

Conclusion

Setting up an approval workflow with Microsoft Power Automate significantly improves efficiency, reduces manual errors, and ensures consistent tracking of approvals. Whether you're handling expense reports, purchase orders, or project requests, Power Automate provides flexible options to meet your business needs.

In the next section (**6.1.2 Multi-Step Approval Processes**), we will explore how to create complex multi-tiered approval workflows with multiple decision-makers and conditions.

6.1.2 Multi-Step Approval Processes

Introduction to Multi-Step Approval Processes

In many business scenarios, a single approval step is not enough to ensure the correct decision-making process. Complex workflows often require multiple layers of review before final approval. Multi-step approval processes in Microsoft Power Automate allow businesses to implement structured, hierarchical decision-making workflows that involve multiple approvers, conditions, and actions.

For example, a leave request might require:

1. **Manager's approval** (Immediate supervisor)

2. **Department head's approval** (For budget concerns)

3. **HR team's approval** (For final processing)

By leveraging multi-step approval workflows, organizations can ensure compliance, maintain transparency, and improve decision-making efficiency.

How Multi-Step Approvals Work in Power Automate

A multi-step approval process consists of the following key components:

- **Triggers:** Events that start the approval workflow (e.g., a form submission, an email request, or a document upload).

- **Approval Actions:** Steps where designated individuals or groups approve or reject the request.

- **Conditional Logic:** Determines the flow's path based on approval/rejection outcomes.

- **Notifications and Alerts:** Keeps all stakeholders informed of approval statuses.

Power Automate provides various approval types:

- **Sequential approvals:** Requests move step by step in a specific order.

- **Parallel approvals:** Multiple approvers review the request simultaneously.

- **Custom approvals:** Complex workflows with mixed sequential and parallel steps.

Creating a Multi-Step Approval Process in Power Automate

Step 1: Define the Workflow Requirements

Before building the approval process, outline the required steps:

- Who are the approvers?

- In what order should approvals be made?

- What happens if an approval is rejected?

- Should approvals be time-sensitive?

Step 2: Start with a Trigger

1. **Log in to Power Automate** and create a new flow.

2. Choose a **trigger**, such as:

   o "When an item is created" (for SharePoint or Dataverse entries).

   o "When a new response is submitted" (for Microsoft Forms submissions).

   o "When an email is received" (for requests via email).

Step 3: Add the First Approval Action

1. Click **New Step** → Search for **Start and wait for an approval**.

2. Choose **Approval Type**:

   o **Everyone must approve** (for unanimous approval).

   o **First to respond** (for faster approvals).

3. Set the **Approver** as the **First-Level Manager**.

4. Configure the **Approval Message** (e.g., "A new leave request needs your approval").

Step 4: Add Conditional Logic for Next-Level Approval

Once the first approver gives approval:

1. **Add a Condition**: Check if the response is **"Approved"**.

2. If **Yes** → Proceed to the second approval step.

3. If **No** → Stop the process and notify the requester.

For the **Second-Level Approval (Department Head)**:

1. Add another **"Start and Wait for an Approval"** action.

2. Assign the **Department Head** as the approver.

3. Provide necessary details (e.g., request details, first approver's comments).

Step 5: Configure Final Approval Step

If the department head approves:

1. Add a **Condition** to check approval status.

2. If approved → Proceed to the final approver (e.g., HR team).

3. If rejected → Notify the requester and log the response.

For **HR Team Approval**:

1. Assign HR personnel or a team.

2. Once approved, trigger final actions (e.g., updating databases, sending confirmation emails).

Step 6: Add Notifications and Logging

Once the final approval is granted:

- **Notify the requester** via email or Teams.

- **Update records** in SharePoint or Dataverse.

- **Log approval history** for tracking and compliance.

Example: Multi-Step Leave Request Approval

Scenario

An employee submits a leave request, which must be approved by:

1. **Immediate Manager**

2. **Department Head**

3. **HR Team**

Power Automate Flow

1. **Trigger:** Employee submits a Microsoft Form.

2. **Step 1:** Manager approval → If rejected, notify the employee.

3. **Step 2:** Department head approval → If rejected, notify the employee.

4. **Step 3:** HR final approval → If approved, send confirmation to the employee.

5. **Logging:** Approval details are stored in SharePoint.

Best Practices for Multi-Step Approvals

1. **Use Dynamic Approvers**: Instead of hardcoding emails, use **Manager Lookup** in Microsoft Entra ID (formerly Azure AD).

2. **Set Time Limits**: Use **Timeout Actions** to escalate requests if an approver does not respond.

3. **Provide Detailed Messages**: Ensure each approver receives **clear instructions** and relevant documents.

4. **Use Adaptive Cards in Teams**: Enable **Teams Approvals** for faster responses.

5. **Enable Logging**: Store approval records for **audit and compliance tracking**.

Troubleshooting Multi-Step Approval Issues

Issue	Possible Cause	Solution
Approvers not receiving emails	Email notifications blocked	Check spam folder or use Teams approvals
Approval stuck at a step	Approver did not respond	Set a timeout and auto-escalate
Incorrect approver assigned	Hardcoded email issue	Use dynamic lookup from Entra ID
Flow errors randomly	API limits exceeded	Optimize flow with fewer actions

Conclusion

Multi-step approval processes in Power Automate help organizations manage complex decision-making workflows efficiently. By following best practices and using dynamic approvals, businesses can streamline operations while maintaining compliance and transparency.

6.1.3 Tracking and Managing Approvals

Introduction

Approval processes are an essential part of business operations, ensuring that key decisions are reviewed and authorized by the right individuals. Power Automate simplifies this process by automating approval requests, routing them to the appropriate stakeholders, and keeping track of their status. However, beyond setting up approvals, managing and tracking them efficiently is crucial for maintaining workflow transparency, preventing bottlenecks, and ensuring timely decision-making.

In this section, we will explore how to track and manage approval requests in Power Automate. You will learn how to monitor approval flows, review pending and completed approvals, manage approval notifications, and optimize the process for better efficiency.

1. Understanding Approval Tracking in Power Automate

Power Automate provides built-in tools to track and manage approval requests efficiently. When an approval request is triggered, it follows a structured process:

1. A request is sent to the designated approver(s).

2. The approver receives a notification via email, Microsoft Teams, or the Power Automate Approval Center.

3. The approver makes a decision (Approve, Reject, or request additional information).

4. The system logs the decision and notifies the requester.

5. The approval flow either proceeds to the next step or ends based on the response.

To manage this process effectively, Power Automate provides various tracking and management options, including **Approval Center, Flow Run History, Power Automate Analytics, and Custom Dashboards**.

2. Tracking Approvals Using the Power Automate Approval Center

What is the Approval Center?

The Approval Center is a centralized hub where users can review, approve, or reject pending requests. It provides an organized interface to track all approval requests, making it easy to manage multiple requests efficiently.

To access the Approval Center:

1. Go to Power Automate.

2. Click on **Approvals** in the left navigation pane.

3. You will see three main tabs:

   o **Received**: Lists all approval requests assigned to you.

   o **Sent**: Displays the approval requests you have created.

   o **History**: Shows past approval requests, including their status (approved, rejected, or expired).

Managing Approvals in the Approval Center

- **Filtering Requests**: Use filters to sort approvals by status, request date, or requester name.

- **Bulk Approvals**: Select multiple approvals and take action simultaneously.

- **Request Details**: Click on an approval request to see its details, including comments and attached documents.

Using the Approval Center ensures that all pending requests are easily accessible, reducing delays in decision-making.

3. Monitoring Approval Flows Using Flow Run History

What is Flow Run History?

Each approval process in Power Automate generates a record in the **Flow Run History**, allowing users to monitor how a flow executes and diagnose any failures.

To access Flow Run History:

1. Open Power Automate.

2. Click on **My Flows** and select the approval flow you want to track.

3. Navigate to the **Run History** tab.

4. Click on a specific run to view detailed logs, including timestamps and response statuses.

Identifying Approval Bottlenecks

Flow Run History helps in:

- **Identifying Pending Approvals**: See which approvals are delayed and who is responsible.

- **Reviewing Decision Logs**: Check who approved or rejected a request and when.

- **Troubleshooting Errors**: Identify failures due to missing data, incorrect configurations, or permissions issues.

By regularly monitoring Flow Run History, you can ensure that approval processes run smoothly without unnecessary delays.

4. Setting Up Notifications for Approval Tracking

Enabling Email and Teams Notifications

To ensure timely responses, Power Automate allows you to send automatic notifications when an approval request is created, approved, or rejected.

Configuring Email Notifications

1. In your approval flow, add a **Send an Email** action after the approval step.

2. Configure the email details:

    o   **To**: The requester or approver's email.

    o   **Subject**: "Approval Request Status Update"

    o   **Body**: Include approval details, status, and next steps.

3. Save and test your flow to ensure email notifications are sent correctly.

Sending Notifications via Microsoft Teams

1. Add the **Post a Message in Teams** action in your approval flow.

2. Select the relevant Teams channel or direct message.

3. Customize the message to display approval details and actions required.

With automated notifications, stakeholders stay informed without needing to check the Approval Center constantly.

5. Managing Expired or Overdue Approvals

Setting Expiration Times for Approvals

By default, approvals remain active indefinitely. To prevent delays, you can set expiration times.

1. In your approval flow, open the **Create an Approval** action.

2. Under the **Timeout** field, set a specific time (e.g., 2 days).

3. Add a condition to handle expired approvals (e.g., escalate to a manager or send reminders).

Escalating Unanswered Approvals

If an approval request remains unanswered, you can escalate it automatically:

1. Add a **Condition** step after the approval action.

2. If no response is received within the deadline, trigger an alternative action, such as:

   o   Sending a reminder email.

   o   Forwarding the request to a higher authority.

6. Optimizing Approval Tracking for Better Efficiency

Using Power BI to Analyze Approval Data

For large organizations handling multiple approvals, Power BI can provide deeper insights.

1. Connect Power Automate data to Power BI.

2. Create dashboards displaying:

    o   Pending approvals by department.

    o   Average response times.

    o   Approval bottlenecks and delays.

3. Use this data to improve workflow efficiency and accountability.

Best Practices for Efficient Approval Tracking

- **Keep Approval Requests Clear**: Provide detailed descriptions and necessary documents.

- **Enable Mobile Notifications**: Use the Power Automate mobile app for on-the-go approvals.

- **Regularly Review Approval Metrics**: Monitor trends and optimize workflows accordingly.

- **Train Users on Approval Processes**: Ensure all stakeholders understand how to access and respond to requests.

Conclusion

Tracking and managing approvals effectively in Power Automate is essential for maintaining workflow efficiency. By leveraging the Approval Center, Flow Run History, automated notifications, and escalation mechanisms, businesses can ensure approvals are processed smoothly without delays.

In the next section, we will explore how Power Automate can be used to **automate data collection and processing**, further streamlining business processes.

📌 **Key Takeaways**

✓ Use the **Approval Center** to review and manage approval requests.

✓ Monitor **Flow Run History** to identify delays and troubleshoot errors.

✓ Enable **email and Teams notifications** to ensure timely responses.

✓ Set **expiration times and escalations** to prevent bottlenecks.

✓ Utilize **Power BI analytics** to optimize approval processes.

6.2 Automating Data Collection and Processing

6.2.1 Extracting Data from Forms and Emails

Data collection is a fundamental part of business operations, but manually extracting and processing information from forms and emails can be time-consuming and prone to errors. With **Microsoft Power Automate**, organizations can **automate data extraction** to improve efficiency, accuracy, and responsiveness.

In this section, we will explore how to use **Power Automate** to extract data from **online forms, email messages, and attachments**. We will also discuss common scenarios, best practices, and step-by-step examples of automating data extraction.

1. Why Automate Data Extraction?

Manual data collection from forms and emails often leads to:

- **Time-consuming processes** – Employees spend hours copying and pasting data.
- **Human errors** – Typing mistakes and overlooked data points cause inaccuracies.
- **Inefficiencies** – Delays in processing incoming information slow down workflows.

By using **Power Automate**, businesses can:

- Automatically **extract structured and unstructured data** from emails and forms.
- Store extracted data in **Excel, SharePoint, SQL databases, or third-party applications**.
- Reduce manual effort and **speed up decision-making**.

2. Extracting Data from Microsoft Forms

Overview of Microsoft Forms Integration

Microsoft Forms allows users to create surveys, quizzes, and feedback forms. By integrating Power Automate with Forms, you can:

- Capture responses in real-time.

- Store form data in Excel, SharePoint, or Dataverse.

- Trigger additional workflows based on form responses.

Setting Up Power Automate to Extract Microsoft Forms Data

Step 1: Create a New Flow in Power Automate

1. Open **Power Automate** and click **Create → Automated cloud flow**.

2. Choose **"When a new response is submitted"** as the trigger.

3. Select the **Microsoft Forms** connector and choose the target form.

Step 2: Retrieve Form Responses

1. Add a new action: **"Get response details"**.

2. Select the **Form ID** and **Response ID** dynamically from the trigger event.

Step 3: Process and Store Data

- **Option 1: Store Data in an Excel File**

  o Use the **"Add a row into a table"** action in the **Excel Online** connector.

  o Select the **target Excel file** in OneDrive or SharePoint.

  o Map form fields to Excel columns.

- **Option 2: Store Data in SharePoint**

  o Use the **"Create item"** action in the **SharePoint** connector.

  o Specify the SharePoint list where responses will be saved.

  o Map form fields to corresponding SharePoint columns.

Step 4: Notify the Team or Take Action

- Add an **Outlook or Teams notification** to inform relevant team members.

- Trigger **conditional logic** to escalate urgent responses.

---

3. Extracting Data from Emails

Common Use Cases

Businesses receive critical data via emails, such as:

- **Customer orders** (order details, shipping requests).

- **Service requests** (support tickets, inquiries).

- **Survey responses** (customer feedback, event registrations).

By using Power Automate, we can **automatically extract data from emails and attachments**, saving time and reducing errors.

Setting Up Email Data Extraction with Power Automate

Step 1: Create an Automated Flow for Incoming Emails

1. Open **Power Automate** → Click **Create** → Select **Automated cloud flow**.

2. Choose **"When a new email arrives"** as the trigger.

3. Select the target email inbox (Outlook, Gmail, etc.).

Step 2: Apply Filters to Identify Relevant Emails

- Use **conditions** to filter emails by subject, sender, or keywords.

- Example: Extract only **customer inquiries** by checking if the subject contains "Inquiry".

Step 3: Extract Data from the Email Body

- Use the **"HTML to Text"** action to remove formatting.

- Apply **regular expressions (RegEx)** or **string functions** to parse key details.

- Example: Extract an **order number** from:

      o   **"Order ID: 12345"** → **Extract "12345"**

Step 4: Extract Data from Email Attachments

- Use the **"Get attachments"** action to retrieve files.

- If attachments are PDFs or images:

  o   Use **AI Builder** to extract text from scanned documents.

- If attachments are Excel files:

  o   Use the **"List rows present in a table"** action to extract structured data.

Step 5: Store Extracted Data

- Save extracted information to **Excel, SharePoint, or a database**.

- Forward important details to **Microsoft Teams or an approval process**.

---

4. Advanced Data Extraction Techniques

Using AI Builder for Intelligent Data Extraction

Power Automate integrates with **AI Builder**, which enables intelligent **document processing**. It can extract data from:

- **Invoices**

- **Receipts**

- **Contracts**

- **Handwritten notes**

How to Use AI Builder in Power Automate

1. Train a **custom AI model** to recognize key fields (e.g., invoice number, total amount).

2. Add an **"Extract information from documents"** action in Power Automate.

3. Process **scanned PDFs and images** to extract structured data.

Using Expressions for Advanced Data Manipulation

Power Automate allows data formatting using **expressions**:

- Extract numbers: replace(body('Get_email')?['body'], '[^0-9]', '')

- Convert text to lowercase: toLower(body('Get_email')?['body'])

- Split email content into structured fields: split(body('Get_email')?['body'], ' ')

5. Best Practices for Automating Data Extraction

✓ Ensure Data Accuracy

- Validate extracted data before storing it.

- Use conditional checks to avoid incorrect entries.

✓ Optimize Flow Performance

- Minimize unnecessary actions to **reduce API calls**.

- Use batch processing for handling **large data volumes**.

✓ Secure Data Processing

- Encrypt sensitive data before storing it.

- Use **role-based access** to restrict unauthorized access.

✓ Monitor and Maintain Flows

- Regularly check **flow run history** for errors.

- Set up **failure notifications** to alert administrators.

6. Conclusion

Automating data extraction from **forms and emails** using Power Automate **reduces manual effort, increases accuracy, and improves business efficiency**. By leveraging

Power Automate's **connectors, expressions, and AI capabilities**, businesses can process data in real-time and integrate it with various applications.

The next section will explore how to **sync extracted data between apps**, ensuring seamless data processing across different systems.

6.2.2 Syncing Data Between Apps

In today's digital landscape, businesses rely on multiple applications to manage different aspects of their operations. Whether it's customer relationship management (CRM), enterprise resource planning (ERP), email services, cloud storage, or marketing tools, these applications need to work together efficiently. **Microsoft Power Automate** provides a seamless way to **sync data between apps**, ensuring consistency and reducing manual effort.

This section will explore how Power Automate enables data synchronization between different applications, its benefits, and step-by-step instructions for setting up automated workflows. Additionally, we'll cover best practices, troubleshooting techniques, and real-world use cases.

Understanding Data Synchronization in Power Automate

What is Data Synchronization?

Data synchronization is the process of ensuring that data remains consistent and up to date across multiple applications. This can involve one-way sync (data moves from one app to another) or two-way sync (data is updated in both apps).

For example:

- When a new contact is added to **Microsoft Outlook**, it is automatically added to **Salesforce**.

- When a customer updates their profile in a **CRM system**, the changes reflect in **Microsoft Excel** for reporting.

- When an invoice is marked as paid in **QuickBooks**, it updates the corresponding record in **SharePoint**.

Why is Data Synchronization Important?

Automating data sync with Power Automate provides several benefits:

- **Eliminates manual data entry**, reducing errors and saving time.

- **Enhances data consistency** across platforms.

- **Improves collaboration** by ensuring all teams have access to the latest data.

- **Increases efficiency** by automating repetitive tasks.

- **Enables real-time updates**, allowing for better decision-making.

Key Components of Data Synchronization in Power Automate

Power Automate uses **triggers, actions, and conditions** to automate data synchronization.

1. Triggers

A trigger starts the automation when a specified event occurs. Some common triggers for data synchronization include:

- **When a new row is added to an Excel table**

- **When a new email arrives in Outlook with an attachment**

- **When a new lead is created in Dynamics 365**

- **When a file is modified in SharePoint**

2. Actions

Actions define what happens after a trigger. Some typical actions for data sync include:

- **Creating a new record in another application**

- **Updating an existing record**

- **Deleting duplicate records**

- **Appending new data to an existing dataset**

3. Conditions

Conditions allow you to **filter** when an action should run. Examples include:

- Only sync data if the customer's email contains a specific domain.

- Only update a record if the **status is marked as "Active"**.

- Sync only records modified within the last 24 hours.

How to Set Up Data Synchronization Between Apps

Example 1: Syncing Customer Data Between Microsoft Excel and SharePoint

Scenario: You have a sales team that logs customer information in an **Excel sheet**. You want this data to automatically sync to a **SharePoint list** for better collaboration.

Step 1: Create a Flow in Power Automate

1. Go to Power Automate and **Sign in**.
2. Click on **Create → Automated cloud flow**.
3. Choose **"When a row is added to an Excel table"** as the trigger.

Step 2: Connect to Excel and SharePoint

1. Select the **Excel file** stored in OneDrive or SharePoint.
2. Choose the correct **table** from the dropdown.
3. Click **New Step** and search for **"Create item"** in SharePoint.
4. Select your **SharePoint site** and the **list** where data should be added.

Step 3: Map Data Fields

1. In the **"Create item"** action, match Excel columns to SharePoint fields.

- o **Customer Name → Title**

- o **Email → Email Address**

- o **Phone → Contact Number**

2. Click **Save** and **Test** your flow.

Step 4: Run and Monitor the Flow

- Add a test entry in Excel and check if it appears in SharePoint.

- If errors occur, check **Flow History** to troubleshoot.

Example 2: Syncing New Leads from Microsoft Forms to Dynamics 365

Scenario: You collect leads using a **Microsoft Forms survey**. You want this data to sync automatically with **Dynamics 365 CRM**.

Step 1: Create a Trigger

1. Open **Power Automate** and click **Create → Automated Flow**.

2. Select **"When a new response is submitted"** (Microsoft Forms).

3. Choose the survey form from the dropdown.

Step 2: Get Form Responses

1. Add a new step **"Get response details"**.

2. Select the **Form ID** and choose **Response ID** as dynamic content.

Step 3: Create a New Lead in Dynamics 365

1. Add a new step **"Create a new record"** in Dynamics 365.

2. Select **Leads** as the table.

3. Map form fields:

- o **Full Name → Lead Name**

- o **Email → Contact Email**
- o **Phone → Business Phone**

4. Save and test the flow.

Step 4: Verify Sync and Automate Follow-ups

- Check if new leads appear in Dynamics 365.

- Add an additional **email notification step** to alert the sales team.

Best Practices for Data Synchronization

1. **Use Scheduled Flows for Large Data Sets**

   - o If syncing thousands of records, avoid real-time sync to prevent performance issues.

2. **Ensure Data Integrity**

   - o Use conditions to **prevent duplicate records**.

3. **Optimize API Calls**

   - o Some services have API limits (e.g., Salesforce, Google Sheets). Optimize flow runs to **avoid hitting limits**.

4. **Implement Error Handling**

   - o Add retry policies and failure notifications to catch errors in real-time.

5. **Monitor and Improve Performance**

   - o Regularly check Power Automate's **run history** and optimize slow-performing flows.

Troubleshooting Common Issues

Issue 1: Flow Fails to Sync Data

- Check API limits for connected apps.

- Ensure authentication credentials are correct.

Issue 2: Duplicate Records Appear

- Add a **"Check if record exists"** condition before creating new data.

Issue 3: Slow Data Synchronization

- Use **batch processing** instead of real-time triggers.

Real-World Use Cases

1. **Syncing HR Data**: Employee records from **Workday** to **Microsoft Teams** for better collaboration.

2. **Inventory Management**: Syncing **Shopify orders** with an **Excel dashboard**.

3. **Marketing Automation**: Syncing **Mailchimp contacts** with a **CRM system**.

4. **Finance Data Sync**: Updating **QuickBooks invoices** in **SharePoint**.

Conclusion

Syncing data between applications using Power Automate helps businesses automate workflows, reduce errors, and improve productivity. By following the steps outlined in this chapter, users can set up automated data sync processes tailored to their business needs.

6.2.3 Generating and Sending Reports

Introduction

In business operations, reporting is a critical component that helps organizations analyze performance, make informed decisions, and maintain transparency. Microsoft Power Automate simplifies the process of generating and sending reports by automating data collection, formatting, and distribution. Instead of manually gathering data from various sources, compiling it into a document or spreadsheet, and sending it to stakeholders, Power Automate can perform these tasks efficiently and consistently.

This section will guide you through the process of setting up automated workflows for generating and distributing reports, integrating Power Automate with various tools such as Microsoft Excel, Power BI, SharePoint, and email services. We will cover different report formats, scheduling options, and best practices to ensure smooth and efficient reporting automation.

1. Understanding Automated Report Generation

Why Automate Report Generation?

Manual report generation is time-consuming, prone to errors, and inefficient, especially when dealing with large datasets or frequent updates. Automating this process provides several benefits:

- **Time Efficiency** – Saves time by eliminating manual data entry and formatting.

- **Consistency** – Ensures reports are generated in a standardized format every time.

- **Accuracy** – Reduces human errors in data processing and presentation.

- **Real-Time Insights** – Enables faster decision-making with up-to-date information.

- **Scheduled and On-Demand Reports** – Allows reports to be generated periodically or triggered by specific events.

Types of Reports You Can Automate

Power Automate supports a variety of reporting formats, depending on business needs:

- **Excel Reports** – Data pulled from databases, SharePoint lists, or APIs, formatted into Excel spreadsheets.

- **Power BI Reports** – Automated refresh and distribution of Power BI dashboards and reports.

- **PDF Reports** – Generated reports converted into PDFs for easy sharing.

- **Email Summaries** – Brief data reports sent as emails, containing insights or key metrics.

2. Integrating Power Automate with Reporting Tools

Power Automate and Microsoft Excel

Microsoft Excel is one of the most widely used tools for data reporting. Power Automate can automate Excel report generation by:

- Fetching data from SharePoint, SQL databases, or APIs.

- Creating a new Excel file and populating it with data.

- Applying formulas and formatting automatically.

- Saving or sharing the report via email or cloud storage.

Example: Automating a Weekly Sales Report in Excel

1. **Trigger:** The workflow runs on a scheduled basis (e.g., every Monday morning).

2. **Action:** Power Automate fetches sales data from a SharePoint list.

3. **Action:** It writes the data into a pre-formatted Excel template stored in OneDrive or SharePoint.

4. **Action:** The Excel file is emailed to the sales team.

Power Automate and Power BI

Power BI is a powerful tool for creating interactive dashboards and data visualizations. Power Automate can be used to:

- Refresh Power BI datasets automatically.

- Export Power BI reports as PDFs or images.

- Distribute reports via email or upload to SharePoint.

Example: Sending a Monthly Performance Report from Power BI

1. **Trigger:** The report is generated on the first day of each month.

2. **Action:** Power Automate exports a Power BI dashboard to a PDF file.

3. **Action:** The report is emailed to department heads and stored in SharePoint.

Power Automate and SharePoint

Many organizations use SharePoint lists to store business data. Power Automate can:

- Extract data from SharePoint lists and generate reports.

- Format SharePoint list data into tables or charts in Excel.

- Send reports to stakeholders automatically.

Example: Generating a Compliance Report from SharePoint

1. **Trigger:** A compliance report is generated when a new entry is added to a compliance tracking list.

2. **Action:** Power Automate retrieves relevant data from the SharePoint list.

3. **Action:** The data is structured in an Excel or PDF report.

4. **Action:** The report is emailed to compliance officers.

3. Automating Report Distribution

Sending Reports via Email

Once a report is generated, Power Automate can automatically send it via email.

- Attach Excel or PDF reports to emails.

- Personalize email messages with dynamic content.

- Schedule recurring report emails.

Example: Sending a Daily Financial Report via Email

1. **Trigger:** The report workflow runs every morning at 8 AM.

2. **Action:** Power Automate generates an Excel report with financial data.

3. **Action:** The report is attached to an email with a summary message.

4. **Action:** The email is sent to the finance team.

Uploading Reports to Cloud Storage

Instead of sending reports via email, Power Automate can upload them to cloud storage solutions such as:

- **SharePoint** – Store and organize reports in SharePoint document libraries.

- **OneDrive** – Save reports for personal access or sharing.

- **Google Drive/Dropbox** – Upload reports to third-party cloud storage.

Example: Storing a Weekly Employee Performance Report in SharePoint

1. **Trigger:** Every Friday at 5 PM, a report is generated.

2. **Action:** Power Automate formats and saves the report as a PDF.

3. **Action:** The report is uploaded to a designated SharePoint folder.

Sending Reports to Microsoft Teams

Power Automate can integrate with Microsoft Teams to:

- Send report summaries to Teams channels.

- Notify users when a new report is available.

- Allow users to request reports on demand using Power Automate bots.

Example: Sharing a Weekly Marketing Report in Teams

1. **Trigger:** The report is generated every Monday at 9 AM.

2. **Action:** Power Automate creates a summary message with key insights.

3. **Action:** The message and report file are posted in a Teams channel.

4. Best Practices for Report Automation

To ensure efficient and reliable report automation, follow these best practices:

Optimize Data Sources

- Use structured data sources such as SQL databases or well-organized SharePoint lists.

- Ensure data consistency to prevent reporting errors.

Manage File Storage Efficiently

- Organize report files in dedicated folders for easy access.

- Implement version control to track changes.

Use Scheduled Flows Wisely

- Avoid excessive report generation that may overwhelm users.

- Use Power Automate's built-in scheduling options to control execution times.

Test and Monitor Report Flows

- Run test flows to identify errors before full deployment.

- Monitor flow performance using Power Automate analytics tools.

Conclusion

Automating report generation and distribution with Power Automate enhances business efficiency, ensures accuracy, and saves valuable time. Whether generating financial summaries, compliance reports, or sales insights, Power Automate streamlines the process by integrating with Excel, Power BI, SharePoint, and Teams. By following the strategies outlined in this section, businesses can create a reliable and effective reporting system that delivers critical data to the right people at the right time.

6.3 Automating Notifications and Alerts

6.3.1 Email and Teams Notifications

In today's fast-paced digital environment, timely notifications and alerts are essential for maintaining smooth business operations. Microsoft Power Automate provides a robust way to automate notifications via email and Microsoft Teams, ensuring that users stay informed about critical events without manual intervention. This section explores how to set up automated email and Teams notifications, common use cases, best practices, and troubleshooting techniques.

1. Understanding Automated Notifications in Power Automate

Notifications serve as a vital communication tool in businesses. They can alert employees about approvals, system failures, completed tasks, upcoming deadlines, and more. With Power Automate, you can automate these notifications using various triggers and conditions, ensuring they are sent to the right recipients at the right time.

Power Automate supports two primary notification channels:

1. **Email Notifications** – Sending alerts via Outlook, Gmail, or other email services.

2. **Microsoft Teams Notifications** – Sending messages to specific users or Teams channels for collaboration.

Each method has its strengths and is suited for different business scenarios. While emails are great for formal communications, Teams notifications enable instant and interactive messaging.

2. Setting Up Email Notifications in Power Automate

Choosing the Right Trigger for Email Notifications

Email notifications in Power Automate typically begin with a trigger that detects an event requiring an alert. Some common triggers include:

- **"When a new response is submitted" (Microsoft Forms)** – Notify someone when a form submission occurs.

- **"When an item is created or modified" (SharePoint, Excel, or Dataverse)** – Alert users when a record is updated.

- **"When an email is received" (Outlook or Gmail)** – Forward important emails to specific recipients.

- **"When a file is added" (OneDrive, SharePoint)** – Notify someone when a document is uploaded.

- **"When an approval is required" (Approvals)** – Send an email alert to approvers.

Configuring an Email Notification Flow

To create a basic email notification in Power Automate, follow these steps:

Step 1: Create a New Flow

1. Open Power Automate and click on **Create**.

2. Choose **Automated cloud flow** and give it a meaningful name (e.g., "New Task Notification").

3. Select a trigger based on your requirements (e.g., "When an item is created in SharePoint").

Step 2: Add an Email Action

1. Click **New Step** and search for "Send an email (Outlook 365)" or "Send an email (Gmail)".

2. Configure the email fields:

   o **To:** Enter recipient(s) (e.g., a manager, team member, or department).

   o **Subject:** Define a clear subject (e.g., "New Task Assigned to You").

   o **Body:** Include dynamic content such as the task name, due date, and description.

3. (Optional) Attach files, format the email with HTML, or add inline images.

Step 3: Save and Test the Flow

1. Save the flow and click **Test**.

2. Trigger the action (e.g., create a new SharePoint item).

3. Verify that the email notification is received correctly.

3. Setting Up Microsoft Teams Notifications in Power Automate

Microsoft Teams is widely used for collaboration, and automating notifications within Teams channels or direct messages helps streamline communication.

Choosing the Right Trigger for Teams Notifications

Similar to email notifications, Teams notifications start with an event trigger. Some common triggers include:

- **"When a new message is posted in a Teams channel"** – React to incoming messages.

- **"When an item is created in SharePoint"** – Notify a Teams channel about updates.

- **"When an approval is requested"** – Notify approvers in Teams.

- **"When a new response is submitted in Forms"** – Alert a team about form submissions.

Configuring a Teams Notification Flow

Follow these steps to automate Teams notifications:

Step 1: Create a New Flow

1. Open Power Automate and click **Create**.

2. Choose **Automated cloud flow** and name it (e.g., "Task Notification in Teams").

3. Select an appropriate trigger (e.g., "When an item is created in SharePoint").

Step 2: Add a Teams Message Action

1. Click **New Step** and search for **"Post a message in a chat or channel"** (Microsoft Teams).

2. Configure the message:

   o **Post as:** Choose **Flow bot** or **User**.

   o **Post in:** Select **Chat with Flow bot** or a **Teams channel**.

   o **Message:** Include dynamic content (e.g., "A new task has been assigned: [Task Name]").

Step 3: Save and Test the Flow

1. Save the flow and click **Test**.

2. Trigger the action (e.g., create a SharePoint item).

3. Verify that the message appears in the selected Teams channel.

4. Best Practices for Automated Notifications

To maximize the effectiveness of email and Teams notifications, follow these best practices:

Avoid Notification Overload

- Ensure users receive only necessary notifications.

- Use conditions to filter notifications (e.g., notify only if priority = "High").

Personalize and Format Messages

- Use dynamic content to make messages relevant.

- Format messages using HTML in emails or adaptive cards in Teams.

Ensure Timely Delivery

- Use instant triggers for time-sensitive notifications.

- Implement retry policies for failed notifications.

Maintain Security and Compliance

- Avoid sending sensitive data in plain-text emails.

- Use encrypted connections and authentication for API-based notifications.

5. Troubleshooting Common Issues

Emails Not Being Sent

- Check if the Power Automate service is running.

- Verify that the email address is correct and accessible.

- Ensure the account has proper permissions to send emails.

Teams Messages Not Appearing

- Ensure the Flow bot has access to the Teams channel.

- Check for any throttling limits on Teams notifications.

Delayed or Duplicate Notifications

- Optimize triggers to prevent duplicate messages.

- Implement conditional checks to reduce redundant alerts.

Conclusion

Automating email and Teams notifications in Power Automate improves communication, enhances productivity, and ensures critical events receive timely attention. Whether you need to notify a team about project updates or alert management about approvals, Power Automate provides a powerful, flexible, and scalable solution.

By following best practices, troubleshooting common issues, and optimizing flow performance, you can create highly effective notification systems that enhance collaboration and efficiency in your organization.

6.3.2 SMS and Push Notifications

In today's fast-paced digital world, timely communication is critical for business operations. Whether it's sending alerts to employees, notifying customers about updates, or keeping teams informed about workflow progress, SMS and push notifications play a crucial role in business process automation. Microsoft Power Automate provides seamless integration with SMS services and push notification systems, enabling businesses to automate real-time communication efficiently.

This section explores how to configure and use SMS and push notifications within Power Automate, covering essential concepts, common use cases, and step-by-step implementation techniques.

1. Understanding SMS and Push Notifications in Power Automate

What are SMS and Push Notifications?

- **SMS (Short Message Service)**: A text messaging service that allows businesses to send short messages (typically 160 characters) to mobile devices. SMS is widely used for critical alerts, authentication, and customer engagement.

- **Push Notifications**: Notifications that appear on a user's device (mobile or desktop) even when an app is not actively running. They are commonly used by mobile apps, web applications, and services like Microsoft Power Automate to deliver real-time information.

Why Use Automated SMS and Push Notifications?

Automating notifications with Power Automate helps organizations:

- **Improve efficiency**: No need for manual updates; notifications are triggered based on real-time events.

- **Enhance user engagement**: Keeps employees, customers, and stakeholders informed about important updates.

- **Reduce response time**: Immediate notifications allow for quick decision-making and action.

- **Ensure consistency**: Automated messages reduce human error and ensure standardized communication.

2. Sending SMS Notifications in Power Automate

Choosing an SMS Provider

Power Automate does not natively provide SMS functionality but integrates with third-party SMS providers such as:

- Twilio

- Plivo

- Vonage (formerly Nexmo)

- Azure Communication Services

Before setting up an SMS notification, ensure you have an account with one of these services and obtain the necessary API keys.

Setting Up an SMS Notification Flow

Follow these steps to create an automated SMS notification flow:

Step 1: Create a New Flow

1. Navigate to Power Automate and sign in.

2. Click **Create → Automated cloud flow**.

3. Name the flow (e.g., "Send SMS Alert") and choose a trigger (e.g., "When a new response is submitted in Microsoft Forms").

Step 2: Configure the Trigger

- Select a suitable trigger based on your use case (e.g., form submission, database update, SharePoint list change).

- Configure the trigger conditions if necessary.

Step 3: Add an SMS Action

1. Click **New Step → Search for Twilio (or another SMS provider)**.

2. Select the "Send an SMS" action.

3. Enter the required details:

   o **From**: Your Twilio phone number.

   o **To**: The recipient's phone number (can be dynamic, retrieved from a database).

   o **Message**: The text of the notification (can include dynamic content from the trigger).

Step 4: Test and Deploy

- Run a test to ensure the SMS is sent correctly.

- Deploy the flow for real-time use.

Common Use Cases for SMS Automation

- **System alerts**: Notifying IT teams about server downtime.

- **Customer engagement**: Sending appointment reminders.

- **Transaction confirmations**: Notifying customers of completed payments.

- **Two-factor authentication**: Sending verification codes.

3. Sending Push Notifications in Power Automate

Push Notification Options

Power Automate supports various push notification methods:

- Power Automate mobile app notifications

- Microsoft Teams notifications

- Third-party push notification services (Firebase, OneSignal, Pusher, etc.)

Setting Up a Push Notification Flow

Step 1: Create a Flow with a Trigger

1. Open Power Automate.

2. Click **Create → Automated cloud flow**.

3. Select a trigger (e.g., "When a new file is uploaded to SharePoint").

Step 2: Add the Push Notification Action

- Click **New Step → Search for 'Notifications'**.

- Select "Send me a mobile notification."

- Enter the notification details:

  o **Message**: The content of the notification.

  o **Title**: A brief heading for the notification.

  o **Link (Optional)**: A URL users can click for more information.

Step 3: Test and Deploy

- Ensure you have the **Power Automate mobile app** installed.

- Run a test flow to verify notifications are received correctly.

- Deploy the flow for continuous operation.

Common Use Cases for Push Notification Automation

- **Employee notifications**: Alerting staff about meeting changes.

- **Security alerts**: Notifying administrators of suspicious login activity.

- **Workflow approvals**: Informing managers when an approval is needed.

- **Customer service updates**: Sending order status updates.

4. Advanced Notification Features

Customizing Notification Content

- Use **dynamic content** from triggers (e.g., user name, order details).

- Format messages for better readability.

- Use conditional logic to modify message content.

Integrating with Microsoft Teams for Better Notifications

Instead of sending SMS or push notifications, businesses can use Microsoft Teams for real-time updates:

- Send automated messages to Teams channels.

- Tag specific users for critical alerts.

- Embed actionable buttons for quick responses.

Example: Sending a Teams Notification

1. Add a **New Step** in Power Automate.

2. Search for **"Microsoft Teams"** and select **"Post a message in a chat or channel"**.

3. Configure message details (Channel, Content, Mentions).

4. Save and test the workflow.

Combining SMS and Push Notifications with Other Automation Features

- **Approval workflows**: Send notifications when approvals are required.

- **Database triggers**: Notify users when data is updated.

- **Multi-step processes**: Use conditions to determine notification type.

---

5. Best Practices for SMS and Push Notification Automation

- **Use clear and concise messages**: Avoid long texts that may overwhelm users.

- **Personalize notifications**: Include names or specific details for relevance.

- **Avoid over-notification**: Too many alerts can be annoying.

- **Ensure compliance**: Follow data protection laws like GDPR for SMS communications.
- **Monitor delivery performance**: Track failed messages and adjust configurations.

6. Conclusion

Automating SMS and push notifications in Power Automate enhances efficiency and improves real-time communication across various business processes. Whether used for customer engagement, internal alerts, or system monitoring, these notifications provide an essential tool for modern enterprises. By following best practices and leveraging Power Automate's integration capabilities, organizations can build powerful and reliable notification workflows that drive better decision-making and user experience.

6.3.3 Monitoring Triggers for Alerts

Introduction to Monitoring Triggers for Alerts

In modern business environments, real-time notifications are essential for staying informed and responsive. Microsoft Power Automate enables users to automate alerts based on specific triggers, ensuring that critical events do not go unnoticed. Whether tracking system updates, monitoring data changes, or receiving security alerts, automated notifications help teams react promptly and improve workflow efficiency.

This section explores how to set up trigger-based alerts in Power Automate, best practices for monitoring workflow performance, and real-world applications for various industries.

1. Understanding Triggers for Alerts

What Are Triggers in Power Automate?

Triggers in Power Automate are predefined conditions that start a flow. They act as event listeners, waiting for specific activities before initiating an automated workflow.

There are three main types of triggers:

- **Automated triggers:** Activated by external events such as receiving an email or updating a database.

- **Instant triggers:** Manually started by users, often for quick notifications.

- **Scheduled triggers:** Activated at specified intervals, useful for periodic monitoring tasks.

For monitoring alerts, automated triggers are the most relevant, as they ensure real-time responses to key events.

Types of Alerts in Power Automate

Power Automate allows for the creation of various alerts, including:

- **System alerts:** Notifications triggered by system status changes, such as server downtimes or API failures.

- **Data alerts:** Triggered by modifications in data, such as changes in a SharePoint list, a new entry in an Excel file, or updates in a CRM system.

- **Security alerts:** Used for monitoring unauthorized access, failed login attempts, or suspicious activities in business applications.

- **Performance alerts:** Notifies users about slow response times, failed workflows, or exceeded resource limits.

Choosing the right type of alert depends on business requirements and operational needs.

---

2. Setting Up Triggers for Alerts in Power Automate

Selecting the Right Trigger

To create an automated alert system, selecting the right trigger is essential. Power Automate provides built-in connectors with triggers for various applications, including:

- **Microsoft 365 Apps:** Outlook, Teams, SharePoint, OneDrive

- **Third-party Apps:** Slack, Trello, Salesforce, Twitter

- **Databases and Cloud Storage:** SQL Server, Google Drive, Azure Blob Storage

For example, to monitor changes in a SharePoint list, users can select the "When an item is created or modified" trigger.

Configuring Trigger Conditions

Not every event requires an alert. To avoid unnecessary notifications, users can define trigger conditions:

- **Filter specific changes:** Only trigger alerts for significant updates, such as high-priority tickets in a help desk system.

- **Set value-based triggers:** Monitor numerical thresholds, such as inventory levels dropping below a specified limit.

- **Use boolean logic:** Combine multiple conditions to refine alert triggers, ensuring more relevant notifications.

Using Expressions for Advanced Monitoring

Power Automate allows users to create expressions using Power Fx to enhance trigger logic. Examples include:

- Sending an alert only if an invoice amount exceeds $1,000.

- Notifying managers only when an employee requests more than three days of leave.

- Triggering security alerts for multiple failed login attempts from the same IP address.

Expressions add flexibility and customization, making monitoring more intelligent and effective.

---

3. Automating Notification Delivery

Choosing Notification Channels

Once a trigger is activated, Power Automate sends alerts through different communication channels. Common options include:

- **Email notifications:** Using Outlook, Gmail, or Exchange to send alerts.

- **Microsoft Teams notifications:** Sending messages directly to a specific team or user.

- **Push notifications:** Using Power Automate's mobile app to send real-time alerts.

- **SMS alerts:** Sending text messages via Twilio or other messaging services.

Each channel has advantages based on urgency, audience, and accessibility.

Customizing Alert Messages

Effective alert messages should be concise, informative, and actionable. Key elements of a well-structured alert include:

- **Clear subject line:** Identifies the type of alert (e.g., "URGENT: Server Downtime Detected").

- **Relevant details:** Provides context about the triggered event.

- **Actionable instructions:** Guides recipients on necessary steps.

For example, a well-crafted alert for low stock levels in an inventory system might look like this:

Subject: Low Stock Alert: Item XYZ
Message: Stock for Item XYZ has dropped below the minimum threshold (5 units remaining). Please reorder immediately.

Adding Dynamic Content to Notifications

Power Automate allows dynamic content insertion, ensuring that each alert is contextually relevant. This includes:

- **User names and email addresses** (e.g., "Hello [UserName], your approval is required.")

- **Time and date stamps** (e.g., "Alert triggered on [TriggerDate].")

- **Custom fields from connected apps** (e.g., "New lead generated: [LeadName], [CompanyName].")

Using dynamic content makes alerts more informative and reduces the need for manual follow-ups.

4. Monitoring and Managing Alerts

Tracking Alert History

To ensure accountability and track system performance, Power Automate logs all triggered flows. Users can:

- **View run history:** Access logs to see when and why an alert was triggered.
- **Check execution details:** Identify which actions succeeded or failed.
- **Audit user responses:** Monitor if and when recipients acted on the alerts.

Handling Alert Failures

Not all alerts function flawlessly. Common failure points include:

- **API rate limits exceeded:** Too many triggers in a short period.
- **Incorrect conditions:** Misconfigured logic preventing the trigger from firing.
- **Delivery issues:** Emails marked as spam, or Teams notifications failing due to permission errors.

To mitigate failures, users should:

- Implement retry policies for failed notifications.
- Set up backup alert channels in case the primary method fails.
- Regularly review and refine trigger conditions.

Optimizing Alert Performance

To enhance efficiency, businesses should follow best practices, such as:

- **Grouping related alerts:** Reducing excessive notifications.
- **Using dashboards for aggregated alerts:** Instead of multiple messages, summarize alerts in Power BI.
- **Integrating with AI-based anomaly detection:** Identifying unusual patterns that require attention.

By optimizing alerts, users prevent "alert fatigue" and ensure that only critical notifications are sent.

5. Real-World Applications of Monitoring Triggers for Alerts

IT and Security Monitoring

- Alerting IT teams about unauthorized access attempts.

- Notifying admins about server performance issues.

Customer Support and Service Management

- Sending alerts when high-priority support tickets are created.

- Monitoring customer complaints and escalating urgent cases.

Sales and Marketing Automation

- Notifying sales teams when a high-value lead submits a form.

- Alerting marketing teams when social media engagement spikes.**HR and Employee Engagement**

- Notifying HR when employees submit time-off requests.

- Sending reminders for upcoming performance reviews.

Conclusion

Monitoring triggers for alerts in Power Automate is a powerful way to automate business processes, improve response times, and enhance operational efficiency. By carefully selecting triggers, refining alert conditions, and optimizing notification delivery, businesses can ensure that critical events are detected and addressed promptly.

By applying these techniques, users can transform Power Automate from a simple automation tool into a proactive monitoring system that keeps teams informed and productive.

PART VII
Managing and Optimizing Your Flows

7.1 Monitoring Flow Performance

7.1.1 Viewing Flow Run History

Monitoring the performance of your flows in Microsoft Power Automate is essential for ensuring they run smoothly and efficiently. One of the key ways to track how your flows are performing is by reviewing their **Flow Run History**. This feature provides a detailed log of every instance a flow has been executed, allowing you to identify successful runs, failures, and potential performance issues.

In this section, we will explore:

- What **Flow Run History** is and why it matters
- How to access **Flow Run History**
- How to interpret run details
- Understanding different flow statuses
- How to troubleshoot common issues using run history

What is Flow Run History?

Flow Run History is a record of every time your flow has been executed. Each run includes details such as:

- **Start and completion times** – When the flow started and finished running.

- **Status of execution** – Whether the flow **succeeded**, **failed**, or is **running**.

- **Trigger and action details** – Information on which trigger initiated the flow and the actions it performed.

- **Error messages** – If the flow failed, details about what went wrong.

- **Duration of execution** – How long the flow took to complete.

This data helps users analyze performance trends, detect issues, and optimize workflows for efficiency.

How to Access Flow Run History

To view the **Flow Run History** in Power Automate, follow these steps:

1. Navigate to Power Automate

1. Open **Microsoft Power Automate** by visiting flow.microsoft.com.

2. Sign in using your Microsoft account.

2. Locate the Flow

1. In the left navigation panel, click **My flows** to see a list of your created flows.

2. Find the flow you want to review and click on it to open its details page.

3. View Run History

1. On the flow details page, navigate to the **Run History** section.

2. Here, you will see a list of recent executions of the flow. Each row represents a different instance where the flow was triggered.

3. The table includes columns for:

   - **Start Time** – When the flow started running.

   - **Duration** – How long the flow took to complete.

   - **Status** – Whether the flow **Succeeded**, **Failed**, or is **Running**.

   - **Trigger Name** – The event that started the flow.

> o **Action Details** – A breakdown of the steps executed in the flow.

4. Open a Specific Flow Run

1. Click on any row to open detailed logs of that specific run.

2. You will see a **step-by-step breakdown** of how the flow was executed, including:

   o The **trigger event** that initiated the flow

   o The **data inputs and outputs** for each action

   o Any errors encountered during execution

Understanding Different Flow Run Statuses

Power Automate provides different **statuses** for each flow run. Understanding these statuses is key to diagnosing issues:

1. Succeeded

- **Meaning**: The flow executed all actions correctly.

- **What to do**: No action needed unless you're optimizing for performance.

2. Failed

- **Meaning**: One or more actions in the flow encountered an error.

- **What to do**: Open the run details, locate the failed action, and review the error message.

3. Running

- **Meaning**: The flow is still in progress.

- **What to do**: Wait for completion or check for actions that may be taking longer than expected.

4. Skipped

- **Meaning**: Certain actions were bypassed due to conditions not being met.

- **What to do**: Review the logic of your flow and verify conditions are correct.

5. Canceled

- **Meaning**: The flow execution was manually stopped or encountered a system failure.

- **What to do**: Investigate the reason for cancellation and restart the flow if necessary.

Interpreting Flow Run Details

Once you open a flow run, you will see a **visual representation** of all the steps executed. Here's how to analyze key sections:

1. Trigger Details

- This shows **which event initiated the flow** and the data associated with it.

- Example: If your flow starts when an email arrives in **Outlook**, this section will display the email's subject, sender, and content.

2. Action Details

- Every action in your flow will be listed along with:

  - **Input data** (what information was provided to the action)

  - **Output data** (what the action returned)

  - **Execution time** (how long the action took to run)

- Example: If you have an action that creates a new row in **Excel**, you can verify what data was written to the spreadsheet.

3. Error Messages and Troubleshooting Tips

- If an action fails, you will see a red **error icon**. Clicking on it will reveal:

  - A detailed **error message** explaining what went wrong

  - Error **codes** that can be used for troubleshooting

- Common error messages:

  - **"Action timed out"** → The action took too long to execute.

- o **"Authentication failed"** → The flow may have lost permissions to access an external system.

- o **"Invalid input"** → The data provided to an action did not match expected parameters.

Troubleshooting Common Issues Using Flow Run History

1. Identifying Bottlenecks

- If a flow takes too long to execute, check which **action** has the highest duration.

- Optimize by:

  - o Reducing **API calls**

  - o Avoiding unnecessary loops

  - o Using **parallel branching** where possible

2. Fixing Authentication Errors

- If a flow fails due to authentication:

  - o Reauthorize the connection under **Data** → **Connections**.

  - o Ensure the connected service (e.g., Outlook, SharePoint) has **valid credentials**.

3. Resolving Skipped Actions

- If an action was **skipped**, check if any **conditions** were not met.

- Example: If a condition requires an email to contain **"Urgent"**, but the email didn't, the action won't run.

4. Debugging Loops and Conditions

- Use **"Compose" actions** to inspect values being passed into conditions and loops.

- If a loop runs infinitely, consider adding a **counter variable** to limit iterations.

Conclusion

The **Flow Run History** in Microsoft Power Automate is a powerful tool for monitoring, diagnosing, and optimizing automation processes. By regularly checking flow performance, identifying potential issues, and making necessary adjustments, you can ensure your workflows run efficiently and reliably.

In the next section, we will explore how to **manage flow ownership and permissions**, ensuring smooth collaboration within teams.

7.1.2 Troubleshooting Flow Failures

Microsoft Power Automate is a powerful tool for automating workflows, but like any automation system, issues and failures can arise. Troubleshooting flow failures effectively ensures that your processes remain smooth, reliable, and efficient. In this section, we will explore the common causes of flow failures, how to diagnose them, and best practices for resolving issues.

1. Understanding Flow Failures

A flow failure occurs when a workflow encounters an error that prevents it from executing successfully. These failures can happen for various reasons, including configuration issues, permission restrictions, API limitations, or data inconsistencies.

When a flow fails, Power Automate provides error messages, run history details, and debugging tools to help identify the root cause of the problem. Understanding these errors is the first step in troubleshooting effectively.

2. Common Causes of Flow Failures

Incorrect Trigger Configuration

Triggers are essential in Power Automate as they initiate the workflow. If a trigger is misconfigured, the flow may not start at all or may not capture the intended data.

Common Issues:

- Using the wrong trigger type (e.g., an "Automated" trigger instead of an "Instant" trigger).

- Failing to configure required parameters (e.g., missing a required value in a SharePoint trigger).

- Exceeding API limits for trigger-based flows.

Troubleshooting Steps:

1. Verify the trigger type and ensure it matches the intended automation use case.

2. Check the trigger settings and ensure all required fields are correctly configured.

3. Review the Power Automate **Run History** to see if the trigger is being fired correctly.

Missing or Insufficient Permissions

Flows often fail due to permission issues, especially when working with Microsoft 365 apps like SharePoint, Outlook, or Teams.

Common Issues:

- The user creating the flow does not have the correct access rights to a connected service.

- A service account used in the flow has expired or lost permissions.

- A user who shared a flow has left the organization, breaking the connection.

Troubleshooting Steps:

1. Check the **Connections** section in Power Automate to ensure all accounts are authenticated.

2. Verify user permissions in the respective service (e.g., SharePoint access levels).

3. If a flow owner has left the organization, transfer flow ownership to an active user.

API Rate Limits and Throttling

Power Automate has API limits that can restrict the number of requests a flow can make within a specific period. When these limits are exceeded, the flow may fail or be delayed.

Common Issues:

- Too many requests sent to a service in a short time.

- Power Automate throttling API requests due to high usage.

- External services rejecting requests due to their own API limits.

Troubleshooting Steps:

1. Reduce the frequency of the flow by adding delays between actions.

2. Use batch processing where possible instead of individual API calls.

3. Check Microsoft's official **Power Automate limits and licensing documentation** to ensure compliance.

Data Format and Validation Errors

Flows often interact with multiple services that require data in specific formats. If the data structure does not match the expected format, the flow may fail.

Common Issues:

- Sending a string where a number is expected.

- Formatting issues in date/time fields.

- Missing required fields in an API request.

Troubleshooting Steps:

1. Use the **Run History** to examine the data being passed between actions.

2. Add **"Compose"** actions to inspect data at different steps in the flow.

3. Use **Expression Functions** (e.g., formatDateTime(), int(), string()) to ensure correct formatting.

Conditional Logic and Loops Errors

Flows that use loops (Apply to each) and conditional branches (Condition action) can run into issues if not configured properly.

Common Issues:

- Infinite loops causing a flow to exceed execution limits.

- Conditional expressions evaluating incorrectly due to data mismatches.

- The loop iterating over an empty dataset, causing unexpected results.

Troubleshooting Steps:

1. Test conditions using sample data to verify logic before deploying.

2. Use the **Terminate** action to exit loops that may run indefinitely.

3. Add **Logging Steps** (e.g., "Send Email" or "Append to Array") to track loop behavior.

3. Diagnosing Flow Failures with Power Automate Tools

Using the Run History and Flow Checker

Power Automate provides built-in tools to help diagnose and troubleshoot issues in flows.

Run History

- Located in the **My Flows** section, Run History logs every execution of a flow.

- Shows success, failure, and duration for each run.

- Allows users to click on a failed step to view error details.

Flow Checker

- Analyzes flows for configuration issues before execution.

- Highlights potential errors, missing fields, and best practice recommendations.

- Provides direct links to correct misconfigured actions.

Debugging Flows with Test Runs

Power Automate allows users to perform test runs before deploying flows into production.

Running a Flow in Test Mode

- Use the **Test** button in Power Automate to simulate different inputs.

- Select "Use data from previous runs" to test with real-world data.

Using "Compose" Actions for Debugging

- Insert **Compose** actions at key points in the flow to inspect data values.

- Helps verify whether conditions are evaluating correctly.

Monitoring Flow Execution Logs

- Use **Power Automate Analytics** to analyze execution patterns and failure rates.

4. Best Practices for Avoiding Flow Failures

To minimize flow failures, follow these best practices:

Keep Flows Simple and Modular

- Avoid overly complex workflows with too many actions.

- Break large flows into smaller, manageable flows.

Implement Error Handling and Retries

- Use **Scope Actions** to group steps and implement error handling.

- Enable **Retry Policy** for API-based actions to handle temporary failures.

Document and Maintain Flows

- Add comments to explain logic for future reference.

- Regularly review and update flows to adapt to system changes.

5. Conclusion

Troubleshooting Power Automate flows is an essential skill for ensuring reliable automation. By understanding common causes of failures, utilizing built-in diagnostic tools, and following best practices, users can minimize disruptions and maintain efficient workflows. Effective troubleshooting not only resolves issues but also improves overall automation strategies, making Power Automate an even more powerful tool in day-to-day operations.

7.1.3 Optimizing Flow Execution Time

Microsoft Power Automate is a powerful tool for automating tasks and streamlining business processes. However, as flows become more complex, they can sometimes take longer to execute than expected. Optimizing flow execution time ensures that automation remains efficient, responsive, and scalable. This section covers best practices, techniques, and strategies to reduce execution time, improve efficiency, and prevent performance bottlenecks.

1. Understanding Flow Execution Time

Flow execution time refers to the total duration required for a flow to complete all its actions from start to finish. This duration can be affected by several factors, including:

- The number of actions in a flow

- The complexity of conditions and loops

- The response time of connected services (e.g., SharePoint, Outlook, APIs)

- Network latency and data processing speeds

- The execution mode (synchronous vs. asynchronous)

Understanding the factors that impact execution time allows users to identify bottlenecks and apply optimization strategies.

2. Key Factors Affecting Flow Execution Time

Number of Actions in a Flow

Each additional action in a flow increases execution time. Redundant or unnecessary actions can slow down performance, so it's crucial to minimize them.

Optimization Tips:

- Remove unnecessary actions that do not contribute to the final outcome.

- Combine multiple actions into one where possible (e.g., use **"Compose"** to merge text instead of multiple concatenation actions).

- Use parallel branches to run actions simultaneously when tasks do not depend on each other.

API and Service Response Times

Many flows rely on external services such as SharePoint, Outlook, or custom APIs. If these services respond slowly, the entire flow slows down.

Optimization Tips:

- Use **"Get"** operations instead of **"List"** operations where possible to retrieve only the necessary data.

- Implement caching mechanisms (e.g., store frequently used data in a variable rather than fetching it repeatedly).

- Optimize API queries by filtering results before retrieving them.

- Avoid unnecessary API calls by using conditions to check if an action is needed.

Loops and Conditions

Loops (e.g., **"Apply to Each"**) and conditions can significantly impact performance, especially when processing large datasets.

Optimization Tips:

- Use **"Filter Array"** before loops to minimize the number of iterations.

- Leverage **"Select"** and **"Map"** actions to transform data efficiently instead of iterating over it.

- Consider using **bulk actions** (e.g., **Batch processing in SharePoint**) instead of looping through individual records.

- Reduce nesting levels by simplifying complex conditional logic.

Connection Limits and Throttling

Power Automate enforces service limits and throttling to prevent overuse of resources. If a flow exceeds API call limits, it may slow down or fail.

Optimization Tips:

- Use **"Retry Policy"** to handle temporary throttling errors.

- Reduce API calls by **combining multiple actions into one request** (e.g., using batch requests).

- Consider **Power Automate Premium Plans** if execution limits are consistently exceeded.

3. Best Practices for Faster Flow Execution

Using Parallel Branching

Parallel branching allows multiple actions to execute simultaneously rather than sequentially, reducing overall execution time.

How to Implement Parallel Branching:

1. Identify actions that do not depend on each other.

2. Use **"Parallel Branch"** to create separate execution paths.

3. Monitor execution time to ensure improved performance.

Example:

Instead of sending three separate emails sequentially, create parallel branches to send them simultaneously.

Reducing Dependencies Between Actions

Dependencies between actions force the flow to execute sequentially. Reducing dependencies speeds up execution.

Optimization Tips:

- Use **"Scope"** actions to group related tasks and process them independently.

- Store frequently used data in **variables** to avoid repeated calculations or API calls.

- Minimize data lookups by **retrieving necessary fields only**.

Using Triggers Efficiently

Triggers define when a flow runs. Poorly configured triggers can cause unnecessary executions, consuming resources and slowing down processes.

Optimization Tips:

- Use **filter conditions** in triggers to prevent flows from executing unnecessarily.

- For scheduled triggers, choose the right frequency (e.g., avoid checking for new data every minute if hourly is sufficient).

- Use **"Change Detection"** in SharePoint instead of querying all records.

Optimizing Data Processing and Storage

Processing large datasets in Power Automate can slow down flows.

Optimization Tips:

- Process **data in batches** instead of one-by-one.

- Use **"Select"** to transform data efficiently instead of multiple actions.

- Store frequently used data in **Excel, SharePoint, or Dataverse** for quick access.

- Avoid unnecessary data conversions.

4. Troubleshooting Slow-Running Flows

If a flow is running slower than expected, follow these troubleshooting steps:

Step 1: Identify Slow Actions

- Go to **Flow Run History** and check execution times for each action.

- Look for actions with the highest execution time.

Step 2: Check API Call Limits

- Review Power Automate's **Flow Analytics** to see if throttling is affecting execution.

- Reduce unnecessary API calls or optimize queries.

Step 3: Simplify Logic and Reduce Loops

- Refactor complex conditions to reduce nesting.

- Replace **"Apply to Each"** loops with bulk actions when possible.

Step 4: Use Debugging Tools

- Enable **"Run After"** conditions to handle failures efficiently.

- Log execution details using **"Compose"** and **"Scope"** actions for better debugging.

5. Advanced Optimization Techniques

Using Power Automate Premium Connectors

Premium connectors offer faster execution and improved reliability. Consider upgrading if high performance is critical.

Combining Power Automate with Power Apps and Power BI

- Use **Power Apps** for real-time processing instead of running multiple Power Automate flows.
- Use **Power BI** for data visualization instead of retrieving large datasets in a flow.

Leveraging Azure Logic Apps for Heavy Workloads

For enterprise-level automation, **Azure Logic Apps** provide greater scalability and advanced processing capabilities.

6. Conclusion

Optimizing flow execution time in Power Automate is crucial for maintaining efficiency and ensuring smooth automation. By reducing unnecessary actions, optimizing loops and conditions, leveraging parallel processing, and managing API calls effectively, users can significantly improve the performance of their flows.

Regular monitoring, troubleshooting, and best practices help ensure that Power Automate workflows run efficiently, delivering the best results with minimal execution time.

Next Steps:

- Review **Flow Run History** to identify performance bottlenecks.
- Apply **parallel processing** and **batch operations** to speed up execution.
- Optimize API calls and reduce **unnecessary actions**.
- Monitor execution times regularly to keep workflows efficient.

By implementing these strategies, Power Automate users can create faster, more reliable, and more efficient automation workflows.

7.2 Managing Flow Ownership and Permissions

As you create and refine your workflows in Microsoft Power Automate, managing access and ownership becomes crucial, especially in collaborative environments. Ensuring that the right people have access to your flows helps maintain efficiency, prevent disruptions, and secure sensitive information. This section explores how to effectively manage flow ownership and permissions.

7.2.1 Sharing Flows with Your Team

Sharing flows is a fundamental feature in Power Automate that enables teams to collaborate on workflow automation. Instead of recreating similar workflows, team members can leverage shared flows to enhance efficiency and consistency.

Why Share Flows?

There are several key reasons why sharing flows is beneficial:

1. **Collaboration** – Team members can co-manage flows, troubleshoot issues, and improve workflows together.

2. **Business Continuity** – If the original creator leaves the organization or changes roles, shared ownership ensures that workflows continue running.

3. **Efficiency** – Avoiding duplicated efforts by reusing well-designed flows saves time and reduces redundancy.

4. **Scalability** – Teams can scale automation efforts by allowing multiple users to refine and extend existing workflows.

Types of Flow Sharing in Power Automate

When sharing a flow, you need to decide what level of access others should have. Power Automate provides several options for sharing flows:

1. Adding Co-Owners

Adding a co-owner allows another user to edit, update, and manage the flow. This is useful when multiple team members need administrative control over a workflow.

- Co-owners can modify triggers and actions.

- They can view flow run history and troubleshoot issues.

- They can disable or delete the flow if necessary.

2. Assigning Run-Only Permissions

Run-only permissions allow users to execute the flow but not modify it. This is useful when:

- You want employees to use a workflow without altering it.

- A flow is designed for data collection (e.g., an approval process or a form submission flow).

- A flow interacts with sensitive data, and modification rights need to be restricted.

3. Sharing via a Power Automate Team Flow

A **Team Flow** allows multiple people to co-own and collaborate on automation. This is ideal for scenarios where a department or group is responsible for a workflow rather than an individual.

- Any owner can edit or manage the flow.

- If the original creator leaves the organization, the flow remains active.

- Changes made by any co-owner are automatically applied for all users.

How to Share a Flow in Power Automate

Sharing a flow is a straightforward process in Power Automate. Follow these steps to grant access to other users:

Step 1: Open the Flow You Want to Share

1. Sign in to Power Automate.

2. Go to **My Flows** in the left navigation menu.

3. Locate the flow you want to share and click on it to open the details page.

Step 2: Add Co-Owners

1. Click on the **Share** button at the top right of the flow page.

2. In the **Manage owners** section, enter the names or email addresses of the users you want to add.

3. Click **Add** to grant them access.

4. The users will now appear as co-owners, and they can edit and manage the flow.

Step 3: Assign Run-Only Permissions

1. If you only want users to run the flow, navigate to the **Run-Only Users** section.

2. Click **+ Add a user** and select the appropriate people or groups.

3. Choose whether they need to sign in before running the flow.

4. Save the settings to apply changes.

Step 4: Confirm Permissions and Test

1. Review the list of co-owners and run-only users.

2. Ask a team member to test the flow to ensure that permissions work as expected.

Best Practices for Sharing Flows

1. Define Access Levels Clearly

Before sharing a flow, decide whether users need full control or only run access. Giving unnecessary edit permissions can lead to unintended changes or errors.

2. Use Groups Instead of Individuals

Instead of adding individual users, consider sharing flows with a **Microsoft 365 Group** or **Security Group**. This makes management easier when team members join or leave.

3. Monitor Shared Flows Regularly

- Regularly check who has access to your flows.

- Remove users who no longer need access to prevent security risks.

4. Document Flow Ownership

Maintain a record of who owns and manages critical flows. If a key owner leaves the company, reassign ownership before they lose access.

5. Avoid Personal Accounts for Business Flows

- Use a shared service account or a designated automation account instead of an individual user's account.

- This prevents issues when a person leaves the company.

Common Issues and Troubleshooting

1. Shared Users Cannot See the Flow

- Ensure the user is added as a co-owner in the sharing settings.

- Refresh the Power Automate dashboard after sharing.

2. Flow Stops Running After Owner Leaves

- Before a user departs, transfer flow ownership to another co-owner.

- Use **Power Automate Team Flows** to prevent dependency on a single owner.

3. Run-Only Users Cannot Execute the Flow

- Check if **trigger authentication** is required (e.g., some API-based flows need additional sign-in permissions).

- Ensure that the **run-only access** is correctly set up for their user role.

4. Co-Owners Cannot Modify the Flow

- Ensure the user is assigned as a **co-owner**, not just a run-only user.

- Verify if the flow is part of a **Solution**, as some solution-based flows require different permission settings.

Conclusion

Sharing flows in Power Automate is an essential skill for collaboration, efficiency, and business continuity. By carefully assigning co-owners and run-only users, teams can work together effectively while maintaining control over automation processes.

In the next section (**7.2.2 Managing Flow Permissions and Access**), we will dive deeper into advanced access control settings, including role-based permissions and governance best practices.

7.2.2 Managing Flow Permissions and Access

Microsoft Power Automate is a powerful tool for workflow automation, but managing who can access, edit, and run flows is crucial for maintaining security, collaboration, and operational efficiency. In this section, we'll explore the different aspects of managing flow permissions, how to control access levels, best practices for securing flows, and how to handle flow ownership changes effectively.

1. Understanding Flow Permissions in Power Automate

Power Automate allows users to share and manage flows with different permission levels. Permissions determine who can view, edit, or run a flow, ensuring that automation processes are secure and accessible only to the right individuals or teams.

Types of Flow Permissions

When managing flow permissions, Power Automate provides three primary levels of access:

1. **Owner** – Full control over the flow, including editing, running, sharing, and deleting the flow.

2. **Co-owner (Editor)** – Can edit and run the flow but cannot delete or transfer ownership.

3. **User (Run-Only Access)** – Can only trigger and execute the flow without modifying its structure.

Each permission level plays a key role in ensuring that workflows are accessible to the right users without compromising security.

Where Are Flow Permissions Applied?

Flow permissions are applied in different scenarios:

- **Personal flows** – Created by an individual and not shared with others.

- **Team flows** – Shared with multiple team members for collaboration.

- **Organizational flows** – Used across departments or the entire organization.

Each scenario requires different permission settings to ensure security and collaboration are balanced.

2. Managing Permissions in Power Automate

Properly managing permissions ensures that users have the necessary access while preventing unauthorized modifications.

How to Manage Flow Permissions

To manage flow permissions, follow these steps:

Step 1: Open the Flow in Power Automate

- Navigate to Power Automate.

- Click on **My flows** and locate the flow you want to manage.

Step 2: Access Flow Sharing Settings

- Click on the **three-dot menu (⋮)** next to the flow.

- Select **Share** to open the permissions management window.

Step 3: Add or Remove Users

- Enter the name or email of the user you want to add.

- Assign the appropriate permission level: **Owner, Co-owner, or Run-only user**.

- Click **Share** to save the changes.

Step 4: Reviewing Existing Permissions

- View the list of current users and their permission levels.

- Remove unnecessary users to ensure security.

This method ensures that only authorized personnel have access to your flows, reducing security risks.

3. Setting Up Run-Only Users

What Are Run-Only Users?

Run-Only Users are individuals who can **execute** a flow without modifying it. This is useful for workflows like:

- Approving requests

- Submitting forms

- Generating reports

Configuring Run-Only Access

To set up Run-Only access:

1. Open the flow in **Power Automate**.

2. Click on **More (⋮) > Manage Run-Only Users**.

3. Add users or groups.

4. Select whether they **must sign in** or can use a **shared connection**.

5. Click **Save**.

4. Managing Flow Ownership and Role-Based Access

Assigning Co-Owners for Collaboration

Co-owners (Editors) can modify a flow without having full ownership. To assign a co-owner:

1. Open the **Share** settings of the flow.

2. Add the user and assign the **Co-owner** role.

3. Click **Save**.

This is ideal for team-based automation workflows where multiple users need modification access.

Role-Based Access Control (RBAC) in Power Automate

RBAC ensures that users only have access to flows relevant to their roles. Best practices include:

- **Use Microsoft Entra ID (formerly Azure AD)** for centralized access management.

- **Group users by roles (Admin, Editor, Operator, Viewer)**.

- **Limit the number of Owners and Co-Owners** to prevent unauthorized modifications.

5. Best Practices for Securing Flow Permissions

To enhance security and collaboration, follow these best practices:

Grant the Least Privilege Necessary

- Avoid giving **Owner** access unless necessary.

- Use **Run-Only access** for users who only need to execute flows.

Review and Audit Flow Permissions Regularly

- Periodically check who has access to flows.

- Remove users who no longer need permissions.

Use Power Automate Environment Controls

- Create separate environments for development and production.

- Limit flow creation rights to authorized personnel.

Implement Data Loss Prevention (DLP) Policies

- Prevent unauthorized data sharing by restricting flow connectors.

- Set up policies in **Microsoft Power Platform Admin Center**.

6. Handling Flow Ownership Changes

Flow ownership might need to be transferred if the original owner leaves the organization or moves to another role.

Transferring Flow Ownership

To transfer flow ownership:

1. Open Power Automate and navigate to **My Flows**.

2. Locate the flow and click **Share**.

3. Add the new owner as a **Co-owner**.

4. After confirmation, remove the old owner from the list.

What Happens When a Flow Owner Leaves?

If a flow owner leaves, the flow might **stop running** if it depends on their credentials. To prevent disruptions:

- Use service accounts instead of individual accounts.

- Transfer ownership before offboarding.

- Migrate flows to shared environments.

7. Conclusion

Managing permissions and access in Power Automate is essential for maintaining **security, efficiency, and collaboration**. By implementing proper **role-based access**, reviewing permissions **regularly**, and setting up **best practices**, organizations can ensure their workflows run **smoothly** while preventing **unauthorized changes and security risks**.

7.2.3 Transferring Flow Ownership

Introduction

As organizations grow and workflows evolve, the need to transfer ownership of Power Automate flows becomes increasingly important. Whether an employee is leaving, changing roles, or simply handing off responsibility, transferring flow ownership ensures that automation processes continue without disruption. Proper management of flow ownership is critical for maintaining operational efficiency, security, and compliance.

In this section, we will explore why ownership transfers are necessary, different methods for transferring ownership, and best practices to ensure a seamless transition.

Understanding Flow Ownership in Power Automate

What is Flow Ownership?

Flow ownership refers to the user or entity responsible for managing, maintaining, and executing a Power Automate flow. The owner has full control over the flow, including editing, sharing, and monitoring its performance.

Types of Flow Ownership in Power Automate

Power Automate allows two primary types of ownership:

1. **Individual Ownership** – A flow is owned by a single user who created it. This user has complete control and can add co-owners if needed.

2. **Team/Service Account Ownership** – A flow is shared with a team or managed by a service account, which allows multiple users to maintain the automation.

Why Transfer Flow Ownership?

Ownership transfers are necessary in several situations, including:

- **Employee Departure** – When an employee leaves the company, their flows need to be reassigned to prevent disruptions.

- **Role Change** – If a user moves to a different department, they may no longer be responsible for maintaining certain flows.

- **Process Ownership Change** – Business processes evolve, and new teams or individuals may take over automation responsibilities.

- **Ensuring Continuity** – Transferring ownership ensures that workflows continue running smoothly even if the original owner is unavailable.

Methods for Transferring Flow Ownership

There are multiple ways to transfer ownership in Power Automate. Below, we explore the most common methods.

Method 1: Adding a Co-Owner

The simplest and most effective way to transfer ownership is by adding a co-owner. A co-owner has full access to edit, manage, and monitor the flow.

Steps to Add a Co-Owner:

1. **Go to Power Automate:**

   o Open Power Automate and sign in with your Microsoft account.

2. **Locate the Flow:**

   o Click on "My Flows" to see a list of flows you own.

3. **Open Flow Details:**

   o Click on the flow you want to transfer ownership of.

4. **Manage Owners:**

   o Select the "Share" option.

   o Enter the email address of the person you want to add as a co-owner.

      o   Click "Save" to confirm.

After adding a co-owner, the new owner can modify the flow as needed. However, the original owner still retains ownership unless they manually remove themselves.

Method 2: Exporting and Reimporting the Flow

If direct ownership transfer is not feasible, another option is exporting the flow as a package and reimporting it under a different user account.

Steps to Export a Flow:

1. Go to Power Automate and Open "My Flows"

2. Select the Flow to Transfer

3. Click on "Export" → "Package (.zip)"

4. Configure Package Details:

        o   Assign a name to the exported package.

        o   Define dependencies such as connected services and variables.

5. Click "Export" and Download the File

Steps to Reimport a Flow:

1. Sign in as the New Owner

2. Go to Power Automate and Select "Import"

3. Upload the Exported Package

4. Configure Connections and Assign a New Owner

5. Click "Import" to Finalize the Process

This method effectively transfers ownership but requires manual intervention to restore all settings and permissions.

Method 3: Using Power Automate Management Connectors

For organizations managing multiple flows, Microsoft provides **Power Automate Management Connectors**, which allow administrators to reassign ownership programmatically.

Using Power Automate Management API:

1. Access Power Automate Management API:

   o Open Power Automate Management API

2. Use the "Update Flow Owner" API Call

3. Specify the Flow ID and New Owner Details

4. Execute the API Request to Transfer Ownership

This method is recommended for IT administrators handling enterprise-wide automation governance.

Method 4: Assigning Flows to a Service Account

A best practice for business-critical flows is to assign ownership to a **service account** rather than an individual user.

Benefits of Using a Service Account:

- **Prevents Disruptions** – Flows remain active even if an employee leaves.

- **Enhances Security** – Permissions are controlled centrally.

- **Facilitates Team Collaboration** – Multiple users can access and manage flows under the service account.

To implement this:

1. Create a Service Account in Microsoft 365

2. Assign the Account as a Co-Owner of Business-Critical Flows

3. Restrict Access to Authorized Personnel Only

Best Practices for Ownership Transfers

Transferring flow ownership is a critical task that should be done systematically to avoid workflow disruptions. Below are best practices to follow:

1. Plan Ownership Transfers in Advance

- Do not wait until an employee leaves. Assign co-owners proactively.

2. Maintain Documentation

- Keep a record of all flows, their owners, and associated permissions.

3. Use Service Accounts for Long-Term Stability

- For mission-critical automation, avoid assigning ownership to a single user.

4. Regularly Review Flow Ownership

- Conduct periodic audits to ensure the correct people manage the right flows.

5. Test the Flow After Ownership Transfer

- Run the flow after transferring ownership to confirm it works correctly.

6. Communicate Ownership Changes

- Notify team members of any updates to avoid confusion.

Troubleshooting Ownership Transfer Issues

Issue 1: Co-Owner Cannot Edit or Manage Flow

- **Solution:** Ensure the co-owner has the required permissions in Power Automate and connected services.

Issue 2: Flow Stops Running After Ownership Transfer

- **Solution:** Update authentication credentials for all connected services.

Issue 3: Exported Flow Fails to Reimport

- **Solution:** Verify dependencies and connections before importing the package.

Issue 4: API Transfer Fails Due to Permissions

- **Solution:** Ensure the user executing the API call has **Power Automate Administrator** privileges.

Conclusion

Transferring ownership of Power Automate flows is a vital process that ensures automation continuity in an organization. By using the appropriate transfer method—whether adding a co-owner, exporting and reimporting flows, using management APIs, or assigning flows to a service account—users can maintain workflow stability and security.

Following best practices such as planning ahead, maintaining proper documentation, and regularly reviewing flow ownership can help organizations prevent disruptions and optimize their automation strategies.

With a structured approach, ownership transfers in Power Automate can be executed seamlessly, ensuring that business processes remain efficient and uninterrupted.

7.3 Best Practices for Efficient Automation

7.3.1 Reducing Unnecessary Steps in Flows

Introduction

One of the key principles of automation is efficiency. A well-optimized flow should accomplish its goal with minimal steps while maintaining accuracy and reliability. Overcomplicated flows can lead to performance issues, increased maintenance, and unnecessary API calls, which can slow down execution and consume system resources.

This section explores strategies to streamline your flows, remove redundant actions, and ensure your automation is as efficient as possible. Whether you're working with simple workflows or complex business processes, optimizing your flow's structure can lead to faster execution times, reduced costs, and improved reliability.

1. Understanding the Impact of Unnecessary Steps

Before optimizing, it's crucial to recognize how redundant steps affect your flow:

- **Increased Execution Time** – Every unnecessary step adds processing time, leading to slower automation.

- **Higher API and Connector Usage** – Many connectors have usage limits; excessive steps can cause throttling or additional costs.

- **Maintenance Complexity** – The more steps a flow has, the harder it is to troubleshoot, modify, and scale.

- **Error Propagation** – Unnecessary actions increase the likelihood of failures, complicating debugging and error handling.

2. Strategies to Reduce Unnecessary Steps

Using Built-In Expressions Instead of Extra Actions

Power Automate provides built-in functions that can replace multiple actions. Instead of adding extra steps for simple operations, leverage expressions in the **Expression Editor** within dynamic content.

Example 1: Avoiding Multiple 'Compose' Actions

Bad Practice:

- Using multiple **Compose** actions to modify a string.

Better Practice:

- Use a single expression in **Compose** or directly in the action that needs the result.

Example: Instead of:

1. **Compose** – Convert value to uppercase

2. **Compose** – Trim spaces

3. **Compose** – Concatenate another string

Use:

toUpper(trim(concat(variables('InputString'), ' - Processed')))

This removes unnecessary actions and achieves the same result in one step.

Example 2: Combining Conditions

Bad Practice:

- Using multiple **Condition** actions for similar checks.

Better Practice:

- Combine multiple conditions using logical operators (AND, OR) in a single condition action.

Instead of:

1. **Condition 1**: If "Status" = "Approved"

2. **Condition 2**: If "Amount" > 1000

3. **Condition 3**: If "Region" = "US"

Use:

- A single condition:

(Status = 'Approved') AND (Amount > 1000) AND (Region = 'US')

Eliminating Redundant Data Retrieval Actions

When working with data sources like SharePoint, Excel, or SQL databases, retrieving data multiple times increases execution time and API usage.

Example: Optimizing Data Queries

Bad Practice:

- Using separate **Get Items** actions for different conditions.

Better Practice:

- Use OData filters or advanced queries to fetch only necessary data in one action.

Example: Instead of:

1. **Get Items** – Retrieve all records
2. **Filter Array** – Remove unwanted items

Use:

- OData query in **Get Items**:

Status eq 'Active' and Region eq 'North America'

This reduces the dataset returned, improving speed and efficiency.

Avoiding Unnecessary Loops

Loops (Apply to Each) are powerful but can slow down execution, especially with large datasets.

Example 1: Using Array Functions Instead of Loops

Bad Practice:

- Iterating over an array just to extract specific values.

Better Practice:

- Use Select or Filter Array actions to transform data without loops.

Example: Instead of looping through a list to extract email addresses:

1. **Apply to Each** – Extract Email
2. **Append to Array** – Add Email to list

Use:

- A single **Select** action:

map(Body('Get_Items'), 'Email')

Example 2: Bulk Processing Instead of Step-by-Step Iteration

Bad Practice:

- Updating records one by one in a loop.

Better Practice:

- Use batch processing whenever possible. Many connectors (e.g., SharePoint, Dataverse) support bulk updates, reducing API calls.

Removing Unnecessary Variables

Using variables is essential, but excessive variables increase memory usage and complexity.

Example: Declaring and Using Variables Efficiently

Bad Practice:

1. **Initialize Variable** – Counter = 0

2. **Apply to Each** – Increment Counter in every iteration

3. **Set Variable** – Store the final count

Better Practice:

- Use **Length()** function instead:

length(Body('Get_Items'))

This eliminates the need for a counter variable altogether.

Consolidating Actions into a Single Step

When designing a flow, look for opportunities to combine actions.

Example: Combining String Operations

Bad Practice:

1. **Compose** – Extract substring

2. **Compose** – Convert to uppercase

3. **Compose** – Trim spaces

Better Practice:

- Use a single expression:

toUpper(trim(substring(variables('Text'), 0, 10)))

Using Default Values to Avoid Extra Steps

Some actions require default values, and many flows use conditional checks to handle missing data. Instead of adding extra conditions, use **coalesce()** or **default values** in expressions.

Example: Instead of checking for null:

if(empty(variables('Data')), 'Default Value', variables('Data'))

Use:

coalesce(variables('Data'), 'Default Value')

This removes unnecessary conditional logic.

---

3. Conclusion

Reducing unnecessary steps in Power Automate flows is essential for improving efficiency, reducing execution time, and minimizing API usage. By leveraging expressions, optimizing data retrieval, eliminating redundant loops, and consolidating actions, you can create streamlined workflows that are easier to maintain and scale.

When designing a flow, always ask:
✓ Can this be done in fewer steps?
✓ Can I use an expression instead of an action?
✓ Can I retrieve only the necessary data?
✓ Can I process records in bulk instead of iterating?

By following these best practices, you ensure that your automation remains powerful, scalable, and cost-effective.

7.3.2 Managing API Limits and Performance

Microsoft Power Automate is a powerful tool for automating workflows by integrating multiple services and applications. Many of these integrations rely on **APIs (Application Programming Interfaces)**, which allow different systems to communicate with each other. However, APIs come with limitations, such as **rate limits, request quotas, and throttling policies**, which can impact the performance and reliability of automated workflows.

In this section, we will explore:

- What API limits are and how they work in Power Automate

- How to monitor and troubleshoot API usage

- Strategies to optimize API performance

- Best practices for managing API-based integrations

1. Understanding API Limits in Power Automate

What Are API Limits?

API limits, also known as **rate limits** or **quotas**, define the maximum number of API requests that a system can process within a specific time frame. These limits are put in place to ensure that a service remains stable and does not get overwhelmed by excessive requests.

For Power Automate, API limits depend on various factors, including:

- **The type of Power Automate license** (free, premium, enterprise)

- **The type of connector used** (standard vs. premium)

- **The API policies of external services** (e.g., Microsoft Graph, SharePoint, Salesforce)

How API Limits Affect Workflows

When an API limit is exceeded, Power Automate may:

- **Throttle** the flow, slowing down requests until the limit resets.

- **Fail** the request, causing the flow to stop or produce an error.

- **Queue** requests, delaying execution until the system is ready to process them.

Understanding these behaviors is crucial for designing efficient and reliable automation solutions.

2. Monitoring and Troubleshooting API Usage

To effectively manage API limits, it is essential to monitor API usage and identify potential issues before they disrupt workflows.

Checking Flow Run History for API Usage

Power Automate provides a **Flow Run History** feature that helps users analyze API activity and performance. To access it:

1. Go to **Power Automate Portal** (https://flow.microsoft.com).

2. Navigate to **My flows** and select the flow you want to inspect.

3. Click on **Run history** to view detailed logs of executed flows.

Key insights you can gather:

- The number of API calls made per flow run.

- The response time for each API request.

- Errors related to API limits, such as **429 Too Many Requests** (rate limit exceeded).

Identifying Throttling Issues

If your flows are experiencing delays or failures, it may be due to **throttling**. This occurs when Power Automate temporarily restricts API calls to prevent excessive usage.

Symptoms of throttling include:

- Flows taking longer than expected to execute.

- Errors like **"Rate limit exceeded"** or **HTTP 429 responses**.

- Unexpected failures when interacting with external services.

Using Power Automate Analytics for API Performance

Power Automate offers built-in **Analytics and Insights** that provide a high-level view of API usage across multiple flows. To access:

1. Open the **Power Automate Admin Center**.

2. Navigate to **Analytics > Flows**.

3. Review performance metrics, including execution times, success rates, and API call counts.

3. Strategies to Optimize API Performance

To avoid hitting API limits and improve workflow efficiency, consider the following optimization strategies:

Reducing Unnecessary API Calls

One of the most effective ways to manage API limits is to minimize redundant API calls. Here's how:

- Use batch processing: Instead of making multiple API calls for each item, group them into a single batch request where possible.

- Filter data before fetching: Apply queries and filters to retrieve only the necessary data instead of pulling entire datasets.

- Store frequently used data locally: Use variables or dataverse tables to cache data and reduce repeated API calls.

Implementing Retry and Error Handling Mechanisms

To handle API rate limits effectively:

- Use built-in retry policies in Power Automate to automatically retry failed API calls.

- Introduce exponential backoff to progressively increase wait time between retries.

- Use 'Try-Catch' error handling techniques to prevent flows from failing abruptly.

Leveraging Parallel Execution for Efficiency

If your flow performs multiple independent API calls, you can speed up execution using parallel branching.

- Power Automate allows you to split flows into multiple branches that run simultaneously.

- This prevents sequential API calls from slowing down the workflow.

Using Premium Connectors for Higher Limits

Microsoft provides premium connectors that often come with higher API quotas and improved performance.

- Example: Standard SharePoint API calls may have stricter limits compared to Premium SharePoint Connectors.

- Evaluate whether upgrading to a higher-tier Power Automate license can provide better API allowances.

Scheduling Flows During Low-Traffic Hours

If your automation makes frequent API requests to an external system, consider running it during off-peak hours.

- Many APIs enforce rate limits per hour or per day, so scheduling tasks at less busy times helps prevent throttling.

---

4. Best Practices for Managing API-Based Integrations

To maintain efficient and sustainable API integrations, follow these best practices:

Document API Usage and Limits

- Maintain an internal document listing API limits, request quotas, and best practices for each service you integrate with.

- Stay updated with Microsoft Power Automate documentation and API provider policies.

Use Service Accounts for Critical Flows

- Instead of running flows with personal accounts, use dedicated service accounts to manage API calls.

- This reduces the risk of exceeding personal quotas and improves security.

Monitor API Consumption Regularly

- Set up alerts and notifications to detect excessive API usage before it impacts workflows.

- Consider using Power BI dashboards to visualize API performance trends.

Implement API Key Rotation and Security Measures

- Regularly rotate API keys and authentication tokens to maintain security.

- Store sensitive credentials securely using Azure Key Vault or Power Automate environment variables.

5. Conclusion

Managing API limits and optimizing performance is essential for maintaining reliable and efficient Power Automate workflows. By understanding API constraints, monitoring usage, and applying best practices, you can reduce errors, improve automation speed, and ensure long-term sustainability of your flows.

Key Takeaways:

✓ Understand API limits and how they impact workflows.
✓ Monitor API usage using Flow Run History and Analytics.
✓ Reduce unnecessary API calls through batching and filtering.
✓ Use retry mechanisms and parallel processing to handle throttling.
✓ Upgrade to premium connectors for higher API limits.
✓ Follow best practices for secure and efficient API integration.

By applying these strategies, you can **maximize the potential of Power Automate while staying within API limits**, ensuring smooth and scalable automation.

7.3.3 Securing Sensitive Data in Flows

Introduction

As automation becomes a crucial part of business operations, ensuring the security of sensitive data in Power Automate workflows is more important than ever. Many flows handle confidential information such as customer records, financial data, employee details, and proprietary business processes. If not properly secured, these flows can become a potential security risk.

This section will guide you through best practices for securing sensitive data in Power Automate, covering authentication, data encryption, access controls, compliance considerations, and real-world strategies to prevent data breaches.

1. Understanding Sensitive Data in Power Automate

Before securing your flows, it's essential to recognize the types of sensitive data that Power Automate may process. These include:

- **Personally Identifiable Information (PII):** Names, addresses, phone numbers, Social Security Numbers, etc.

- **Financial Data:** Bank account numbers, credit card details, invoices, payroll data, etc.

- **Health Information:** Medical records, insurance details, patient information (especially relevant to HIPAA compliance).

- **Business Secrets:** Trade secrets, proprietary processes, unpublished reports, intellectual property.

Knowing what data is at risk will help you implement the right security measures.

2. Using Secure Authentication Methods

Implementing Multi-Factor Authentication (MFA)

Multi-Factor Authentication (MFA) adds an extra layer of security by requiring users to verify their identity beyond just a password. Enforcing MFA in Power Automate:

- **Enable MFA for Microsoft 365 Accounts**: Use the Microsoft Entra ID (formerly Azure AD) security settings.

- **Require MFA for Admin and Sensitive Accounts**: Restrict flow editing or creation to users with additional authentication layers.

- **Use Conditional Access Policies**: Limit login access based on location, device, or risk level.

Utilizing Service Accounts for Critical Flows

Instead of personal accounts, use dedicated **service accounts** to run automated workflows. Benefits include:

- **Controlled Access:** Service accounts can have limited permissions.

- **Reduced Exposure:** If an employee leaves, flows remain functional.

- **Improved Monitoring:** Service accounts can be tracked more effectively.

Ensure that these accounts follow **least privilege principles**, meaning they only have the minimum access required to perform their tasks.

3. Implementing Role-Based Access Control (RBAC)

Power Automate allows administrators to define different permission levels, ensuring that only authorized users can access or modify flows.

Assigning Appropriate Roles and Permissions

Use Microsoft Entra ID (Azure AD) and Power Platform Admin Center to assign roles:

- Flow Owners: Can edit, delete, and share flows.

- Flow Users: Can run flows but cannot modify them.

- Flow Administrators: Manage all flows in an environment.

Keep access **restricted** based on business needs and ensure that only essential personnel have elevated permissions.

Implementing Data Loss Prevention (DLP) Policies

Microsoft Power Platform provides **DLP policies** that help prevent unauthorized data sharing.

How to Set Up DLP Policies in Power Automate:

1. Access the Power Platform Admin Center and navigate to Data Policies.

2. Define policy categories:

- o Business Data: Internal applications (e.g., SharePoint, OneDrive, Dataverse).

- o Non-Business Data: External applications (e.g., Twitter, Dropbox).

3. Restrict connectors from interacting with each other to prevent sensitive data leaks.

4. Monitor and refine policies based on user activities and compliance needs.

Managing Flow Ownership Securely

When transferring ownership of a flow:

- Avoid assigning individual user accounts as owners.

- Use Power Automate Teams or Groups for better role-based control.

- Revoke access when employees leave the organization.

4. Encrypting and Masking Sensitive Data

Encryption ensures that data remains unreadable to unauthorized users, even if intercepted.

Enforcing Data Encryption

Power Automate relies on **Microsoft's built-in encryption standards**:

- Data at Rest: Stored data is encrypted using Azure Storage encryption (AES-256).

- Data in Transit: Information traveling between services is secured via TLS (Transport Layer Security) 1.2.

For additional security:

- Use Azure Key Vault to manage encryption keys instead of storing credentials in flows.

- Enable Microsoft Purview Compliance Center for additional encryption controls.

Masking Sensitive Data in Logs and Notifications

When logging or sending notifications, sensitive data should not be exposed.

Best practices include:

- Using placeholders instead of raw data (e.g., "****" for credit card numbers).

- Storing logs in a secured SharePoint or Azure location instead of exposing details in emails.

- Configuring Power Automate connectors to obfuscate sensitive fields before processing.

Example: Instead of sending a full SSN in an email alert, send only the last four digits:

Masked SSN: ***-**-1234

5. Monitoring and Auditing Flow Security

Enabling Audit Logging

Ensure that all Power Automate activities are logged in Microsoft Purview (formerly Compliance Center). Logs should capture:

- Flow Execution Details: Who ran the flow and when?

- Data Access Records: Which data sources were accessed?

- Modifications and Ownership Changes: Who modified or transferred ownership of a flow?

Setting Up Alerts for Unauthorized Activity

Create custom alerts in Microsoft Defender or Power Automate itself to notify admins of:

- Unusual login attempts or MFA bypasses.

- Flows accessing unauthorized data sources.

- Sudden permission changes to critical flows.

Conducting Regular Security Reviews

- **Quarterly Flow Audits**: Review who has access to each flow and revoke unnecessary permissions.

- **Incident Response Planning**: Have a plan for handling security breaches involving Power Automate.

- **User Training & Awareness**: Educate employees on security risks and best practices for flow management.

6. Compliance Considerations for Secure Automation

Organizations must ensure that Power Automate flows comply with industry standards and regulations.

Aligning with Compliance Standards

- **GDPR** (General Data Protection Regulation) – Ensuring user data is handled correctly.

- **HIPAA** (Health Insurance Portability and Accountability Act) – Protecting healthcare data.

- **ISO 27001** – International standard for information security.

Using Microsoft Compliance Manager

Microsoft Compliance Manager helps assess risks and recommend improvements in Power Automate security.

- Provides a Compliance Score based on security configurations.

- Suggests actions to improve security posture.

- Allows tracking of compliance-related tasks and documentation.

Conclusion

Securing sensitive data in Power Automate is a **multi-layered approach** involving authentication, access control, encryption, monitoring, and compliance. By implementing these best practices, you can:

✓ Protect sensitive information from unauthorized access.
✓ Prevent data breaches and compliance violations.
✓ Ensure that Power Automate workflows remain reliable, secure, and efficient.

Security should never be an afterthought—make it a fundamental part of your automation strategy.

PART VIII
Real-World Use Cases and Case Studies

8.1 Automating HR and Employee Onboarding

Human Resources (HR) departments handle numerous repetitive tasks, from recruiting and onboarding new employees to managing benefits and performance evaluations. By leveraging **Microsoft Power Automate**, HR teams can streamline and automate various processes, reducing manual effort and improving efficiency. One of the most impactful areas where **Power Automate** can be utilized is **employee onboarding**.

This section explores how **Power Automate** can transform onboarding by automating key steps such as collecting employee information, setting up accounts, sending welcome emails, and tracking training progress.

The Challenges of Manual Employee Onboarding

Traditional employee onboarding often involves multiple manual steps, such as:

- Collecting employee information via email or paper forms
- Creating accounts in multiple systems (email, HR software, payroll, security access)
- Assigning IT resources (laptops, software licenses, VPN access)
- Sending welcome emails and introductory documents
- Scheduling orientation meetings and training sessions

These manual processes can be time-consuming, prone to errors, and create inconsistent onboarding experiences. Additionally, delays in setting up necessary tools can lower employee productivity and engagement.

Power Automate eliminates these inefficiencies by **automating** these processes, ensuring that new hires receive the necessary resources and information seamlessly.

Key Automation Scenarios for HR and Employee Onboarding

Here are some common ways **Power Automate** can enhance the employee onboarding process:

1. Automating Employee Data Collection and Processing

Scenario: A company hires new employees and needs to collect their personal and professional details.

Solution Using Power Automate:

- A Microsoft Forms survey is sent automatically to the new hire, collecting necessary details such as full name, date of birth, emergency contact, and tax information.

- When the form is submitted, Power Automate triggers a workflow that:

    o Saves the data to a SharePoint list or Excel file.

    o Notifies HR and IT teams via Microsoft Teams or Outlook.

    o Creates an entry in the HR system (e.g., Workday, SAP, or Dynamics 365).

2. Automating Account Creation and System Access

Scenario: IT teams manually create user accounts for new employees, which is time-consuming and prone to errors.

Solution Using Power Automate:

- Once HR submits a new hire request in SharePoint, Power Automate:

    o Automatically creates an Azure Active Directory (AAD) account.

    o Assigns the employee to appropriate security groups for access to internal systems.

    o Sends a confirmation email to HR and IT with account details.

    o Generates a temporary password and sends it securely to the new hire.

3. Sending Welcome Emails and Documentation

Scenario: New employees often receive scattered and delayed emails with company policies, HR guides, and IT setup instructions.

Solution Using Power Automate:

- As soon as a new hire's account is created, Power Automate:

    o Sends a personalized welcome email with important documents attached.

    o Shares links to company resources, such as an employee handbook, code of conduct, and benefits enrollment forms.

    o Schedules a Teams meeting with HR for orientation.

4. Assigning Onboarding Tasks and Tracking Progress

Scenario: HR and managers manually track onboarding tasks, leading to miscommunication and incomplete steps.

Solution Using Power Automate:

- Once an employee joins, Power Automate:

    o Creates a checklist in Microsoft Planner for onboarding tasks (e.g., IT setup, policy review, benefits enrollment).

    o Assigns tasks to HR, IT, and the hiring manager.

    o Sends automated reminders to ensure tasks are completed on time.

    o Updates a SharePoint dashboard with onboarding progress.

5. Automating Training and Compliance Tracking

Scenario: New hires need to complete compliance training and acknowledge company policies.

Solution Using Power Automate:

- Power Automate:

    o Enrolls new employees in an LMS (Learning Management System) such as Microsoft Viva Learning or LinkedIn Learning.

    o Sends reminders until the training is completed.

    o Tracks completion status and updates HR records in SharePoint.

o   Notifies managers when training is finished.

6. Streamlining Equipment and Resource Allocation

Scenario: New hires require laptops, software licenses, and office equipment, often leading to delays.

Solution Using Power Automate:

- When HR submits a request in Microsoft Forms, Power Automate:

    o   Notifies the IT and Facilities team to allocate resources.

    o   Creates a service ticket in ITSM **tools** like ServiceNow or Jira.

    o   Updates HR when equipment is assigned.

Step-by-Step Guide to Building an Automated Onboarding Flow

Here's how you can build a **basic employee onboarding workflow** in Power Automate:

Step 1: Trigger the Flow with Employee Information Submission

- Use **Microsoft Forms** to collect new hire data.

- Create a **Power Automate flow** that triggers when a form response is submitted.

Step 2: Store Data in SharePoint or Excel

- Add an action to save the employee details to a **SharePoint List** or **Excel file**.

Step 3: Send Welcome Email

- Add an **Outlook action** to send a **welcome email** with key information.

Step 4: Create an Azure AD User Account

- Use the **Azure AD connector** to create a user account.

- Assign appropriate **security groups** for system access.

Step 5: Assign Onboarding Tasks

- Use **Microsoft Planner** to create a checklist for HR, IT, and managers.

Step 6: Schedule Orientation Meetings

- Use the **Microsoft Teams connector** to schedule a welcome meeting.

Step 7: Track Progress in Power BI

- Create a **Power BI dashboard** to monitor onboarding status.

Benefits of Automating Employee Onboarding

1. Time Savings

- Reduces manual data entry and repetitive tasks.

- Speeds up account creation and equipment allocation.

2. Improved Accuracy

- Eliminates human errors in data entry.

- Ensures new hires receive accurate and timely information.

3. Consistency in Onboarding

- Standardizes the onboarding experience.

- Ensures all employees receive the necessary documents, training, and resources.

4. Enhanced Employee Experience

- Provides a smooth and engaging onboarding process.

- Helps new hires integrate into the company culture faster.

5. Increased HR and IT Productivity

- Frees HR and IT teams from repetitive tasks.

- Allows HR to focus on strategic initiatives.

Conclusion

Automating the **HR onboarding process** with **Microsoft Power Automate** can significantly improve efficiency, reduce errors, and enhance the employee experience. By integrating Power Automate with **Microsoft 365 tools, HR systems, and IT service**

management platforms, businesses can streamline workflows and ensure a smooth transition for new employees.

In the next section, we will explore how Power Automate can be used to **streamline IT support and help desk operations**.

8.2 Streamlining IT Support and Help Desk Operations

IT support and help desk operations are essential components of any organization, ensuring that employees and customers receive timely technical assistance. However, these operations often involve repetitive tasks, ticket management, approvals, and troubleshooting workflows that can be time-consuming if handled manually.

Microsoft Power Automate can significantly streamline IT support by automating ticket management, system monitoring, incident response, and communication processes. In this section, we will explore how Power Automate can enhance IT help desk efficiency, improve response times, and reduce workload for IT teams.

Automating IT Ticket Management

One of the primary functions of an IT help desk is managing support tickets. Traditional ticket management systems require manual logging, categorization, and assignment of tickets, which can delay response times and increase workload. With Power Automate, organizations can automate various aspects of ticket handling, from ticket creation to resolution.

Creating Support Tickets Automatically

Power Automate can integrate with popular IT service management (ITSM) platforms like ServiceNow, Zendesk, and Microsoft Dynamics 365. Automated flows can be set up to:

- Capture support requests from emails, chatbots, or web forms.

- Create tickets in the ITSM system automatically.

- Categorize tickets based on keywords or priority levels.

- Assign tickets to the appropriate IT support teams.

Example Use Case

A company receives IT support requests via email. With Power Automate, an email trigger can scan incoming messages for specific keywords (e.g., "network issue," "VPN problem"), extract relevant information, and create a support ticket in ServiceNow. The ticket is then assigned to the appropriate technician based on the issue type.

Automating Ticket Escalation

Some IT issues require urgent attention or need to be escalated to higher-level support teams. Power Automate can:

- Monitor ticket statuses and automatically escalate unresolved issues beyond a specified timeframe.

- Notify IT managers via Microsoft Teams or email if a critical ticket is pending.

- Trigger additional workflows, such as restarting a service or running a diagnostic script.

Example Use Case

If a server-related ticket remains unresolved for over 4 hours, Power Automate sends an automatic alert to the IT supervisor and reassigns the ticket to a senior engineer.

Enhancing Incident Response and System Monitoring

IT teams are responsible for monitoring systems, networks, and applications for potential failures or security threats. Instead of relying solely on manual monitoring, Power Automate can integrate with monitoring tools to automate responses and alerts.

Automated Incident Notifications

Power Automate can listen for alerts from monitoring platforms like Microsoft Azure Monitor, Splunk, or Nagios and take automated actions, such as:

- Sending real-time alerts to IT teams via Microsoft Teams or SMS.

- Logging incidents in a database for tracking and analysis.

- Restarting a failed service automatically.

Example Use Case

An organization using Azure Monitor detects a server failure. Power Automate immediately logs an incident in ServiceNow, notifies the IT team via Microsoft Teams, and attempts an automated restart of the affected server.

Self-Healing IT Systems

Advanced automation with Power Automate allows IT teams to create self-healing mechanisms, where systems automatically resolve minor issues without human intervention. Examples include:

- Restarting a crashed application when a failure is detected.

- Clearing temporary files if disk space runs low.

- Resetting VPN connections when frequent disconnections are detected.

Example Use Case

If a company's web server experiences high CPU usage, Power Automate triggers a script to terminate unnecessary background processes and send a performance report to the IT team.

Automating IT Support Communications

Timely communication is crucial in IT support, whether it's informing users about system outages, providing status updates on their requests, or sending security alerts. Power Automate can enhance communication efficiency in multiple ways.

Automating IT Support Acknowledgments

Instead of manually acknowledging support requests, Power Automate can:

- Send an automated confirmation email when a new ticket is logged.

- Provide estimated resolution times based on ticket priority.

- Direct users to self-service knowledge base articles if applicable.

Example Use Case

A user submits a ticket about a slow internet connection. Power Automate automatically responds with troubleshooting steps from the IT knowledge base and assigns the ticket to a network specialist.

Automated Outage Notifications

During major outages or system downtime, Power Automate can:

- Detect service failures through monitoring tools.

- Send mass notifications to employees via email, SMS, or Microsoft Teams.

- Provide estimated restoration times and updates as issues are resolved.

Example Use Case

If Microsoft 365 services experience downtime, Power Automate pulls status updates from the Microsoft Service Health Dashboard and sends them to employees via Teams and email.

Automating Password Resets and User Access Requests

One of the most common IT support requests is password resets and account access issues. These requests often take up a significant portion of help desk resources. Power Automate can integrate with Microsoft Entra ID (Azure AD) and security systems to streamline user account management.

Self-Service Password Reset Automation

With Power Automate, organizations can enable self-service password resets by:

- Verifying user identity through multi-factor authentication (MFA).

- Resetting passwords in Active Directory or cloud-based directories.

- Notifying users via email or SMS with new credentials.

Example Use Case

A user forgets their corporate password. Instead of submitting a ticket, they fill out a form with identity verification steps. Power Automate verifies their details, resets the password in Azure AD, and sends them the updated credentials.

Automating Employee Onboarding and Offboarding

New employees often require multiple system access permissions, while departing employees need access revoked. Power Automate can:

- Create user accounts and assign permissions automatically.

- Provision access to corporate applications based on job roles.

- Disable or delete accounts when employees leave the company.

Example Use Case

A new IT support engineer joins the company. Power Automate automatically sets up their email, grants access to the IT help desk system, and adds them to relevant Teams channels.

Reporting and Analytics for IT Support Operations

IT teams rely on data to track performance, identify bottlenecks, and improve service quality. Power Automate can integrate with Power BI and other analytics tools to generate reports automatically.

Generating Weekly IT Support Reports

Power Automate can:

- Collect ticket resolution times, success rates, and common issues.

- Generate weekly reports in Power BI or Excel.

- Send reports to IT managers via email or Teams.

Example Use Case

Every Monday morning, Power Automate compiles a report on IT help desk performance and sends it to IT leadership for review.

Conclusion

By automating IT support and help desk operations with Microsoft Power Automate, organizations can significantly reduce manual workloads, improve response times, and enhance overall efficiency. Whether it's ticket management, incident response, communication, or system monitoring, Power Automate empowers IT teams to focus on higher-value tasks while ensuring seamless support for users.

By leveraging automation, businesses can create a more proactive and self-sufficient IT support environment, ultimately leading to better user experiences and operational effectiveness.

8.3 Enhancing Sales and Marketing Workflows

Introduction

Sales and marketing teams are constantly handling repetitive and time-consuming tasks such as lead management, customer follow-ups, campaign tracking, and data analysis. Microsoft Power Automate offers a powerful solution to streamline these workflows, reducing manual effort and increasing efficiency.

By automating sales and marketing processes, businesses can ensure timely responses, improve customer engagement, and gain valuable insights from their data. In this chapter, we'll explore how Power Automate can be used to enhance sales and marketing workflows with real-world use cases, step-by-step implementation, and best practices.

Automating Lead Capture and Management

Challenges in Lead Management

Managing leads effectively is critical to increasing conversion rates. However, many businesses struggle with:

- Manually collecting leads from different sources (web forms, social media, email inquiries).

- Keeping lead information updated in CRM systems.

- Assigning leads to the right sales representatives in a timely manner.

How Power Automate Can Help

Power Automate can automate lead collection, categorization, and distribution, ensuring that leads are processed efficiently.

Example: Capturing Leads from Web Forms and Storing Them in CRM

Many companies use web forms to collect leads. With Power Automate, you can:

1. Trigger an automation when a new lead submits a form (e.g., through Microsoft Forms, HubSpot, or a WordPress plugin).

2. Extract lead details such as name, email, and inquiry details.

3. Store the information in a CRM system like Dynamics 365, Salesforce, or HubSpot.

4. Assign the lead to a sales representative based on predefined rules (e.g., region, product interest).

5. Send an automatic confirmation email to the lead, acknowledging their inquiry.

This process ensures that leads are not lost and that sales teams can respond promptly.

Automating Lead Scoring

Power Automate can integrate with AI-powered tools to score leads based on engagement, demographics, and behaviors. The workflow can:

- Analyze past interactions with the lead.

- Assign a score based on predefined rules.

- Notify sales teams when a lead reaches a high score threshold.

Streamlining Email Marketing Campaigns

Challenges in Email Marketing

Marketing teams often spend hours managing email campaigns, including:

- Sending bulk emails at scheduled intervals.

- Tracking open rates and engagement.

- Following up with potential customers who interacted with emails.

How Power Automate Can Help

By integrating with Microsoft Outlook, Mailchimp, or other email platforms, Power Automate can:

- Schedule and send personalized emails automatically.

- Track email opens and clicks to measure engagement.

- Segment contacts based on their interactions for targeted follow-ups.

Example: Automated Follow-Ups for Email Campaigns

1. Trigger: When a recipient opens an email but does not click on a call-to-action (CTA) link.

2. Condition: If the recipient has engaged with previous campaigns, mark them as a warm lead.

3. Action: Send a follow-up email with additional details or a limited-time offer.

This automation ensures that potential customers remain engaged without requiring manual follow-ups.

Social Media Automation for Brand Engagement

Challenges in Social Media Management

Marketers often struggle to manage multiple social media accounts and ensure timely responses to customer interactions.

How Power Automate Can Help

By integrating with platforms like Twitter, LinkedIn, and Facebook, Power Automate can:

- Schedule posts in advance.

- Monitor brand mentions and customer comments.

- Automatically respond to inquiries or escalate issues to the support team.

Example: Monitoring Brand Mentions and Engaging with Users

1. Trigger: When a user mentions your brand on Twitter.

2. Action: Store the tweet in a SharePoint list for tracking.

3. Condition: If the tweet contains a question, send an automated response or assign it to the customer support team.

This workflow ensures that the brand maintains an active presence and engages with potential customers efficiently.

Automating Sales Reporting and Insights

Challenges in Sales Reporting

Sales teams often need to generate reports from multiple sources, which can be time-consuming and prone to errors.

How Power Automate Can Help

By connecting Power Automate with Power BI and CRM systems, businesses can:

- Aggregate sales data from multiple sources.

- Generate real-time sales dashboards.

- Send automated performance reports to stakeholders.

Example: Automating Weekly Sales Reports

1. Trigger: Every Monday at 8 AM.

2. Action: Collect sales data from Dynamics 365 and Excel.

3. Action: Generate a Power BI report with updated sales performance metrics.

4. Action: Email the report to the sales team and management.

This automation ensures that decision-makers have the latest insights without manual effort.

Managing Customer Feedback and Surveys

Challenges in Gathering Customer Feedback

Collecting and analyzing customer feedback manually can be inefficient and lead to missed insights.

How Power Automate Can Help

With Power Automate, businesses can:

- Automatically send feedback surveys after a purchase or interaction.

- Collect and analyze responses in real-time.

- Trigger follow-up actions based on feedback scores.

Example: Automating Post-Purchase Surveys

1. Trigger: When a customer completes a purchase.

2. Action: Send a survey link via email or SMS.

3. Condition: If the customer rates the service below 3 stars, create a support ticket for resolution.

4. Action: Store feedback in a SharePoint list or Power BI dashboard for analysis.

This ensures that businesses can quickly act on customer feedback and improve their services.

Automating Contract and Proposal Approvals

Challenges in Sales Proposal Approvals

Sales teams often face delays in getting proposals and contracts approved, affecting deal closures.

How Power Automate Can Help

By integrating with SharePoint, Outlook, and Teams, Power Automate can:

- Route proposals for approval automatically.

- Send notifications and reminders to approvers.

- Track approval status in real-time.

Example: Automating Contract Approvals

1. Trigger: When a sales proposal is uploaded to SharePoint.

2. Action: Assign approval requests to the legal and finance teams.

3. Condition: If no action is taken within 48 hours, send a reminder email.

4. Action: Notify the sales team once approval is completed.

This ensures a faster and more efficient approval process, reducing sales cycle time.

Conclusion

By leveraging Microsoft Power Automate, businesses can significantly enhance their sales and marketing workflows. From lead management to social media engagement, reporting, and contract approvals, automation reduces manual effort, improves efficiency, and allows teams to focus on strategic growth.

In the next chapter, we'll explore how Power Automate is transforming industries like healthcare and education, providing even more opportunities for business process automation.

8.4 Automating Finance and Accounting Processes

Introduction

Finance and accounting teams are responsible for managing transactions, tracking financial records, ensuring compliance, and generating reports. Many of these tasks are repetitive, time-consuming, and prone to human error. Microsoft Power Automate provides a powerful solution to automate finance and accounting processes, enabling professionals to focus on higher-value activities such as financial analysis and strategic planning.

This chapter explores how Power Automate can streamline financial operations, improve efficiency, reduce errors, and enhance compliance. We will cover common automation use cases, workflow examples, and best practices for implementing automation in finance and accounting.

Common Finance and Accounting Tasks That Can Be Automated

Finance and accounting involve numerous recurring tasks that can be streamlined using automation. Below are some of the key processes that Power Automate can optimize:

1. Invoice Processing and Approval

- Automatically extract invoice details from emails or scanned documents.
- Route invoices for approval based on predefined conditions (e.g., amount thresholds).
- Integrate with accounting software (QuickBooks, Xero, SAP) to record transactions.
- Send notifications when an invoice is approved, rejected, or needs further review.

2. Expense Management and Reimbursement

- Capture receipts and expense reports from employees via Microsoft Forms or email.
- Validate expense claims against company policies using automated rules.

- Route expense reports for approval to the appropriate managers.

- Sync approved reimbursements with payroll systems for processing.

3. Payment Processing and Vendor Management

- Automate the payment approval process to ensure compliance with company policies.

- Generate and send payment confirmations to vendors.

- Maintain vendor records by syncing data between Power Automate and ERP systems.

4. Bank Reconciliation

- Fetch transaction data from bank statements via API integration.

- Compare bank transactions with internal financial records.

- Flag discrepancies for manual review.

5. Financial Reporting and Data Consolidation

- Generate automated financial reports and dashboards.

- Aggregate data from multiple sources (Excel, SQL, SharePoint, etc.).

- Distribute reports via email or upload them to SharePoint for easy access.

6. Compliance and Audit Trail Management

- Maintain an audit log of approvals and financial transactions.

- Automate documentation storage for regulatory compliance.

- Send alerts for policy violations or missing documentation.

Automating Invoice Processing with Power Automate

One of the most common finance workflows that can be automated is invoice processing. Traditional invoice handling involves receiving invoices via email, extracting data, obtaining approvals, and recording transactions in accounting software. This manual process is not only time-consuming but also susceptible to human error.

Step-by-Step Power Automate Workflow for Invoice Processing

Step 1: Capture Incoming Invoices

- Create a Power Automate flow that monitors an email inbox for invoices.
- Use AI Builder to extract invoice details (vendor name, invoice number, amount, due date).

Step 2: Validate Invoice Data

- Check for missing or incorrect fields.
- Compare the invoice details with purchase orders stored in SharePoint or an ERP system.

Step 3: Route for Approval

- If the invoice amount is below a threshold (e.g., $1,000), auto-approve the invoice.
- If the amount exceeds the threshold, route it to a manager for approval using Microsoft Approvals.

Step 4: Record the Approved Invoice

- Once approved, push the invoice data to an accounting system such as QuickBooks or SAP.
- Store a digital copy of the invoice in SharePoint for audit purposes.

Step 5: Notify Stakeholders

- Send email notifications to the finance team confirming that the invoice has been processed.
- Notify vendors about payment status updates.

Expense Management Automation

Processing employee expenses manually can be inefficient and lead to delays in reimbursements. Power Automate can streamline the entire process, from submission to approval and payment.

Example Workflow for Expense Reimbursement

Step 1: Submission of Expense Reports

- Employees submit expenses through Microsoft Forms or Power Apps.

- Power Automate extracts and categorizes expense data.

Step 2: Policy Validation and Approval Routing

- The system checks expenses against company policies.

- If within policy limits, expenses are auto-approved; otherwise, they are sent for manager review.

Step 3: Payment Processing

- Approved expenses are recorded in an accounting system.

- The finance team receives a summary report before releasing payments.

Step 4: Employee Notification and Record Keeping

- Employees receive an email confirming the status of their reimbursement.

- Expense records are archived for auditing purposes.

Automating Bank Reconciliation

Bank reconciliation ensures that financial records match bank statements. Manual reconciliation can be slow and error-prone. Power Automate can help by:

- Pulling transaction data from banks via API integration or file uploads.

- Comparing transactions with accounting records.

- Flagging discrepancies and sending alerts to finance teams.

Example Bank Reconciliation Workflow

Step 1: Import Transactions

- Retrieve bank transactions from an API or CSV file.
- Store the data in a structured format (Excel, SQL, or SharePoint).

Step 2: Match Transactions

- Compare bank transactions with financial records.
- Identify missing or duplicate transactions.

Step 3: Generate Reconciliation Report

- Summarize matched and unmatched transactions.
- Alert accountants about discrepancies for further investigation.

Best Practices for Finance Automation

To ensure successful automation of finance processes, consider these best practices:

1. Maintain Data Accuracy

- Use AI-powered tools like AI Builder to minimize errors in data extraction.
- Validate financial data before processing transactions.

2. Implement Approval Workflows

- Set up multi-level approvals for high-value transactions.
- Use Microsoft Approvals to ensure proper authorization.

3. Ensure Compliance and Security

- Encrypt sensitive financial data.
- Store audit logs for compliance tracking.

4. Monitor Performance and Optimize Workflows

- Regularly review flow run history and fix performance issues.

- Optimize API calls to stay within system limits.

Conclusion

Microsoft Power Automate offers powerful automation capabilities for finance and accounting teams. By leveraging automation, organizations can reduce manual effort, improve accuracy, and enhance compliance. Whether it's invoice processing, expense management, or bank reconciliation, Power Automate can transform finance operations, making them faster and more efficient.

By implementing best practices and continuously optimizing workflows, finance teams can ensure seamless automation that delivers long-term benefits. In the next section, we will explore how Power Automate is being used in **healthcare and education** to streamline critical processes.

8.5 Power Automate in Healthcare and Education

Introduction

Microsoft Power Automate has revolutionized workflow automation across various industries, including **healthcare and education**. These two sectors involve extensive administrative tasks, documentation, and communication processes that can be optimized with automation.

In **healthcare**, Power Automate can streamline patient data management, automate appointment scheduling, and ensure compliance with medical regulations. Meanwhile, in **education**, the tool can help with grading automation, student record management, and communication between students, teachers, and administrators.

This chapter explores **practical applications** of Power Automate in healthcare and education, providing real-world **use cases, benefits, and best practices** for leveraging automation effectively.

Power Automate in Healthcare

Challenges in Healthcare Administration

The healthcare industry is known for its **complex and time-sensitive operations**, including:

- **Manual data entry** leading to errors in patient records.

- **Time-consuming appointment scheduling** and follow-ups.

- **Compliance and regulatory requirements** needing strict documentation.

- **Inefficient communication** between healthcare professionals, patients, and insurance providers.

By integrating Power Automate, hospitals and clinics can **automate repetitive tasks, reduce paperwork, and improve patient care efficiency**.

Use Cases of Power Automate in Healthcare

1. Automating Patient Appointment Scheduling

Problem: Manual scheduling of patient appointments is time-consuming and prone to errors.

Solution: Power Automate can integrate with Microsoft Outlook, Teams, and electronic health records (EHR) systems to automate scheduling.

- When a **new appointment request** is submitted via an online form, Power Automate can:
    - Check **available slots** in the hospital's scheduling system.
    - **Send automated confirmation emails or SMS** to patients.
    - **Create calendar events** for doctors and notify staff.
    - **Trigger reminders** to reduce no-show rates.

2. Streamlining Patient Data Management

Problem: Healthcare professionals must update patient records manually, leading to errors and inefficiencies.

Solution: Power Automate can **integrate with electronic medical records (EMR) systems** to ensure automatic data synchronization.

- When a new patient registration form is filled out, Power Automate can:
    - Extract relevant information and update the hospital's database.
    - Generate and store digital copies of patient documents.
    - Notify relevant departments (e.g., billing, pharmacy).

3. Automating Prescription Refill Requests

Problem: Patients frequently request prescription refills, which require administrative approval.

Solution: Power Automate can create a workflow that connects patients, doctors, and pharmacies.

- Patients submit a prescription refill request online.

- Power Automate sends the request to the doctor for approval.

- Once approved, the pharmacy is notified automatically to prepare the prescription.

- The patient receives an email or SMS notification when the medication is ready for pickup.

4. Compliance and Regulatory Reporting

Problem: Healthcare organizations must submit compliance reports regularly, which involves manual data collection.

Solution: Power Automate can:

- Extract relevant compliance data from multiple sources.

- Automatically generate reports in Excel or Power BI.

- Send reports to regulatory bodies via email or secure portals.

Benefits of Power Automate in Healthcare

- Reduces administrative burden, allowing healthcare workers to focus on patient care.

- Enhances data accuracy by eliminating manual entry errors.

- Improves patient engagement through automated communication.

- Ensures regulatory compliance with automated reporting and tracking.

Power Automate in Education

Challenges in Education Administration

Educational institutions manage large volumes of student data, schedules, and communications, leading to:

- Time-consuming manual grading and attendance tracking.

- Inefficient communication between students, teachers, and administrators.

- Difficulties in managing student enrollment and records.

By implementing Power Automate, schools and universities can automate repetitive tasks, enhance learning experiences, and improve operational efficiency.

Use Cases of Power Automate in Education

1. Automating Student Enrollment and Registration

Problem: Manual processing of student enrollments is slow and error-prone.

Solution: Power Automate can integrate with Microsoft Forms, Excel, and student databases to:

- Automatically collect and validate student information.

- Generate student IDs and email confirmations.

- Update school records and notify administrators.

2. Automating Attendance Tracking

Problem: Teachers often have to manually record attendance, which can be tedious.

Solution:

- Power Automate can integrate with Microsoft Teams and Excel to automatically log attendance from virtual meetings.

- If a student is absent for multiple days, the system can send an automated email notification to parents.

3. Automating Assignment Grading and Feedback

Problem: Teachers spend significant time grading assignments and providing feedback.

Solution: Power Automate can:

- Extract student responses from Microsoft Forms.

- Automatically grade multiple-choice questions.

- Send personalized feedback to students via email.

4. Enhancing Communication Between Students and Staff

Problem: Schools need an efficient way to send announcements and updates.

Solution: Power Automate can:

- Send automated reminders for upcoming exams or deadlines.

- Distribute newsletters via email or Microsoft Teams.

- Enable chatbot responses for student inquiries.

5. Automating Financial Aid and Scholarship Processing

Problem: Processing scholarship applications involves multiple departments.

Solution: Power Automate can:

- Collect applications via Microsoft Forms.

- Automatically verify eligibility criteria.

- Notify applicants of approval or rejection.

Benefits of Power Automate in Education

- **Saves teachers' time** by automating grading and attendance.

- **Improves communication** with automated notifications and updates.

- **Enhances student engagement** through faster feedback and assistance.

- **Reduces administrative workload** by streamlining enrollment and records management.

Best Practices for Implementing Power Automate in Healthcare and Education

To ensure successful adoption of Power Automate:

1. Identify High-Impact Use Cases

- Focus on time-consuming, repetitive tasks that can benefit from automation.

- Prioritize workflows that improve accuracy and efficiency.

2. Ensure Compliance and Security

- Implement **role-based access control (RBAC)** to protect sensitive data.

- Regularly audit automated workflows to maintain compliance.

3. Train Users and Monitor Performance

- Provide **training for staff and educators** to use Power Automate effectively.

- Regularly review workflow performance and optimize processes.

Conclusion

Power Automate offers game-changing automation solutions for both healthcare and education, reducing administrative burdens and improving efficiency, accuracy, and communication. By leveraging Power Automate, hospitals, clinics, schools, and universities can focus more on patient care and education while reducing manual tasks.

This chapter has explored real-world examples and best practices to help organizations implement automation successfully. The next step is to start building your own automated workflows and unlock the full potential of Power Automate!

Appendices

A. Power Automate Keyboard Shortcuts

Microsoft Power Automate is a powerful tool that enables users to automate repetitive tasks and streamline workflows across multiple applications. While most users interact with Power Automate through its graphical interface, keyboard shortcuts can significantly improve efficiency and productivity. Mastering these shortcuts allows users to navigate the platform faster, execute actions with minimal effort, and enhance their overall automation experience.

This appendix provides a comprehensive list of keyboard shortcuts for Power Automate, including those available in the **Power Automate web portal**, **Power Automate Desktop**, and **related Microsoft 365 applications** that integrate with Power Automate. Additionally, we'll explore best practices for using keyboard shortcuts, customization options, and practical examples of how these shortcuts can optimize workflow automation.

1. Why Keyboard Shortcuts Matter in Power Automate

Keyboard shortcuts are essential for enhancing productivity in any software environment. In Power Automate, they offer several key benefits:

- **Faster Navigation** – Move between screens and execute actions without relying on the mouse.

- **Efficiency in Flow Creation** – Quickly add, edit, and manage automation steps.

- **Reduced Click Fatigue** – Minimize repetitive clicking, which can slow down workflow development.

- **Accessibility** – Improve usability for users who prefer or require keyboard-based interactions.

For Power Automate users, leveraging shortcuts can significantly cut down the time spent configuring flows, debugging processes, and managing automation components.

2. Essential Keyboard Shortcuts in Power Automate Web Portal

The Power Automate **web portal** is where users design, manage, and monitor automated workflows. Below are key shortcuts that enhance workflow management:

2.1 General Navigation

Action	Shortcut
Open Power Automate Home	Alt + Shift + H
Open My Flows	Alt + Shift + M
Open Create Flow Page	Alt + Shift + C
Open Templates Page	Alt + Shift + T
Open Connectors Page	Alt + Shift + O
Open AI Builder	Alt + Shift + A
Navigate Between Sections	Tab
Navigate Back	Shift + Tab
Search for Flows	Ctrl + F
Open Help and Support	F1

2.2 Flow Editing Shortcuts

Action	Shortcut
Create a New Flow	Ctrl + N
Save Flow	Ctrl + S
Undo Last Action	Ctrl + Z
Redo Last Action	Ctrl + Y

Action	Shortcut
Delete Selected Action	Del
Duplicate Selected Action	Ctrl + D
Move Up in Flow Editor	Arrow Up
Move Down in Flow Editor	Arrow Down
Expand/Collapse Action Details	Space

2.3 Flow Testing and Debugging

Action	Shortcut
Run a Flow Manually	Ctrl + R
Open Flow Run History	Ctrl + H
View Flow Details	Enter
Open Flow Logs	Ctrl + L
Stop Running Flow	Esc

3. Power Automate Desktop Keyboard Shortcuts

Power Automate Desktop enables users to automate local computer tasks. Since it operates separately from the web-based Power Automate, it has its own set of shortcuts.

General Navigation in Power Automate Desktop

Action	Shortcut
Open Power Automate Desktop	Win + Shift + P
Open a New Flow	Ctrl + N
Open an Existing Flow	Ctrl + O

Action	Shortcut
Save Flow	Ctrl + S
Close Power Automate Desktop	Alt + F4

Working with Actions

Action	Shortcut
Add a New Action	Ctrl + A
Edit Selected Action	Enter
Delete Action	Del
Copy Action	Ctrl + C
Paste Action	Ctrl + V
Move Action Up	Ctrl + Up Arrow
Move Action Down	Ctrl + Down Arrow

Running and Debugging Desktop Flows

Action	Shortcut
Run Flow	F5
Step Through Flow	F10
Pause Execution	Ctrl + P
Stop Execution	Shift + F5

4. Power Automate and Microsoft 365 Shortcuts

Many Power Automate users work with Microsoft 365 applications like Outlook, Excel, and Teams. Understanding relevant shortcuts in these apps can improve automation workflows.

Outlook Shortcuts for Power Automate Users

Action	Shortcut
Open New Email	Ctrl + N
Send Email	Ctrl + Enter
Reply to Email	Ctrl + R
Forward Email	Ctrl + F
Search Emails	Ctrl + E

Excel Shortcuts for Power Automate Users

Action	Shortcut
Open Workbook	Ctrl + O
Save Workbook	Ctrl + S
Insert Row	Ctrl + Shift + +
Delete Row	Ctrl + -
Select Entire Column	Ctrl + Space

Microsoft Teams Shortcuts for Automation

Action	Shortcut
Open Chat	Ctrl + 2
Start a New Chat	Ctrl + N
Open Teams Tab	Ctrl + 3
Search in Teams	Ctrl + E

5. Customizing Keyboard Shortcuts in Power Automate

Currently, Power Automate does not provide built-in options for customizing shortcuts, but users can use third-party tools like **AutoHotkey** or Windows PowerToys to create custom keyboard shortcuts.

Using AutoHotkey for Custom Shortcuts

- Install AutoHotkey and create a script with custom shortcuts.

- Example: Assign Alt + P to open Power Automate web portal.

Using Windows PowerToys to Remap Keys

- Open PowerToys Keyboard Manager.

- Assign custom key mappings for frequent actions.

6. Best Practices for Using Keyboard Shortcuts Effectively

To maximize efficiency, users should:

- Memorize the most frequently used shortcuts for navigation and editing.

- Create cheat sheets for quick reference.

- Practice daily to develop muscle memory.

- Combine shortcuts with automation for even greater efficiency.

7. Conclusion

Mastering keyboard shortcuts in Power Automate can significantly improve productivity and workflow efficiency. Whether you're navigating the web interface, working in Power Automate Desktop, or integrating automation with Microsoft 365 apps, these shortcuts save time and effort.

By incorporating keyboard shortcuts into your daily automation tasks, you can streamline processes, reduce manual effort, and enhance your overall experience with Power Automate.

B. Troubleshooting Common Errors

Power Automate is a powerful tool that enables users to automate workflows across multiple applications. However, like any software, users may encounter errors that can disrupt automation processes. Understanding common errors, their causes, and troubleshooting steps can help resolve issues efficiently.

This appendix provides a **comprehensive guide** to troubleshooting errors in Power Automate, covering:

1. **Understanding Power Automate Error Messages**

2. **Common Errors and How to Fix Them**

    o   Flow Execution Errors

    o   Connection and Authentication Issues

    o   Trigger and Action Failures

    o   Data Formatting and Transformation Errors

    o   API and Connector Limitations

3. **Debugging and Testing Your Flows**

4. **Best Practices to Prevent Errors**

5. **Advanced Troubleshooting Tools**

---

1. Understanding Power Automate Error Messages

When a flow fails in Power Automate, an error message is usually displayed. These messages provide details about what went wrong and may include:

- **Error Code:** A unique identifier for the error.

- **Error Message:** A description of the issue.

- **Suggested Actions:** Recommendations for fixing the issue.

- **Flow Run History:** A log of previous runs with error details.

By reviewing these messages, users can diagnose problems and apply the correct fixes.

2. Common Errors and How to Fix Them

Flow Execution Errors

These errors occur when a flow fails to execute as expected.

Error	Cause	Solution
Flow failed to run	The flow was not triggered, or execution stopped unexpectedly.	Check the **Flow Run History** for errors. Ensure the trigger conditions are met.
Action skipped	A condition prevented an action from running.	Review conditions and expressions. Modify logic if necessary.
Infinite loop detected	A flow is continuously triggering itself.	Add **Trigger Conditions** to prevent unnecessary executions. Use **Delay** actions if needed.

Connection and Authentication Issues

Errors related to authentication, expired tokens, or missing permissions.

Error	Cause	Solution
Invalid connection	Authentication token expired or connection is broken.	Re-authenticate and update the connection under **Data > Connections**.
Access denied	The user lacks permissions to access a resource.	Verify that the correct permissions are granted for the service.

Error	Cause	Solution
Connector limit exceeded	The API or service has reached its request limit.	Reduce the number of requests or upgrade to a premium plan if necessary.

Trigger and Action Failures

Issues that occur when a trigger doesn't start the flow or an action fails to execute.

Error	Cause	Solution
Trigger not firing	The event does not match trigger conditions.	Adjust the trigger conditions or test with different data.
Invalid trigger schema	The trigger expects a different data structure.	Verify the JSON schema in the **Trigger settings**. Use **Peek Code** to inspect inputs.
Action failed	Required fields are missing or contain invalid values.	Check the action's input parameters and ensure they are correctly formatted.

Data Formatting and Transformation Errors

Errors caused by incorrect data types or formatting issues.

Error	Cause	Solution
Invalid JSON format	The input JSON is incorrectly structured.	Use a JSON validator to check for syntax errors.
Expression evaluation failed	A formula or expression has incorrect syntax.	Review the expression in **Peek Code**. Use **Power Automate Expression Tester**.

Error	Cause	Solution
Data type mismatch	An action expects a number, but received text.	Convert data types using **formatNumber()**, **concat()**, or similar functions.

API and Connector Limitations

Some services have rate limits or restrictions on API calls.

Error	Cause	Solution
429 Too Many Requests	API rate limit exceeded.	Reduce API calls, use **Retry Policies**, or introduce delays.
Unsupported action in connector	Some actions are unavailable in a connector.	Check the connector's documentation for supported actions. Consider alternatives.
Timeout error	API request took too long to respond.	Optimize the request, increase timeout settings, or retry later.

3. Debugging and Testing Your Flows

Using Flow Run History

- Navigate to **My Flows > Run History**.
- Review **Failed Runs** to identify errors.
- Expand actions to check input/output details.

Adding Logging for Troubleshooting

- Use **Compose Actions** to inspect variables.
- Enable **Logging in SharePoint or Excel** to track flow execution.

- Use the **"Terminate" action** to stop a flow if certain conditions are met.

Testing with Sample Data

- Use **Test Mode** to debug flows before full deployment.

- Validate inputs by manually triggering the flow.

4. Best Practices to Prevent Errors

- **Use Error Handling Actions:** Implement **"Configure Run After"** settings to handle failures.

- **Implement Retry Policies:** Set retry attempts in action settings.

- **Validate Inputs:** Use conditions to check for null or incorrect values.

- **Optimize Flow Performance:** Avoid unnecessary loops and optimize API calls.

5. Advanced Troubleshooting Tools

Microsoft Power Automate Monitor

- Provides real-time logs and analytics for debugging.

- Helps track API calls and system events.

Power Automate Expression Tester

- Allows testing of functions like **concat()**, **formatDateTime()**, etc.

- Available within the Power Automate **Expression Builder**.

Power Platform Admin Center

- Monitors organization-wide flow performance.

- Identifies system-wide service outages or connector issues.

6. Conclusion

Troubleshooting Power Automate errors is crucial for ensuring smooth automation processes. By understanding common error messages, implementing best practices, and utilizing debugging tools, users can quickly resolve issues and optimize their workflows.

By applying these troubleshooting steps, you can build **reliable, efficient, and error-free** automation solutions in Power Automate.

C. Troubleshooting Common Errors

As you continue to explore and master Microsoft Power Automate, leveraging additional learning resources can help you stay updated with new features, best practices, and real-world applications. This appendix provides a curated list of **official documentation, online courses, community forums, blogs, and books** to support your learning journey.

1. Official Microsoft Resources

Microsoft provides extensive documentation, tutorials, and training courses to help users at all levels.

Microsoft Power Automate Documentation

- **Official Docs:** Power Automate Documentation
- Includes step-by-step guides, API references, troubleshooting tips, and feature updates.

Microsoft Learn – Power Automate Learning Paths

- **Free self-paced courses** on Microsoft Learn: Power Automate Learning Paths
- Covers beginner to advanced topics, including building flows, integrating with Microsoft 365, and automation best practices.

Microsoft Power Automate Blog

- **Stay updated with the latest features and improvements**: Power Automate Blog
- Includes announcements, case studies, and expert insights.

Power Automate Community Forums

- Engage with other users and get help from experts: Power Automate Community
- Share experiences, ask troubleshooting questions, and find solutions.

Microsoft Power Platform YouTube Channel

- Watch video tutorials and deep-dive sessions: <u>Microsoft Power Platform YouTube</u>
- Covers automation use cases, demos, and expert tips.

---

2. Online Courses and Tutorials

If you prefer structured learning through video tutorials and guided courses, consider these platforms:

Udemy – Power Automate Courses

- **Popular courses on Udemy** include:
    - *Microsoft Power Automate: Learn Power Automate from Scratch*
    - *Power Automate Fundamentals for Beginners*
    - *Advanced Power Automate Workflows for Microsoft 365*
- Courses range from beginner to advanced levels, with hands-on exercises.

Pluralsight – Power Automate Training

- Pluralsight offers **professional-level courses** on automation and Power Platform integration.
- Focuses on **real-world scenarios**, including business process automation and Power Automate with Power Apps.

LinkedIn Learning – Microsoft Power Automate

- **Courses taught by industry professionals**, including:
    - *Learning Microsoft Power Automate*
    - *Business Process Automation with Power Automate*
    - *Advanced Workflow Automation with Power Automate*

Coursera & EdX – Microsoft Power Platform Specializations

- Some universities and training organizations offer **Power Platform courses** covering automation, Power Apps, and AI Builder integration.

3. Books on Power Automate and Automation

If you prefer in-depth learning through books, these are excellent resources:

Microsoft Power Automate Step by Step – by Carl Chatfield

- A beginner-friendly guide covering basic to intermediate Power Automate features with practical use cases.

Automate Your Work with Microsoft Power Automate – by Aaron Guilmette

- Explores automation strategies, best practices, and business process improvement using Power Automate.

Hands-On Microsoft Power Automate – by Anders Jensen

- A practical book focusing on real-world workflow automation and integrating Power Automate with Microsoft 365 services.

The Power Automate Cookbook – by Paul Papanek Stork

- A collection of pre-built automation recipes and advanced troubleshooting techniques.

4. Community and Social Media Groups

Power Automate Subreddit (r/PowerAutomate)

- **Reddit Community**: r/PowerAutomate
- Discuss workflows, troubleshoot errors, and share automation ideas.

Power Automate LinkedIn Groups

- **Join Power Automate professional groups** on LinkedIn to network and learn from industry experts.

Twitter & Hashtags to Follow

- Follow Microsoft Power Automate experts and influencers:

- o @MSPowerAutomate
- o @PowerPlatform
- o @JSteadman (Power Automate expert)
- Use hashtags **#PowerAutomate, #MSFlow, #PowerPlatform** to discover automation insights.

5. Advanced Resources for Developers and IT Professionals

Power Automate for Developers (REST API & SDK)

- If you are a developer looking to extend Power Automate capabilities, explore:
    - o Power Automate API Reference: Microsoft Power Automate API
    - o Power Automate SDK for custom connectors and automation logic.

Microsoft Dataverse & Power Automate

- Learn how to use Power Automate with Dataverse for enterprise-level automation:
    - o Dataverse and Power Automate

Power Automate with AI Builder

- Explore **AI-powered automation** with Microsoft AI Builder:
    - o AI Builder in Power Automate

6. Conclusion

Whether you're a beginner looking for foundational knowledge or an advanced user optimizing complex workflows, these resources will help you continue your learning journey with Power Automate.

To stay up to date:
✅ Follow Microsoft's official blog & community forums
✅ Take structured courses & read expert books

✅ Engage with Power Automate communities on LinkedIn, Reddit, and Twitter
✅ Explore advanced topics like AI Builder, Dataverse, and API automation

Automation is constantly evolving, and with continuous learning, you can unlock new possibilities for optimizing workflows and improving business processes.

Acknowledgments

First and foremost, thank you for choosing *Microsoft Power Automate Essentials: Automate Your Day-to-Day Tasks*. I truly appreciate your time, trust, and effort in exploring this book, and I hope it serves as a valuable resource in your automation journey.

Writing this book has been a rewarding experience, and my goal has always been to simplify the learning process and make Power Automate accessible to everyone—whether you're just getting started or looking to refine your skills. Your decision to invest in this book is a testament to your commitment to efficiency, productivity, and continuous learning, and I sincerely hope it helps you unlock new possibilities in your workflows.

A special thanks to the Power Automate community, whose discussions, insights, and shared experiences continue to inspire and shape the way automation evolves. Microsoft's ongoing improvements to the Power Platform also deserve recognition, making automation more powerful and user-friendly every day.

Lastly, to you—the reader, whether you're an individual professional, a business owner, an IT expert, or someone simply curious about automation: thank you! Your support and enthusiasm for learning drive the creation of resources like this one.

If you found this book helpful, I'd love to hear your feedback. Feel free to share your thoughts, connect on professional networks, or leave a review—it helps me continue creating better content for learners like you.

Wishing you success in your Power Automate journey, and may automation bring you efficiency, productivity, and more time to focus on what truly matters.

Happy automating!